Soundies Jukebox Films and the Shift to Small-Screen Culture

TMI TECHNIQUES of the MOVING IMAGE

Volumes in the Techniques of the Moving Image series explore the relationship between what we see onscreen and the technical achievements undertaken in filmmaking to make this possible. Books explore some defined aspect of cinema—work from a particular era, work in a particular genre, work by a particular filmmaker or team, work from a particular studio, or work on a particular theme—in light of some technique and/or technical achievement, such as cinematography, direction, acting, lighting, costuming, set design, legal arrangements, agenting, scripting, sound design and recording, and sound or picture editing. Historical and social background contextualize the subject of each volume.

Murray Pomerance
Series Editor

Jay Beck, *Designing Sound: Audiovisual Aesthetics in 1970s American Cinema*
Lisa Bode, *Making Believe: Screen Performance and Special Effects in Popular Cinema*
Wheeler Winston Dixon, *Death of the Moguls: The End of Classical Hollywood*
Nick Hall, *The Zoom: Drama at the Touch of a Lever*
Andrea J. Kelley, *Soundies Jukebox Films and the Shift to Small-Screen Culture*
R. Barton Palmer, *Shot on Location: Postwar American Cinema and the Exploration of Real Place*
Murray Pomerance, *The Eyes Have It: Cinema and the Reality Effect*
Colin Williamson, *Hidden in Plain Sight: An Archaeology of Magic and the Cinema*
Joshua Yumibe, *Moving Color: Early Film, Mass Culture, Modernism*

Soundies Jukebox Films and the Shift to Small-Screen Culture

ANDREA J. KELLEY

Rutgers University Press
New Brunswick, Camden, and Newark, New Jersey, and London

Library of Congress Cataloging in Publication Control Number: 2017055032

A British Cataloging-in-Publication record for this book is available from the British Library.

∞ The paper used in this publication meets the requirements of the American National Standard for Information Sciences—Permanence of Paper for Printed Library Materials, ANSI Z39.48-1992.

www.rutgersuniversitypress.org

Manufactured in the United States of America

For Izzy

Contents

Soundies Jukebox Films and the Shift to Small-Screen Culture

Introduction

Soundies Jukebox Films

> Why not bring the art of the cinema to bars, restaurants, lunch wagons, station waiting-rooms, drug stores, wherever idle people congregate with time on their hands and minds athirst for esthetic experience?
> —"Jimmie's Peep Shows," *Time*, March 4, 1940[1]

> Just as record players have gotten around so that now one can hardly get into a hot-dog stand without finding one, talking pictures are about to pursue us.
> —Lee Shippey, *Los Angeles Times*, November 23, 1940[2]

The short musical film *Clancy* (1945) features the Dinning Sisters singing around an NBC microphone at a radio station. Aping the vocal style of the more popular Andrews Sisters, the trio harmonizes as they deliver a light-hearted song about an Irish cop who works in Harlem. They sing, "He was transferred up to Harlem by the chief of police . . . How'd that Irish copper get that boogie beat?" The film cuts from the Dinning Sisters to a staged street scene with two policemen dancing in front of a 145th Street and Lenox Avenue street sign. *Clancy*'s filmed rendition of a popular song is typical 1940s musical entertainment fare, blending vocal performance with a novelty dance number in a staged theatrical setting. As a stand-alone short film, *Clancy* may be considered little more than a novelty relic of 1940s popular culture, providing a small dose of musical entertainment history. *Clancy*, though, is not an isolated fragment of media ephemera but one of 1,850 Soundies produced in the United States during the 1940s. Soundies were 16mm short films that circulated exclusively for play in coin-operated movie jukeboxes called Panorams that were located in bars, train stations, and other ordinary spaces of leisure and transit. In both their musical representations and their circulation in coin machines, Soundies jukebox films evidence the integration of popular screen media into everyday practices, spaces, and routines.

As a singular, but not atypical, example of a Soundie, *Clancy* invites questions about how media were reimagined as small-screen entertainment during the 1940s. The film's staging of a popular music performance as both a reenactment of a vocal performance and a comedic dance number illustrates how songs could be visualized for the jukebox screen. Long before the MTV era, Soundies experimented with various modes of presenting popular music as small-screen entertainment. Second, *Clancy*'s appeal hinges on the comical

FIGURE 1 "How'd that Irish copper get that boogie beat?" Production still from *Clancy* (1945). From Soundies Distributing Corporation of America photographs of the Margaret Herrick Library, Academy of Motion Picture Arts and Sciences.

construction of a presumed novelty figure, Clancy, the boogie-woogie Irish cop. With the song's lyrics and the visual backdrop of the Harlem street sign, Clancy is presented as a strange mash-up figure by appropriating and inhabiting black popular culture through the authority of being a white police officer stationed in Harlem. Such hybrid cultural caricatures circulated widely in Soundies jukebox films and point to larger racial dynamics in the 1940s, where issues of traversing identity were seen as a point of intrigue as well as a source of entertainment.[3] Though this content is embedded in the lyrics of popular songs, Soundies like *Clancy* allowed for these figures to be seen and to circulate on movie screens in everyday spaces. Finally, *Clancy* provides a record of 1940s transitional media practices. With its presumed setting in a radio station, *Clancy* makes explicit its connection to broadcast and the Dinning Sisters' past successes on radio. The film presents a representation of a radio broadcast while its own filmic images make the radio broadcast visible. *Clancy*'s visualization of radio broadcast anticipates television's small-screen broadcasts and the expanded circulation of short-form entertainment during the mid-1940s.

As the previous example illustrates, Soundies provide a fertile site for examining the shifting terrain of U.S. screen culture during the 1940s. Cinemagoing in the United States reached its all-time peak in 1946 with weekly theatrical movie attendance reaching eighty-two million.[4] A ritualized part of daily life in the mid-1940s, movie viewing was a central aspect of domestic wartime and the postwar experience. However, theatrical exhibitions of Hollywood features do not represent the entire picture of 1940s screen culture.[5] During the war, 16mm film projection became standard for the U.S. military at home and abroad and continued to spread to other sites that could benefit from the portability and adaptability of 16mm technology.[6] The expanded use of 16mm projectors at public, institutional, educational, and commercial sites during the 1940s contributed to new modes of screen encounters and changing cultural attitudes toward moving images entering into everyday life. As the epigraphs to this chapter attest, the growing presence of films in consumer spaces like restaurants and drugstores by 1940 elicited contested reactions to these new screen presences, ranging from disdain to enrichment. By looking beyond conventional sites of moving images and the dominant industrial practices of Hollywood, this book charts the changes in media viewing through the quotidian spaces of Soundies short musical films playing on coin-operated Panoram film jukeboxes in order to examine how U.S. screen culture became both spectacular and ordinary and almost always within our reach.

A multifaceted screen phenomenon, Soundies constitute their own film genre, technology, and industry—they are at once a vast body of short musical films; a unique, coin-operated playback technology; and an independent, short-lived business practice. From 1940 to 1946, Soundies Distributing

Corporation, Inc. (SDC) circulated their short films in bars, bowling alleys, train stations, hospitals, nightclubs, and cafés and even on domestic military bases. Viewers would pay a dime to watch a Soundie playing on the small (17 × 22½-inch) screens of the Panoram jukebox. Individual films could not be selected from the self-looping reel, so customers had to enjoy their random selection or continue to insert coins to get to a particular film on the eight-film reel. As the machine was large, its walnut cabinet was mounted on wheels so, if needed, it could be moved throughout its screening locale. Its volume also was adjustable so it could accommodate and adapt to the acoustics of various spaces. Presenting top big-band acts, up-and-coming vocalists, drinking songs, and burlesque dances, Soundies' body of short films provides a virtual variety show of 1940s entertainment. The films showcase popular jukebox music like swing, hillbilly, Latin-inspired rhumbas, Irish ballads, and Hawaiian love songs with the added appeal of seeing a performance scenario on the screen. Soundies offer lively musical performances and diverse representations, including several films featuring notable African American artists like Cab Calloway and Dorothy Dandridge. Often produced in a day to accommodate touring musicians, their aesthetics are at once formulaic and low budget but also compelling and even odd in their attempts to visualize popular music for the screen. At their height of popularity in the mid-1940s, almost five thousand Panorams were in circulation throughout the United States.

More than a media novelty or sideshow attraction, Soundies on the Panoram modeled emerging trends in film and media engagement, including the shift from large screens to small, from feature-length films to short formats, from collective to private viewing practices, and from site-specific film venues to ubiquitous screen encounters. Given the cultivation of Panoram Soundies as both a film format and a screen technology, the purpose of this history is to examine two large but intersecting media trends: the profusion of short-form media and the mobilization of small screens. These underlying impulses that shape contemporary screen integration, though evident from the inception of cinematic technologies, become pronounced in Soundies popular discourses and practices just prior to the mainstream arrival of domestic television in the late 1940s. By approaching both of these trends through the history of Soundies, this book provides an intermedial screen history that positions nontheatrical short film as vital to the rising popularity of television and other emergent small-screen technologies from midcentury onward.

A look into the formation of the SDC underscores its ancillary but intersecting positioning to both Hollywood filmmaking and the popular music industry. A messy business practice with several changes in ownership and structure within its seven-year life span, Soundies' corporate history bridges the coin-operated vending industry with independent film production and includes an odd amalgam of cultural figures like FDR's son James "Jimmy"

Roosevelt (Soundies founding executive and first producer), African American football star Fritz Pollard (a casting director and talent scout for one of Soundies' independent film production units), and Cecil B. DeMille (a silent investor). Hoping to capitalize on the popularity of music jukeboxes, motion pictures, and even nascent small-screen television, several inventors tinkered with film-jukebox prototypes during the late 1930s.[7] By 1940, Mills Novelty Company, a prominent Chicago-based manufacturer of coin-operated machines, modeled its designs for a coin-operated 16mm projector encased in a deluxe cabinet and was seeking a film production company to supply its machines with a film product. In February 1940, Jimmy Roosevelt—who then was head of Globe Productions, a small film company that produced the Jimmy Stewart feature *Pot o' Gold* (1941)—agreed to produce musical shorts for these jukeboxes using Globe's current production facilities. Initially called the Mills-Globe Company, they soon renamed their venture to Soundies Distributing Corporation of America, Inc.[8] With Roosevelt overseeing the production of the films and Mills handling the manufacture and sale of Panoram machines and Soundie distribution, the SDC envisioned the Panoram as an extension of the jukebox and hoped to overtake it as the next mainstay in the booming coin-operated amusement business.[9]

In the fall of 1940, the SDC hosted lavish premiere parties in both Los Angeles and New York, which generated a lot of anticipation and speculation within the movie industry about the role of this new moving-image apparatus. Before the SDC could hit its stride, Jimmy Roosevelt was commissioned as captain in the Marine Corps and resigned from his executive post with the SDC. Roosevelt's Globe Productions was taken over by Sam Coslow's company Cameo Productions, which later formed into the aptly named Roosevelt-Coslow-Mills (RCM). RCM remained the primary West Coast Soundies film producer while Minoco Productions in New York, under the direction of Jack Barry, produced Soundies on the East Coast. A few independent production companies also produced Soundies intermittently during the 1940s. Of note is FilmCraft, which, with producer and director William Forrest Crouch and talent scout Fritz Pollard, produced several all-black-cast Soundies.

By early 1941, the SDC began its initial rollout of Panorams and Soundies to regional franchise operators. Soundies did very well during this novelty period, receiving favorable reviews by the press and enough industry interest and curiosity to bolster business. The SDC produced and distributed 379 Soundies in 1941. By the year's end, though, with the attacks on Pearl Harbor and the United States entering into World War II, the SDC was faced with a radically different economic forecast. Wartime production restrictions proved an impediment to new Panoram manufacturing. The ban on aluminum posed immense hurdles for this fledgling company and completely halted

FIGURE 2 FDR's son and first Soundies producer James "Jimmy" Roosevelt. From the core collection biography photographs of the Margaret Herrick Library, Academy of Motion Picture Arts and Sciences.

the production of new Panoram machines in February 1942.[10] Rather than producing their anticipated thirty thousand machines, Mills manufactured roughly five thousand Panorams total, greatly hindering the SDC's capacity to generate profits.

If the constraints of a wartime economy were not debilitating enough to Panoram machine production, resistance posed by the American Federation of Musicians (AFM) further stymied the SDC's access to onscreen talent.

In August 1942, James Petrillo, the AFM's infamous union president, implemented the AFM recording ban, in which union musicians could no longer make recordings except for the motion picture industry and the armed forces. Because of Soundies' associations with the jukebox trade, they were included in the AFM ban. Before the ban was put into place, the SDC rushed to record and stockpile musical films featuring big-band acts, but this still did not make up for the lack of available recording artists. The SDC found innovative ways to repurpose old films and sought nontraditional musicians who were not included in the ban to make up for this loss. Although the SDC still produced 363 films in 1942 and 324 in 1943, the quality and marketability of the films suffered to some degree without well-known musical acts.

The AFM ban was lifted in November 1944, and the SDC greatly anticipated a resurgence in production, especially with the war nearing its end in 1945. However, Soundies film production leveled to roughly 250 films per year, and revenues flatlined. As the novelty of the jukebox film enterprise had by then worn thin, the SDC released its final handful of films in late 1946. After the SDC folded, former Soundies producer and director Crouch briefly continued production under the masthead Soundies Films, Inc. for another year. In 1947, independent 16mm film distribution companies like Blackhawk, Castle, and Official Films (and its developing company Official Television) purchased the rights to Soundies and repackaged them for private collections and nontheatrical film markets and, in some instances, for television distribution. Soundies briefly circulated on television as programming filler in the late 1940s and were featured on a few video deejay programs in the early 1950s. The remaining Panoram machines were adapted and sometimes repurposed into peep-show booths in arcades and sales displays in department stores, travel agencies, and grocery stores. Soon, however, the machines all but disappeared from public use.

Given their industrial constraints throughout the 1940s, the SDC still managed to produce a collection of 1,850 short musical films. A diverse and entertaining collection of filmed popular songs and performances, Soundies traverse music genres and scenarios. Initially, Soundies borrowed their short-film formats from productions like Warner Brothers' jazz shorts from the 1930s, which featured big-band orchestras on sound stages and included a few close-up shots to emphasize musicians' solos. Unlike Soundies on the Panoram, Warner's jazz shorts contained three songs (roughly nine minutes) and would be played in theaters alongside feature films. About a third of all Soundies produced feature similar bandstand scenarios,[11] while also adding in dance routines, comedic gags, or sex appeal to sustain visual interest. As the band genre was the hardest hit by the AFM ban, the SDC extended its musical genres to other popular, commercial styles, including hillbilly, western, Hawaiian, and Irish songs while also incorporating comedy and acrobatic acts. This shift from bandstand Soundies to other genres also changed Soundies visual style to emphasize vocalists and sets that evoked these particular musical genres (i.e., saloons for western songs).

With more than one hundred Latin-themed shorts and almost three hundred exclusively featuring African American performers, Soundies present a range of musical styles and an invaluable collection of cultural forms and character types. As the sheer variety of Soundies complicates simple classification, one of their defining generic characteristics when taken in total is their engagement with multicultural motifs and styles. Hardly anthropological, Soundies employed diversity for visual effect, appealing to exoticism or evoking cultural tourism while drawing on popular music styles. As I discussed earlier with *Clancy*, one of the key motifs of Soundies representations is the ethnic mashup, a conjoining of two or more cultural forms. Often motivated by the style of popular music like Hawaiian love songs or Irish ballads, Soundies identity representations often are made explicit through the staging of their musical content and their literal enactment of a song's lyrics. As part of the gimmick of an ethnically coded song, for instance, not only will performers don outfits to signify some act of identity tourism, but also, as an added visual attraction, the very act of transformation will be shown, usually in a not-so-subtle wipe like in the Soundie *Hula Rumba*'s (1946) metamorphosis of Hawaiian hula dancers into sombrero- and serape-clad Mexicans. While oftentimes sustaining and supporting base stereotypes, Soundies' performances and diversity of performers index 1940s discourses of melting-pot assimilation, racial integration, and wartime patriotism. Soundies' play with ethnic forms also fits well within the often-performative contexts of the musical short, where singers, dancers, and musicians appear on stages in nightclubs or other theatrical venues.

Soundies' short film duration, typically lasting almost three minutes, also is determined by the length of the recorded soundtrack. Prerecorded music provided the organizing structure for these short films and usually was recorded just prior to filming. Unless the songs suggested a narrative structure, Soundies rarely sought to develop a story and more often relied upon the musicians or vocalists to provide the film's action with a dance routine for added interest. Soundies typically relied upon modest settings and only a few camera setups. The films are not only short, but they are also small in the scale of their representation, with a contained and shallow mise-en-scène. Partly because of budgetary restrictions, partly because of a growing awareness of the limitations of small-screen viewing, Soundies often are limited in camera movement and in their settings. As is discussed in chapter 4, Soundies' shift from large bandstand setups to more intimate backdrops like small cafés or domestic living rooms—environs which allow for greater focus on the vocalists—evidences the dovetailing of popular music trends with popular screen representations and practices.

Although Soundies maintain traditional conventions of musical short representations with their emphases on performance rather than abstracted visuals such as those appearing in 1950s avant-garde jazz films or 1980s music videos, they steadily develop a specific style of jukebox film unique to their format and viewing conditions. This cultivated style focuses on intimate vocal delivery and engagement with personality, an emerging small-screen aesthetic that comes to define early televisual representations, particularly 1950s and 1960s variety shows as well as the later-day music video. Their rescaling of the musical short for small-screen viewing perhaps is Soundies' most enduring legacy.

As a historical media phenomenon providing a significant visual record of 1940s musical performances and cultural representations, Soundies offer far more than a collection of short films and their representations but participate in an entire shift in screening practices. This book includes attention to both Soundies and the Panoram's conditions of production, distribution, circulation, and the material aspects of Soundie exhibition at a range of viewing sites to examine this pivotal moment in midcentury screen culture. As Eric Smoodin argues in *Looking Past the Screen: Case Studies in American Film History and Method*, films are not just reflective of a culture but "aspects of a complex system of cultural production."[12] In order to account for this expanded sense of media culture, this book utilizes a range of resource materials (newspapers, magazines, trade press, government documents, industrial discourses, etc.) to locate the sites of Soundies and the cultural discourses that circulate around the emerging encounters with short films and small-screen technologies. Because there has been little scholarly work on Soundies in general and their screen practices in particular, I rely largely on their period coverage in music and film trade publications like *Billboard* and *Variety*, and journalistic accounts of Soundie exhibitions and production practices. With a regular section devoted to coin-machine operations, *Billboard* in particular provides detailed coverage of the machine's initial development and promotion. Of particular note, *Billboard*'s "Movie Machine Reviews" column offered regular listings of new Soundie film releases during their height of popularity in the early to mid-1940s. Not only do these reviews provide information on specific film programs and suggest how the films were paired for distribution into preset programs, they also often present insights into the critical reception of the films, including the perceived quality of the music and the on-screen performances. For instance, during the height of U.S. involvement during the war, patriotic Soundies proliferated, sometimes more than one per reel. *Billboard*'s "Movie Machine Reviews" also indicate the expansive distribution of black-cast Soundies, with at least one African American artist appearing on each reviewed Soundies program.

With trade publications largely oriented around the business of coin-machine operators and the promotion of Panoram Soundies within the industry, records of actual Soundie exhibition sites depicting users engaging with the machines remain scant. Only a few newspaper accounts provide records of site-specific Panoram usage, particularly those made newsworthy due to their screening practices being tied to the war like a Panoram used to play patriotic Soundies in Chicago's city hall during a war loan drive. Needless to say, the war effort proved more newsworthy than the nontheatrical film practices associated with an isolated Soundie viewing, say, in the far corner of a bowling alley in Detroit. Although Soundies' historical framework of the war years lends to an easy romanticizing of its screening practices, the cultural backdrop of World War II informs but does not constitute the entirety of Soundies screen practices. Even in wartime accounts, the discourse surrounding Soundies reveals mundane aspects of emerging small-screen practices.

Beyond trade magazines and journalistic resources, Soundies' 1,850 short films provide their own documentation of the era. With their complex range of identity representations, musical performances, and short film aesthetics, Soundies index and reinforce the cultural discourse that arose around these new small-screen practices. This includes formal considerations of Soundies' representations of spaces, media technologies (including a handful of Soundies which show Panorams in play), consumer interactions, and the sizing and scaling of images for the small screen. All of these textual elements provide insights concerning Soundies' intended modes of exhibition and the discourses that shaped their screen encounters during the 1940s.

Throughout this book, I turn to specific Soundies to illustrate emerging modes of short-film viewing as well as to gauge changing cultural attitudes toward new screen practices. Since not all Soundies are readily available and some exist in fragmentary form, essential Soundies compendia—including Maurice Terenzio, Scott MacGillivray, and Ted Okuda's *The Soundies Distributing Corporation of America: A History and Filmography of their "Jukebox" Musical Films of the 1940s* and Wally Hose's *Soundies*—offer encyclopedic production information on directors and performers, the films' specific release dates, and sometimes descriptions of the films themselves. Further information on the films, including copies of the films themselves, increasingly has become available through the internet. Once hard-to-find films now are accessible via YouTube or Prelinger's Internet Archive. This renewed interest in the preservation and expanded digital circulation of Soundies is significant and makes necessary a better positioning of Soundies viewing practices and of their role in 1940s screen culture. *Soundies* combines methods of historical materialism and textual analysis to situate evasive and mundane moments of Soundies movie machine viewing into a culture of short-form, small-screen media and examines 1940s U.S. media culture within wartime experiences, popular trends, social spaces, and the increasingly banal screen routines of workers, soldiers, diners, and passersby.

This book is organized into two parts, each centralizing an integral dynamic of Soundies and the Panoram. Part 1, "Screen Encounters and Spatial Practices," highlights the material conditions of Soundie viewing, its screen technology, and the cultural spaces through which the Panoram circulated. Part 2, "Short Forms and Enduring Formations," focuses primarily on Soundies films, the aesthetics of the musical short, their racial representations, and their media afterlife and contemporary continuities. Even though each chapter traces a particular strand of Soundies history, each is integrative in its approach to mapping key changes in U.S. screen culture. Chapter 1 foregrounds the technological protocols of the film jukebox to survey the enabling factors for small-screen integration. As the history of Soundies and their screening practices is as much a history of a media technology as it is a history of films in circulation, the Panoram as an object of inquiry opens historical film investigations to questions of mechanism, format, size, and operability. The material mechanisms of the Panoram (its screen size, cabinetry, self-looping rear projector, and coin operation) and the ways that the machine circulates in popular and industrial discourses equally bespeak changes in screen culture and consumer desires for new kinds of moving-image encounters. Particularly, the Panoram's alignment with and similarity to other vending devices informed its screening practices and the ways it was utilized and situated.

Chapter 1 first places Soundies screening practices within the historical and industrial contexts from which they developed by charting the SDC's launch of a new media enterprise and the way it envisioned the juke-film functioning as a new kind of screen practice. This chapter examines the dominant discourses that surrounded the circulation of the Panoram as a jukebox technology, charting how the Panoram and its accompanying film-viewing practices were marketed in trade and industrial accounts. The trade and journalistic accounts of the Panoram also attest to emerging modes of engagement with the screen as a new kind of material, cultural object—a kind of screen awareness not unlike our contemporary, popular discourses on ubiquitous screen presences. In addition to the initial excitement generated over the novelty apparatus, the marketing of the Panoram in the early 1940s reveals a deep ambivalence toward this new screen technology and the ways small, moving-image screens would be encountered in everyday spaces, a wrestling with the role and positioning of screen media throughout the surrounding environs. This ambivalence is echoed in a few Soundies that incorporate images of the Panoram jukebox. This chapter concludes with an analysis of these films to glean how the Panoram's technological and social protocols were imagined in representations of the machine itself.

Whereas the prior chapter examines Soundies through the Panoram and its various discursive constructions as a particular media technology, chapter 2 shifts its investigation to the dynamics of these screens within specific screening sites. Similar to the technological discourses concerning the Panoram as a new kind of multimedia screen technology, Soundies' multiple and varied exhibition locales contribute to an understanding of media culture in the 1940s and further to the cultural import of their screen practices. Panorams performed differing functions at their screening sites (musical entertainment, patriotic bond sales, on-site work training), and their spaces point to a range of viewing dynamics and practices. Soundies screening sites open considerations of new media locales (factories, ferries, bowling allies, etc.) and of how Panorams were situated and integrated into these places. For instance, the Panoram's physical positioning (often in the corner of a room or against the wall of a busy, crowded environ) suggests a decentralized and possibly ambient screen presence or a sideline diversion. Similarly, the Panoram's adjustable volume or its ability to be viewed in a well-lit room also bespeaks variances in its spatial practices. Did audiences sit attentively and quietly in front of these machines, as some photographic evidence illustrates? Did the Panoram incite people to crowd around its screen and maybe dance to the music? Did the passerby even watch the screen at all? Unlike the more contained—though hardly uniform—seating at movie theaters, which strongly suggests particular modes of spectatorship and viewer engagement, Soundie exhibition varies drastically from site to site. Their viewing conditions in places of transit, for instance, may differ greatly from a restaurant or bar or their featured placement at event-oriented sites like war bond rallies.

With all these variations in space and arrangement, site-specific accounts of the Panoram suggest the often-unstable dynamics of screen use, including the large Panoram awkwardly being wheeled from room to room, as well as the mobility of its viewers at spaces of leisure and transport.[13] Analogous to Anna McCarthy's investigation of the "quotidian geography" of television in *Ambient Television Visual Culture and Public Space*, the spaces in which television is not a spectacle but another feature within environments that we inhabit (the tavern, various waiting rooms, shopping centers, transit depots, etc.), Soundies' varied locales suggest multiple modes of media consumption, including often overlooked encounters and happenstance moments of user engagement.[14] This is not to say that Soundies operated in a uniformly ambient mode, fully ensconced as an atmospheric presence in its environs. In fact, Soundies' circulation into quotidian spaces was viewed at times as an invasive screen spectacle and often a novelty. What Soundies evidence and presage historically is an emerging landscape of screen spaces and viewing protocols that index future site-based screens like nondomestic televisions and mobile media devices. Each spatial account provides insights into the shifting role of site-based moving-images screens in the United States during the 1940s as well as to emerging modes of user engagement with screen technologies. Chapter 2 also considers how the representations of space within Soundies interact with their screening sites. Soundies often portray musicians performing in nightclubs and restaurants, spaces suggestive of their own screening spaces. This sometimes mimetic pairing of film settings with possible screening sites (like a bar-themed Soundie, which could have been viewed at a local tavern) forges on-screen space with exhibition space and bespeaks an integration of small screens into their environs. Such films may not document or visualize actual moments of Soundie viewing, but they provide valuable iterations of what was wanted from site-specific screen media.

As the years of Soundie production and Panoram exhibition (1940–1946) encompass the entirety of the United States' involvement in World War II (1941–1945), the brief Soundies enterprise constitutes, albeit inadvertently, a wartime screen practice. Chapter 3 focuses on the installment of Panoram machines in military settings as a wartime technology. As a consumer-oriented screen within institutional spaces, the Panoram still retains its ties to Soundies as an entertaining jukebox technology while also playing instructional films designed for efficient military training. Rather than being placed only in recreational spaces, the Panoram is placed in military classrooms, libraries, hospitals, and on-site training facilities. Couched in discourses ranging from combat to rehabilitation, accounts of U.S. military's deployment of the Panoram expands the role of and possibilities for the small film screen and, by war's end, extends consumer desire for adaptable and automatic small-screen technologies into the postwar market.

Part 2, "Short Forms and Enduring Formations," centralizes Soundies' aesthetics and identity representations as interrelated to their circulation as small-screen, short-form media commodities. The history of Soundies extends beyond the 1940s and beyond the film jukebox and opens wider concerns regarding the continued coupling of short-form media with small-screen technologies. Soundies need to be considered more broadly in terms of their short form to investigate why this film genre is aligned specifically with this kind of exhibition practice and technology. In other words, what made the musical short so conducive to small-screen viewing? This is partly an issue of the duration of the popular song recording rendering the film into a readily digestible media commodity. However, Soundies short forms also support expanding discourses on short-media consumption as a specific practice of small-screen exhibition. With the pairing of short forms with small screens emerging as a dominant mode of media exhibition in the digital era, Soundies as an early iteration of this practice open up historical questions about the role of short media in a pervasive small-screen culture.

As I discuss in chapter 4, Soundies musical genres and evolving formal practices certainly were shaped by trends in the popular music industry such as the rise of the sentimental pop vocalist, the death of big-band orchestra, and the restraints of the AFM recording ban, but their representations were also scaled to their viewing practices and screen technology. By intersecting the conditions (and constraints) of Soundie production with their exhibition practices as codetermining factors in their short-form aesthetics, this chapter examines short media's persistent pairing with small-screen exhibition. Soundies' particular modes of musical representation evidence a pivotal moment in the imaging of popular music for the screen. With their small-screen playback technology and short duration, Soundies on the Panoram organize a popular music viewing experience that emphasizes mood, intimacy, and repeated play while beckoning an era of private and increasingly personalized media consumption. With the relocation of the act of music performance from the expected setting of a performance venue to a range of settings evoking everyday activities and experiences, the changes in Soundies' representational strategies further intersect with broader shifts in 1940s screen viewing, including the rise of domestic-oriented technologies like home movie projectors, record players, and radio and television sets.

Beyond Soundies' emerging juke-film aesthetic of personalized and even domesticated musical shorts, the films also portray an array of racial and ethnic identity performances. Chapter 5 surveys Soundies' representational motifs to grapple with their complex politics of identity. The visualization of popular music in 1940s Soundies expands the scope of film representations by circulating multiple images of diverse identities into diffuse venues like bars, taverns, and restaurants. Soundies' prolific representations of black musicality in particular illuminate the contested identity politics of the war era. Specifically, this chapter focuses on Soundies featuring Dorothy Dandridge, one of Soundies' first burgeoning African American stars. Her films reveal a range of raced identities, including an eroticized primitive dancer, a churchgoer, and even a cowgirl and were marketed for both black and white audiences alike. Through this range of representations, Dandridge's Soundies visualize black musicality through contradictory constructions of racial identity. Treading upon pervasive wartime tensions in articulating and defining an American national identity, Dandridge's performances evince broader racial politics of the 1940s, an era fraught with conflicting and paradoxical attitudes toward African American equality and integration. Soundies' expansive screening sites mobilize these on-screen representations and document a transitional moment in black representation where past stereotypes are brought to the fore and begin to be challenged, oftentimes through highly reflexive and self-conscious performances of racial and ethnic types.

Chapter 6 moves beyond the 1940s and examines the afterlives and relevancies of the Panoram and Soundies as residual media. After the demise of Soundies in 1947, the collection of 1,850 shorts was quickly repackaged for early television programming and for private consumption in the 16mm movie market. The afterlife of the Panoram, however, charts quite a different trajectory, including the repurposing of machines for Times Square peep shows as well as for children's photo booths. This chapter looks to the circulation of the films and the technology beyond the 1940s to consider how both Soundies short-form and small-screen technologies were integrated into midcentury media practices. Despite their failure to sustain as a business entity in the 1940s, the use of Soundies on 1950s television deejay shows and the reboot of automatic film jukeboxes like the Scopitone in the 1960s speaks to ongoing consumer interests in short-form media and the expansion of small-screen culture.

The concluding chapter considers the legacy of Soundies and their screening practices in contemporary screen culture. Soundies' roles in patterning a media landscape of short formats and small-screen placement echoes throughout recent discourse on digital formatting and media portability. With emphasis on both the compressed scale of media content and screen size, contemporary iterations of video jukeboxes from the 1980s through the 2000s reveal that the circulation of musical shorts for small-screen circulation is far from an ephemeral or obsolete practice and is further sustained through the rhetorics of jukebox vending in digital contexts like YouTube and iTunes. This chapter evaluates the shifting scale of music-screen media in both form and format to better understand its development historically while interrogating the consumer-based logics that sustain these assumptions about the circulation of small media commodities.

In their form and circulation, Soundies short musical films and screen practices have played a significant role in constructing popular understandings of contemporary media ubiquity. In an evaluation of current movie culture, *New York Times* film critic A. O. Scott characterizes our media age as that of the screen—not the big screen at the megaplex, but the ubiquitous expansion of screens, both personal and public, throughout our everyday environs.[15] With cell phones, laptops, and a host of handheld mobile media devices, a new screen culture has arrived, or so Scott argues. With this proliferation of multiple screens in smaller formats comes the prominence of the media short—the fragmented, bite-size videos that populate the internet in small doses of spectacle and bursts of entertainment. Although there is a tendency in popular discourse to frame contemporary media practices as the dawn of a new era and something completely different in our viewing habits, small-screen spectacles are no recent anomaly. Our screens may be more prolific, pocket-sized, and portable, but small-screen moving images have populated our everyday spaces well before the iPhone. By foregrounding small-screen technologies, short-film formats, and multiple viewing dynamics, *Soundies* unsettles notions of a saturated, small-screen culture as a recent anomaly or contemporary phenomenon and provides a necessary reorientation to our daily encounters with the screen.

Part I

Small-Screen Encounters and Spatial Practices

1

The Look-Listening Machine

The Panoram Jukebox and New Screen Practices

A Soundie entitled *Frim Fram Sauce* (1945) features a young Nat King Cole sitting alone at a table in a crowded restaurant. As Cole lip-synchs the lyrics to "Frim Fram Sauce," a nonsensical song about ordering food, his gaze falls on a small-screen movie machine placed in the corner of the restaurant. The movie machine, a Panoram, is showing a film of Cole and his trio performing the same song that restaurant Cole is singing. Cole momentarily fixes his attention on the film. In an exchange of shots, the Cole on the screen and the one seated at the café gaze at one another in a moment of surprised and comedic recognition. On the one hand, the projected film of Cole creates a spectacle, a moment of curiosity, as Cole gazes upon his own filmed image. On the other hand, the Panoram machine is underemphasized by its placement in the corner of the restaurant. No one at the restaurant seems to notice the movie machine but Cole himself. The lack of visible interest from the other patrons suggests that the machine is somewhat ordinary, an overlooked fixture in a busy environment, playing atmospheric background music for the crowd with some additional, all-but-unnoticed film accompaniment.

These dual responses of intrigue and familiarity portray certain ambivalences toward the Panoram at the café and suggest broader attitudes concerning the presence of moving-image screens in everyday spaces in the 1940s. The emergence of the Panoram troubles conventional expectations for movie viewing typically associated with theatrical film spectatorship and evidences multiple, and at times conflicting, modes of user engagements with film-screen technologies. As a vending technology, the Panoram initially was marketed for its features of efficiency, automation, and convenience as a media delivery service. As an entertainment machine, it was framed as both a film and music device, as something totally innovative in film projection but also not so different from the more common musical jukebox.[1] In one sense, the Panoram's associations with the jukebox helped naturalize the presence of moving images in new consumer spaces, and yet this positioning also tempered its filmic appeal as a visual spectacle by rendering it into an ambient media device. For example, the varied Panoram viewing habits evidenced in the aforementioned *Frim Fram Sauce* suggest potential constraints in small-screen film viewing in public spaces while also showcasing new possibilities for screen engagement, like watching a film while you wait to place your food order.

This chapter draws upon Panoram promotional materials, industry publications, and Soundies' own representations of Panoram viewing to examine changing attitudes toward the function of moving-image screens in the 1940s. This includes how its producers and manufacturers envisioned the functions and protocols of this new coin-operated amusement machine, its journalistic fanfare in trades like *Billboard* and *Variety* and its initial popular reception. Filmed representations of the Panoram in a handful of Soundies also underscore these discourses surrounding the machine's circulation. They include Spike Jones's *Clink! Clink! Another Drink!* (1942), Al Donahue's *Jumpin' at the Jukebox* (1943), Lawrence Welk's *The Bobby Sox Tune* (1944), Stan Kenton's *Jammin' in the Panoram* (1942), and the aforementioned King Cole Trio's *Frim Fram Sauce* (1945). As reflexive films, these Soundies help imagine how the Panoram may have been used and provide their own historical representations of the Panoram's technological past, including their viewing practices, their physical placement within various venues, and attitudes about film-screen technologies.

Beyond the mechanisms of the Panoram itself, the cultural assumptions that organize the intended usage of the Panoram as a new media technology reveal not just the profit-driven interests of the entertainment industry but shifting cultural assumptions about screen-based media. As Michelle Henning explains, "Those things that are so often identified as changes in media . . . are actually social transformations."[2] Lisa Gitelman similarly defines media technology as "socially realized structures of communication, where structures include both technological forms and their associated protocols."[3] In line with both Gitelman and Henning's claims, the discourses and representations surrounding the circulation of the Panoram provide clear iterations of the machine's intended technological functions alongside the emerging social experiences and engagements with small-screen viewing.

Much of the promotional materials and early reception for the Panoram reveal indeterminate and often contradictory ways for marketing and using this new entertainment machine. Mediating between the ubiquitous music jukebox and the popularity of Hollywood films, the Panoram's promotional discourses often blend and meld their audio and visual platforms, a slipperiness only exacerbated by this technology's presence in various spaces ranging from transit waiting areas to swank nightclubs. At once evidencing its more aural, atmospheric qualities—an "ambient" movie screen that does not need to be watched[4]—Panoram promotional materials and representations concurrently boast its short, moving-image "attractions," to borrow from Tom Gunning, as a new entrainment spectacle.[5] A seemingly paradoxical mode of screen interaction, this dialectic of the ambient attraction pervades the Panoram's brief circulation and indexes a critical negotiation of the role of film-screen technologies into expanding cultural spaces. As Jonathan Sterne explains, "Social forms did not necessarily follow logically from technologies: those connections had to be made. Technologies had to be articulated to institutions and practices to become media."[6] This chapter tends to the "connections" between the Panoram and its cultural uptake to examine how 1940s moving-image screens are articulated to new spaces and practices that include but also exceed film viewing.

Promoting the Panoram

In 1940, Mills Novelty Company, manufacturer of the Panoram and other vending machines, published a promotional booklet for potential Panoram franchise owners entitled *Panoram with Soundies*. Offering a detailed overview of the Panoram's mechanical components, Mills's corporate history, its business partnership with SDC, and Soundies production process, *Panoram* also offers insights into the marketing of the Panoram as a new media technology and the accompanying cultural expectations surrounding it. As would be expected from a self-produced promotional booklet, *Panoram* is enthusiastic about its new product and exuberant in its claims. The booklet's introduction, called "The Changing America," broadly sets the stage for the Panoram's arrival: "The American has no cherished traditions, his worship is only for the new, the more efficient thing—the thing made for today and tomorrow, not for yesterday . . . Into this changing America there now catapults a new amusement device to monopolize millions of American hours of relaxation . . . it is naturally automatic and coin-operated."[7] Within this pitch framing the desire for the new as distinctly American, there also is a sense of a hurried temporality where things must not only be new but also "efficient," where time must be structured, and even leisure activities must be "monopolized" to fit the "ever fast and furious" pace of modern American life. The underlying paradox of efficient leisure becomes the primary need to which the Panoram responds. Little is noted about a desire for more or a new kind of film entertainment but rather for a machine that can deliver a service quickly and automatically. Participating in what Anna McCarthy calls "modernist fantasies of efficiency and mechanization," the new screen technology extends Taylorist discourses of the factory to sites of leisure and consumption.[8]

As *Panoram with Soundies* explains, the Panoram comprises a 16mm rear projector encased in a walnut cabinet that stands more than six and a half feet tall and features mechanisms that allow for the automatic looping of film for repeatable playback. Its 17 × 22½-inch screen displays flashing lights when not in use to attract viewers and a scrolling marquee that lists the song titles and artist names from the particular reel in play. It also boasts an RCA amplifier for controlled sound, an air-conditioning unit to cool the film, and a counter to track usage. Rather than emphasizing the musical films (or justifying why these films should be of a musical variety to begin with), the promotional booklet highlights the Panoram as a technology, a media delivery system providing bursts of efficient entertainment on demand. The booklet primarily defines the films by their short length ("for a period of a few seconds less than three minutes") and somewhat inaccurately asserts, "When one Soundie is through, the next one is ready to play immediately. There is no rewinding at any time—no waiting."[9] For such immediate play to occur, more than one dime would have to be put into the machine in advance. Based on the presumed desire for efficiency, the machine touts quick, mechanized entertainment, attributes that have more to do with the self-looping playback function of the Panoram and little do with its musical films.

These promotional materials frame the Panoram primarily as a new convenience machine and align it with similar vending technologies, while its entertainment function is made secondary. In the back-catalog pages of *Panoram with Soundies*, the other Mills's machines advertised are vending devices that bank on efficient activities of consumption and leisure like gum and candy vending, refrigeration units, ice cream freezers, and coke machines, items expected to be found in break rooms and waiting areas, places where time is often managed and limited.[10] *Panoram with Soundies* foregrounds its status as a vending machine: "Panoram is first, last and always a *coin machine*." Touting the ease of operability, early Panoram marketing emphasized the individual user just popping in a dime and then watching the magic of his or her favorite music to come to life on the screen. Early trade accounts of the Panoram's premiere similarly focus on the user-friendly mechanism of coin operation, which often includes full-length photos of models or celebrities standing alongside the machines with a coin in hand.[11]

The emphasis on the dime for play surely speaks to the potential profitability of the machine for possible owners of Panorams (which cost more than most nickel-in-the-slot devices of the time), but it also targets consumers and their personal interactions with the machine. Notably, the full-length promotional photos of models posed alongside the Panoram provide a sense of the size and proportions of the machine suited for individual or, at most, small group viewing, suggesting the human scale of this new movie viewing technology. *Panoram with Soundies* even features a centerfold poster of the Panoram, lavishly displaying its slick, art-deco cabinetry. Fetishizing the beauty of the machine, the catalog positions the Panoram as a much-desired piece of furniture, an object of beauty comparable to the woman modeling the machine.

Evoking a similar image to these promotional materials, Lawrence Welk's *Bobby Sox Tune*, a Soundie from 1944, also highlights the Panoram as a user-friendly vending machine. Poised around either side of the machine, two teen singers explicitly reference the Panoram and its coin operation in the song's lyrics. The male singer, Bobby Beers, croons, "Hey gents, ten cents! Who's got a dime? Let's have a good time. Be a good sox and slip it into the box . . . ," and the female singer, Jayne Walton, replies, "I start swinging when the Panoram plays." While the song emphasizes the Panoram as a music-delivery technology, the Panoram is ignored as a film technology and even the singers ignore its images. The main purpose of this Soundie is to play music for the dancing crowd, like a jukebox, and no one watches the screen. The film effectively highlights the Panoram as a novelty music machine and not for its films or visual attractions. Rather than emphasizing the visual attractions on the machine itself, *Bobby Sox Tune* focuses on the two singers poised next to the Panoram and the bobbysoxers on the dance floor at the teen hangout. *Bobby Sox Tune* offers a portrait of Panoram usage that has nothing at all to do with film viewing. Rather, *Bobby Sox* centralizes the Panoram's vending delivery and musical function, making its user interactions more akin to the jukebox where people pay to listen to a song and maybe dance along.

This musical-dance function is surprisingly foregrounded throughout early Soundies promotional discourses. In the Soundies film catalog, *Bobby Sox Tune* is promoted "for the jitterbug fans" as a "good band number for dancing or listening," but not necessarily for watching.[12] A photo caption from the Panoram promotional book claims, "When music is played in public, the crowd must dance."[13] Similarly, a *Pittsburgh Courier* article covering the Panoram's premiere party in 1940 explains, "And if you do not look at the pictures . . . you can dance as you do with the jukebox."[14] Rather than trying to compete with or differentiate itself from the more popular jukebox, it rather seeks to align itself with this existing media form and its modes of musical engagement.

Jumpin' at the Jukebox (1943), a Soundie by Al Donahue, features a song about a more common music jukebox, but the Soundie portrays a Panoram-style

FIGURE 3 Teenagers croon alongside the Panoram jukebox in Lawrence Welk's *Bobby Sox Tune* (1944). From Soundies Distributing Corporation of America photographs of the Margaret Herrick Library, Academy of Motion Picture Arts and Sciences.

machine, presenting an interesting technological slippage. Like the other reflexive Soundies, there is a sense of self-promotion, a gimmicky advertisement for the new Panoram technology. Rather than being tucked into an overlooked corner of a bar, here the Panoram takes center stage and literally joins the band. In fact, the presence of the Panoram constitutes the whole gimmick of this Soundie as it is hollowed out with the singer of the band placed inside of it. The film begins with Al Donahue placing a coin into the slot (emphasizing the individual activation of the machine) while the singer Ellen Connor appears inside the box and begins singing. Throughout the film, Al Donahue interacts with Connor. As she bobs her head and tries to dance within the confines of the faux Panoram, her hands clutch the edge of the screen, breaking the wall between supposed filmed and live performance, to the point that you expect her to emerge from the Panoram, but this never happens. She remains encased in the Panoram machine, framed as a screen commodity.[15]

In addition to its odd framing of gender relations as an economic exchange, this Soundie removes the Panoram from its expected viewing context, a leisure space where it supposedly provides a substitute for live musical performance. *Jumpin'* takes this a step further by depicting a literal stand-in performer for the filmed musician, implying that such jukebox technologies are as good as the real thing, since they bring the performers right to you. However, *Jumpin's* attempt to map jukebox interactions onto the Panoram is a bit uneasy. Not only is their Panoram prop not an actual Panoram (it's actually a Phonovision, a less successful, competing brand), it sidesteps its filmic difference by removing the screen image from the setup altogether, as if it just doesn't know what to do with its visual component. These multiple layers of substitution in depicting the Panoram—a live performer instead of the filmed screen image, the bandstand for the space of a bar or restaurant, and the Panoram rather than a jukebox, as the song indicates—illustrates an uncertainty in defining the machine's identity, particularly its visual components, even while trying to promote the machine itself.

Although these visual representations and early promotional materials foreground the Panoram first and foremost as a coin-operated music machine and its film function as secondary, the Panoram also quite self-consciously positions itself in direct relation to the Hollywood film industry. In a section entitled "Two Great Industries Unite," *Panoram with Soundies* reminds the reader that both "the coin-operated business and the movie business started as infant industries in the same family!" with the earliest movie projectors being placed in penny arcades. Having gone their separate paths, these "long-separated brothers, unite once more each giving to the other a new vitalization, excitement and appeal!"[16] Intermingling a shared past with claims of technical innovation and novelty, such discourses call attention to their own uneven historicity, evidencing, as Charles Acland describes, "the way the dynamics of culture bump along unevenly, dragging the familiar into novel contexts."[17] This same dynamic of novelty colliding with obsolescence (or the emerging with the residual) within technological discourses also appears in an early *Billboard Magazine* article written by Soundies producer Jack Barry. Barry echoes this shared history of the film and coin-machine industries while touting the technological novelty of Soundies on the Panoram: "In a way, history is repeating itself . . . for the pioneers of the motion picture industry . . . all came from the coin machine industry. They were arcade operators back in the day of the mutoscope which was the pioneer coin-operated movie."[18] He quickly follows this history lesson by concluding that the Panoram is "blazing a new trail" and "it will continue to make giant strides in the years ahead." By emphasizing these historical continuities, these discourses create an unsteady balancing act between technological novelty and eventual media obsolescence.

In addition to mapping the close ties between the coin machine and the film industry, these promotional materials align themselves with the expansion of cinema culture, an association that disappears soon after the Panoram begins to circulate. Jimmy Roosevelt,[19] the head of Soundies production, claims that Panoram machines would not take money away from movie theaters but rather make "patrons of taverns motion picture–conscious."[20] Roosevelt, as the celebrity spokesperson for Soundies and the Mills Panoram, is clear to nullify any claims that Soundies will pose a competitive threat to Hollywood but rather will aid in the spread of the "art of cinema" by bringing film into a variety of new spaces.[21] Such accounts indicate a zeal toward the proliferation of film images, in this case as art, and for expanding film viewing beyond the theater.

The Ambient Attraction

Early marketing efforts repeatedly align Panoram Soundies with Hollywood fare while making them distinct enough to warrant new practices in film viewing. *Panoram with Soundies* distinguishes the Soundie film from the "regular movie" and even the "fifteen-minute movie short which you have seen in your theatre." Unlike theatrical films "created with the intention of being seen only once," it claims, "Soundies must be so good, so rich in fast and concentrated action . . . that the same persons may want to see the very film fifty or more times!"[22] Soundies are targeted as repeated-play media intended for multiple rounds of viewing. Such accounts also indicate certain expectations for the machine's usage, like repeated viewings, and begin to define expectations for their patterns of exhibition. For example, the translucent Panoram screen "gives faithful reproduction of color and contrast under the most unfavorable light conditions. It is unaffected by atmospheric conditions . . . It is especially made to furnish a sharp, brilliant picture viewed from any angle." Additionally, its RCA amplifier features separate controls for high- and low-frequency tones "to match the acoustic conditions in any location," and the cabinet is designed "to allow the screen to be viewed from the widest angle possible" and to not "distract the attention of the audiences while viewing picture." From such technical descriptions, the proposed conditions of Panoram exhibition may seem vague, and, from a marketing perspective, probably intentionally so. What can be inferred from these descriptions is that the Panoram was framed as an adaptable technology for multiple venues with varying conditions in terms of lighting and sound. Although the marketing suggests small group viewings, rather than just an individual, the Panoram is set in direct contrast to the controlled screening environments of movie theaters with fixed seating, dark lighting, and hidden projection booths. In other words, even in places full of distractions, the Panoram promises to be an amenable attraction.

Such clues to emerging Panoram viewing conditions are also noted by Soundies film producer Jack Barry. Although Barry is concerned with how best to produce an effective musical film, he indicates how the conditions of viewing established by the Panoram's design shape his aesthetic choices in making Soundies. He states, "We have had to tailor our productions with the fact in mind that our customers don't give the screen the prolonged concentration they give the theater screen."[23] While acknowledging the possibilities for viewer distraction, Barry also describes Panoram viewing conditions, with viewers "within 25 feet of the screen at all times—closer than they ever are to the movie screen," as potentially having a greater effect on viewers, if the films are shot accordingly. The Panoram screen's closeness to the viewer, Barry suggests, calls for a greater intimacy in the treatment of the filmed subject, including a reliance on close-up shots of performers.[24] Such claims of intimacy associated with screen proximity would seem to forego the experience of a more ambient, or distracted, viewing, but both modes of spectatorship (distraction and attraction) are introduced as possibilities.

Often straddling the line between ambient media and cinematic attraction,[25] these early accounts of Panoram viewing suggest that Soundies catered to both the transient crowd as well as the ogling, individual spectator. For example, an account of the Panoram premier in Los Angeles claimed that the Panoram would provide a "novelty in brevity entertainment . . . appealing to the public susceptible to its attractions."[26] An anecdotal account from former television personality Joe Franklin cites the spectacle and novelty of the Panoram, with people waiting in line to see a Soundie or watching the Panoram up close, totally transfixed by its images, even whistling at women on the screen. Franklin claims that, with his nose up to the screen, he "got hooked . . . became an addict."[27] Panoram viewing, as Franklin's account reveals, when viewed intimately is an intense, affective experience, especially, it seems, for those wanting to sexualize the cinematic spectacle.

Functioning as attractions, Soundies surely elicited some excitable reactions from audiences, particularly in their infancy, but such anecdotes fail to capture fully the mundane functions and attributes of Panoram exhibition. For example, an article in the *Pittsburgh Courier* compares the Panoram to "regular juke boxes with a two foot screen" that "remind(s) you of television [because it] . . . can be viewed in a lighted room."[28] This comparison to both the jukebox and the early television frame the Panoram as a not-so-novel novelty and perhaps less than spectacular, especially when situated within well-lit, crowded viewing conditions. Complicating neat and tidy models of film spectatorship, Panoram discourses further provide conflicting modes of screen engagement depending on locale.[29] Another early account indicates less-than-attentive engagements from urban crowds well accustomed to live band performances: "In New York, for instance, bandmen think . . . that after one or two looks at the machines in operation few people will bother to divert their attention to concentrate on watching a band they most likely have seen in person many times," but the Panoram will provide more of an "appeal" to "hinterlanders where bands in person are a rarity."[30] Acknowledging differentiated audiences, such discourses rooted in geographic contexts hint at more complex models for imagining nontheatrical screening practices. In considering how geography, in this case the "rusticity" of the "hinterlanders," might shape interactions with the Panoram, a more varied and nuanced portrait of an expanding screen culture emerges.[31]

Further discourses account for Panoram exhibition as a hybrid practice, blending both their ambient and attraction functions as unified modes of consumption. A *Billboard* account from 1944, three years after the Panoram's launch, entitled "The Future of Juke Box Pictures," describes Panoram users involved in a dual activity of "look-listening," an auditory qualification seldom noted in more traditional accounts of film spectatorship.[32] The article claims that the Panoram is "a more specific type of musical service, suitable in locations where the movies can be seen and enjoyed" such as in "the smaller night club and in the high-grade restaurant."[33] Similarly, an article in *Variety* refers to the Panoram as a "Sight and Sound" jukebox,[34] and the *Pittsburgh Courier* calls Soundies "movie-music" (rather than musical movies) "which allows one to both hear and see his favorite group of entertainers."[35] Constructing the Panoram equally as an image and a sound technology, these hyphenated classifications of the Soundie as "movie-music" and the Panoram as a "look-listening" device mediate the critical tension in the Panoram's ambient presence with the Soundies visual screen attractions, acknowledging the Panoram's multimedia functions and various levels of user engagements.

Vividly depicting the Panoram's "look-listening" functions, the Soundie *Clink! Clink! Another Drink!* (1942) features a lively, drunken group involved in a tavern sing-along. Aside from inebriation,[36] the Soundie thematizes music-making, often from unlikely sources like a barmaid lip-synching to the sounds of a horn and the bartender playing percussion on the glasses. These misplaced sonic cues, however, are blended with actual sources of music, such as the presence of the banjo and the trombone players and, of course, the Panoram machine. The joke of music coming from unlikely sources is both aural and visual. In her analysis of the sound and image dynamics in Soundies, Amy Herzog claims that the films are "impossible embodiments" in their attempts to visualize the always-abstract quality of music in their representations. Further, she argues that sound, as opposed to image, dictates the logics of Soundies visual representation.[37]

Herzog locates this disconnect solely within the films themselves; however, these same tensions are evident in the broader discursive tensions surrounding the various modes of Panoram engagement. During the song's chorus, the camera zooms in on a Panoram and then flashes the words to the song on the Panoram screen, suggesting a group sing-along, much like the one already in progress in the film. Although this Soundie suggests the Panoram operates as a sing-along device, it fails to show anyone actually operating it, standing near it, or even watching it. The crowd in *Clink! Clink!* is involved in its musical revelry and hardly seems to heed the promptings on the Panoram screen. Its only function in the scene then is to address the potential viewer of the actual Soundie, presumably the individual who dropped a dime into the machine. This particular representation of the Panoram suggests that Soundies can provide a more collective musical experience, and yet the film features ample sight gags and slapstick to attract more interested viewers. This Soundie thus treads upon the very tension between looking and listening—it seems to say, "Hey! Look at me!" in the address of an attraction but in the same breath, "join your friends in song and dance." In addition, the Panoram screen within this Soundie provides no real visual intrigue, just words on a screen. With its representations of both spectacular and ambient modes of user engagement, *Clink! Clink!* mutually presents both responses to the Panoram as a new screen presence.

These hybrid constructions in Panoram practices even materialize in attempts to merge Panoram technology with the phonograph. A *Billboard* article explains, "Born of the necessity of eliminating the confusion that occurred in some locations where both a movie and a music box were placed side by side and at times played simultaneously," a "hybrid" was developed where one nickel played the phonograph and two the Panoram.[38] Some combinations even feature electric signs to indicate when records are playing so that patrons wouldn't think "the light mechanism of the Panoram was out of order when they heard the music but didn't see the picture." Such accounts of repurposing the technology to fit user protocols or to cater to spatial limitations speak not only to industrial resourcefulness on behalf of the machine operators but to the slipperiness in defining the Panoram as both a music and a film machine.

The often evasive and uncertain positioning of the Panoram as a new media technology is perhaps most apparent in a Soundie entitled *Jammin' in the Panoram* (1942), a film where the Panoram is only a titular presence. *Jammin' in the Panoram* tells the story of Stan Kenton and his band's rise to fame by traversing the spaces of a small nightclub to a barbershop where the crowd listens to their music on the radio and eventually to New York where the band records a hit album. Although *Jammin'* depicts music in the very act of circulation and highlights several places where recorded music would be received, the film never shows Kenton "in" or even near a Panoram, as the song title indicates, nor is the Panoram mentioned in the lyrics of the song. The inclusion of Panoram in the title supposedly refers to the film's own viewing apparatus, but *Jammin*'s failure to depict the Panoram in music or image should seem an odd omission. Appropriate to the machine's brief history and quick demise, the Panoram becomes a present absence in this film. Similar to the

Panoram's inadvertent technological slippage in the Soundie *Jumpin' at the Jukebox*, potential representations of the Panoram are elided, even in their own promotional discourse.

With representations of the Panoram often exposing the machine's categorical slipperiness—questioning whether it is a film or music device, how should it best be utilized (individually or collectively), and how it should be viewed (or not viewed), early Panoram discourse surely suggests some potential shortcomings and opacity in its early marketing efforts. With its technological status shifting between convenience and entertainment, attraction and being overlooked, the discursive fragments that shape the Panoram construct a complicated and often contradictory set of user practices. While such contradictions may predict the Panoram's eventual demise as a novelty technology, these tensions also opened the possibilities for new kinds of screen encounters where the moving image becomes one among many possibilities for the site-specific moving-image screen.

Although a vast body of film scholarship addresses technological components of film production from an industrial standpoint,[39] only recently have media histories engaged with the technological dynamics of film projectors and screens to highlight the cultural import of their technological practices.[40] Media histories oriented around film-screen technologies ask what media technologies can reveal about particular moments of film viewing, including the physical conditions of viewing and particular kinds of screen interactions the machine supports, and how its technological protocols help express and maintain cultural values. As a music-film technology, the Panoram, whose status—even during its heyday—was at best marginally popular is not a mere historical curiosity but pivotal in understanding changes in 1940s screen culture. Even with its short circulation, the Panoram evidences changes in how people interacted with the increasing presence of media playback technologies.

The Panoram's diverse and contested uses, especially given the expanding use of 16mm moving-image projectors throughout the 1940s in both public and private capacities, reveal not just an increase in the popularity of film-viewing technologies but also, as Haidee Wasson posits, "a settling common sense about the place of media and machines in cultural life."[41] Perhaps most vital then to the Panoram's emergence and initial marketing is its status as a machine and not its ties to specific media content. By modernizing antiquated practices in individual film viewing—like the turn-of-the-century Kinetoscope and refiguring moving-image viewing into mechanized vending—the Panoram renders the film screen a small, consumer-oriented interface. Although the movie theater is also a site for economic exchange, it is indirect and, unlike the Panoram, does not organize media viewing as an immediate and automatic point-of-purchase transaction.

This shift to film screens as vending machines certainly mechanizes entertainment by eliminating the need for a film projectionist, but this change is not only technological. The Panoram's consumer-oriented protocols presaged new relationships with media as discrete objects, where a film exists as a singular, contained commodity available at the viewer's discretion. These changes in how consumers (and not just viewers) approach a screen technology reshape expectations for more directed and controlled media interactions. Though circulating sixty years prior to on-demand viewing technologies, the Panoram's automation of film viewing and more precise film selection evidence consumer desires for individualized and controlled screen experiences well before the arrival of digital culture or even playback technologies like the VCR.

Additionally, these emerging attitudes toward the film screen as a vending machine destabilize conventional modes and expectations for theatrical film exhibition. With the screen positioned at the site of consumer exchange, the Panoram expands film viewing from a collective experience to an individualized transaction. As such, the viewer's expectations for media engagement are patterned around variable conditions that exceed sustained viewing of a feature-length film. The Panoram and the short duration of Soundies help organize media encounters that are both brief and intermittent, repackaging entertainment and leisure as efficient consumption while also integrating the act of film viewing into everyday places and activities, something that can be experienced wherever and whenever.

Part of these new media rhythms and increased consumer control of media includes repeated playback and a reliance on recorded media. As the early reviews of the Panoram often indicate, Soundies offered another iteration, or a visual extension, of the record player and the jukebox. The tensions that emerge around the Panoram's initial reception in the 1940s were not so different from the ongoing debates about the role of recorded music and live musicianship throughout the 1930s. Although national radio networks largely resisted relying on records for programming until 1948, record distribution thrived in the jukebox trade. Panoram Soundies were very much participant in these larger trends of recorded media distribution and dispersion that were based on emerging consumer-oriented models of individual selection and repetition. Adopting the logics of musical vending to the moving image, the SDC capitalized on the growing interest in multiple encounters with media, both music and film, as repeated-play consumer objects.

This is not to suggest that people were experiencing their media with greater intensity of engagement just because they could play the films continuously. In fact, as evidenced by both the promotional materials and Soundies' own representations of the Panoram in action, film viewing was often secondary to the screen's more ambient musical function. Rather, this new screen presence suggests diverse modes of multimedia engagement, where the user-oriented screen makes available both film and music as indistinct formats and media. As the previous accounts of the Panoram as a "look-listening" device have illustrated, the Panoram could provide a moving-image "attraction," but, more often than not, accounts of its reception indicate that its repeated play of music-images was overlooked.

The Panoram's hybrid constructions, multiple modes of media "spectatorship," small-screen viewings, and automatic, repeatable playback surely resonate with our contemporary engagements with screen technologies where music and image platforms overlap seamlessly. The Panoram, as a new media vending machine, may have failed in becoming as ubiquitous as the jukebox or television, but its design and user-oriented protocols were participant in cultivating new expectations for media screens and their subsequent integration into our daily activities. However, this technology and the many ways it was employed did not exist in a vacuum. The significances of technology are contingent on and exist alongside multiple codetermining factors, including the social, industrial, and aesthetic. The Panoram's dynamics were shaped by the kinds of spaces in which it circulated, the people who may have encountered the machine within those spaces, the films they may have played, and the social experiences and activities that organized the Panoram's reception within these new screening sites. The following chapter examines these spatial dynamics of the Panoram at its screening sites to situate the machine's uptake within specific locales and cultural practices.

2

The Sites of Soundies

The Dynamics of Space and Screen

A 1944 article from *Billboard* describes Panoram operator M. K. Harner setting up the Panoram machine for his tavern patrons: "Busily engaged in pushing the machine around to get it in the right spot and change position, the watching audience and Harner himself were startled when the machine started off with the reel titled *Move It Over* [1943], singularly apropos of his own exertions."[1] This account surely provided amusing anecdotal fodder for coin-machine operators, especially those who regularly dealt with the cumbersome Panoram cabinetry (about the size of a refrigerator), but the punch line—the Soundie telling the operator to "move it over," however jokingly—constructs a connection between screen content and its viewing site, where film representations interact with their surroundings.

Relations between screen and space are not always this mimetic in accounts of Soundies exhibition practices, but even anecdotal mentions like this reveal the ways that film screens in everyday spaces were imagined to function in the 1940s. Although constitutive of its own unique practices of music playback and film exhibition, Panoram Soundies inform a broader understanding of expanded screen practices during the 1940s, from film exhibitions in schools on highly adaptable and portable 16mm equipment to the rapidly expanding home projector market and, of course, the soon-to-be-ubiquitous television screen.[2] As Haidee Wasson's analysis of the multiple small-screen expositions

FIGURE 4 *Move It Over* (1943) puts song and sex appeal on tour in support of the war effort. From Soundies Distributing Corporation of America photographs of the Margaret Herrick Library, Academy of Motion Picture Arts and Sciences.

(of both film and television) at the 1939 World's Fair shows, the profuse presence of these extratheatrical cinema technologies signals "a paradigmatic shift in film culture, inserting cinema into an important history of mobility and small-scale moving-image display that served an increasingly integral everyday role throughout the interwar period and beyond."[3]

Because of their circulation in everyday locales, including bowling alleys, factory lounges, nightclubs, and train stations, the presence of Soundies on the Panoram jukebox screen poses significant questions about the relationship between screen media and their consequent spaces of exhibition. Their varied locales foreground the often messy dynamics of "media space" in which, according to Anna McCarthy and Nick Couldry, "both the kinds of spaces created by media and the effects that existing spatial practices have on media forms as they materialize in everyday life" can best be explored.[4] Working within the dialectical interchange between space and screen and highlighting what Henri Lefebvre refers to as the "social character of space"—space that is coproduced by institutional planning and by its various users in lived practice—the following accounts of Soundies screening sites examine the material conditions and specific localities of their screen practices.[5]

The spaces for Soundie viewing on the Panoram most often mentioned in popular trade and journalistic accounts are sites of leisure (e.g., restaurants, taverns, and nightclubs), where the small screen caters to more intimate café settings; sites of temporary transit (e.g., train stations and waiting rooms), where the screen provides momentary diversion for people on the go; work sites (e.g., factories and government buildings), where the screen both entertains and motivates the wartime worker; and special-events sites (e.g., war-bond rallies and recruitment sites), where the screen provides an official rally cry for civic-minded viewers. In addition to fragmentary mentions of their exhibition found in popular trade magazines like *Billboard*, Soundies construct their own spatial logics and provide important insights into small-screen discourses of this era. Not just film texts but also dynamic vestiges of their exhibition experiences, Soundies mediate spaces and organize particular viewing modes and social formations. Indexing their exhibition spaces and practices, Soundies would act as "agent(s) in a place's construction," organizing users' experiences and relations to space, whereby, as Anna McCarthy puts it, "the context of the screen greatly determined the effects of the images it displayed."[6] Similar to McCarthy's accounts of television screens in various spaces (taverns, airports, and shopping malls) in *Ambient Television*, the kinds of meanings that Soundies may have generated because, at least in part, of their unique locales is central to examining the cultural shift to small-screen practices.

The ratio between Soundies on-screen spaces and their exhibition sites was never exclusively one-to-one. As Soundies were distributed on reels containing eight different films, each reel could depict several different places and settings (e.g., a street scene, a nightclub, a farm scene, a café) and even a single film could depict a variety of settings. For instance, *Ja-Da* (1942) a Soundie featuring Linda Keene, is a nonsensical song about the transformative power of music featuring the repeating lyric, "Ja-da / ja-da / jing jing jing / That's a funny bit of melody / it's so soothing and appealing to me." The song content is nonspecific to place; it does not presuppose or suggest a possible setting. Moving through three scenes, the Soundie opens at a college graduation ceremony with the band adorned in caps and gowns and students dancing, then shifts to a formal piano concert where the jazzy music surprises the classical music patrons, and ends in an operating room where the presence of music resuscitates the patient undergoing surgery. Each musical scenario speaks to different musical functions ranging from celebration to therapy. By traversing through these locales, *Ja-Da* aptly illustrates the variance of media reception to spatial context and how both location and people can inform each other in articulating the experiences of media. As a large number of Soundies are set in similar spaces of leisure—like restaurants, nightclubs, and arcades, for example—these spaces not only provide a context for their musicality but they also suggest new, viable spaces where people can engage with media. With their representations often correlating to their possible screening spaces, like a tavern Soundie being viewed in a similar setting, the Soundie's screen often is thematically integrated into these various locales and acts as an extension of its screening environs.

Since the years of Soundies and Panoram circulation encompass the entirety of the United States' involvement in World War II (1941–1945), the brief Soundies enterprise constitutes, albeit inadvertently, a wartime, home-front screen practice.[7] While evidence of Soundie exhibition practices incorporate some of the more iconic images of World War II, like accounts of homecoming soldiers arriving in New York, they also point to more mundane viewing spaces and screening practices. Soundie exhibition dynamics at once reveal a culture of participatory patriotism and wartime productivity as well as a sense of limbo and unease—a cultural moment Vivian Sobchack calls "lounge time," where people were waiting, biding their time in transitory public spaces, and

FIGURE 5 Opening with a band playing music in a college quad, *Ja-Da* (1942) integrates music into everyday places. From Soundies Distributing Corporation of America photographs of the Margaret Herrick Library, Academy of Motion Picture Arts and Sciences.

uneasily anticipating a future where they could resume a semblance of the everyday.[8] Soundies echoed these experiences of "lounge time" by providing small doses of entertainment to uncertain audiences on the home front, while their exhibition practices helped integrate small screens into new routines and practices.

Screens at the Table: Sites of Leisure and Consumption

A *New York Post* editorial from February 20, 1940, predicts that the Panoram will cause a "revolution in the atmosphere of diners, bars, bus terminals, roadhouses, and hamburger stands of the nation" by supplanting the "institution" of the jukebox with a movie machine that allows you to not just hear your favorite band but see it as well.[9] Of course, this prediction proved to be erroneous; the jukebox remained the iconic symbol of American roadside amusement, and the Panoram became a quickly rendered obsolescent media technology. What should be noted in this account, though, is the very idea, the possibility, that a new screen presence could alter the landscape so dramatically—even to bring a "revolution" in "atmosphere" to such ubiquitous sites as the hamburger stand. Some motion picture exhibitors who feared the competition of proliferating nontheatrical film attractions also reacted to Soundies in commercial spaces with consternation.[10] As discussed in the prior chapter, popular accounts of the Panoram often managed these tensions over its new screen presence by emphasizing its more ambient functions as a musical playback technology.

Trade publications indicate that Soundies were "most successful in the smaller night club and in the high-grade restaurant," suggesting spatial intimacy at their exhibition sites.[11] Within the spaces of smaller nightclubs and cafés, Soundies could provide a virtual floorshow, either as a supplement to actual live performances or as filler entertainment for nights without in-house entertainment. Although a few exhibition accounts claim the Panoram was used within floor shows themselves, wheeled onto stages previewing coming attractions, most accounts suggest they were placed in smaller, enclosed spaces like lobby areas, adjoining rooms, or the far corners of bars.[12] With Panoram screens functioning as filmic floorshows in the smaller spaces of a performance venue, nightclub attendees could experience big-band performances in an appropriate performance context, where people would dance in front of the screen, much like before a bandstand. One source suggests that such virtual performances would prove popular outside of major cities, where live band performances were less frequent.[13] Like the jukebox, Soundies in rural areas would not just supplement live entertainment but provide a main attraction.

Early Soundies often catered to class-based assumptions about Soundie exhibition spaces with films featuring either classical, orchestral arrangements or big swing bands at black-tie venues. The bandstand Soundie, then, could provide an extension of the performance context, wherein the films of musicians on bandstands were appropriate and even functional to their screen setting. Within such a club setting, it would be fitting to see a Soundie like Will Bradley's bandstand film *When You and I Were Young, Maggie* (1944). Like most bandstand Soundies, *When You and I Were Young* is a performance-oriented Soundie that primarily emphasizes the musicians. Instead of using chorus girls or dancers for an added element of visual appeal, this Soundie includes a (poorly executed) comedic twist, a man in the audience trying to cut through a tough piece of meat. Rather than providing shots from the audience's point of view, the cutaways frame the seated man in a close-up, making his meal as much of an attraction as the band's performance. By simultaneously portraying musical entertainment and dining activities, the film forges these activities of leisurely consumption in which the bandstand has to compete with the man distractedly sawing through a rubbery piece of meat. This example is not unique. Rather than just showing the performance, most nightclub Soundies include cutaway shots of audience members drinking and eating both to emphasize the setting and to suggest a particular mode of musical consumption. These various depictions of on-screen consumption could easily extend to sites of Soundie exhibition where people watching this Soundie also might be enjoying a meal, thereby integrating Soundie viewing as an appropriate activity in such a venue.

Although the performance-oriented big-band Soundies set in nightclubs remained popular throughout Soundies' seven-year circulation on the Panoram, many Soundies, particularly by early 1942, are staged on sets evoking smaller-scale, more intimate venues like restaurants and taverns.[14] These locales provide fitting backdrops for many novelty musical films involving themes of drinking and eating. Several of these restaurant Soundies depict the musicians and performers as customers. The Soundie *Frankie and Johnny* (1942), for instance, stages the band around a small checker-tableclothed table in a café. Although food and drink are in front of them, the band casually plays their instruments instead. This insertion of musical performance into restaurant spaces is developed further in Soundies that thematically integrate food. *One Meatball* (1945), a popular vaudeville-era song, features a cashier-chanteuse (Patti Clayton) narrating the story of a poor man who can afford to order only one meatball from the menu. The screen action consists of close-ups of the cashier singing the song in direct address to the camera and shots of the hungry customer, seated at a table, and a disgruntled waiter. The general mood of the Soundie is sparse, in both film form and in its musical content. With limited camera movement and stationary characters, the pacing is slow and atmospheric as it recounts a simple tale of a "little" hungry man who is humiliated when he "gets no bread" with his one meatball. This downbeat theme of

FIGURE 6 *When You and I Were Young, Maggie* (1944) features a nightclub audience seated at tables around a conventional bandstand setup. From Soundies Distributing Corporation of America photographs of the Margaret Herrick Library, Academy of Motion Picture Arts and Sciences.

hunger and depravity, echoed in other restaurant-themed Soundies like the King Cole Trio's *Frim Fram Sauce* (William Forest Crouch, 1945), pairs appropriately with the restrained atmosphere of restricted wartime consumption.

This sparse and pared-down musical film exemplifies a shift in Soundie representations over their first few years of production, a cultivated juke-film aesthetic that is discussed more fully in chapter 4. As Soundies producer-director Jack Barry explains, Soundies are treated best by "close-up camera treatment . . . elaborate settings for long shots and intricate routines are just as much out of place as they would be in the intimate night club, where the accent must be on intimate delivery."[15] The "intimate" shooting style makes Soundies conducive to small-screen reception dynamics, a lesson quickly learned by soon-to-be early television producers who relied on Soundies as early programming filler.[16] Barry's description further suggests that this trend in Soundies representations also correlates to the migration of Panoram screens from larger performance venues to venues better suited for small screens like ice cream parlors, cafés, and roadside restaurants.[17] With early reviews of Soundie exhibitions claiming that "one must leave a table or a bar to crowd around the miniature screen, and this is figured to hurt drink sales, etc.," Soundies such as *One Meatball* redress this potential problem of the disconnect between film and site by providing restaurant-themed entertainment where, like the man in the film, there is no need to leave the table to get the gist of the film.[18]

Just Passing Through: The Tourist and the Transient Screen

Among the usual list of potential Soundie screening sites alluded to in trade magazines, train and bus stations figure prominently. One source indicates that "locations catering to transients have also proven popular and profitable."[19] A firsthand account from band conductor Van Alexander, who made four Soundies in 1942, tells of watching a Panoram while riding on the Staten Island Ferry, and further evidence indicates that Panorams were at large train stations or in the vicinity of transit sites.[20] In *Pacific Victory, 1945*, military historian Joseph Driscoll provides a rare, descriptive account of one such Soundie's exhibition site: "In a cheap waterfront saloon along San Francisco's picturesque Embarcadero, directly opposite the Southern Pacific Ferry Station, I saw a sign over the bar where longshoremen and their ladies were wolfing turkey sandwiches and guzzling straight shots of rye: JIMMIE ROOSEVELT'S/ SOUNDIES UPSTAIRS."[21] This description situates the space for Soundie viewing on the waterfront and—though not on the actual ferry but across from the ferry station—at a location catering to those in transit, a place for quick entertainment and diversion for the transient passenger or dock worker. In contrast to the more formal nightclub as screening venue, where the film may have provided a virtual floorshow, this depiction of Soundie exhibition is couched in a very casual, unrestrained atmosphere of consumption, where even mundane activities as eating and drinking are framed as animalistic ("wolfing" and "guzzling"). With the screen's further removal to the upstairs of the bar, the account decentralizes Soundie viewing as a marginal activity in an already fringe locale. Driscoll's account of Soundie exhibition is significant in that he does not watch or even mention the specific films. Although he admits that he "didn't bother to climb the creaking stairs" to actually see Soundies, Driscoll acknowledges their atmospheric presence, inserting the small film screen into the cultural landscape of wartime America.[22] Driscoll also mentions other locations of the machines, like "honky-tonks from Alaska to Arizona," giving a sense of the breadth of Panoram and Soundie franchises in the early 1940s.[23]

One can only speculate which Soundies, if any, were being screened in the upstairs of the Embarcadero tavern, but several Soundies portray comparable transient waterfront sites. For example, *He's a Latin from Staten Island* (1941), *Ferry-Boat Serenade* (1941), and *The Man on the Ferry* (1943) are set on ferries and piers, while many other Soundies portray train stations and travel, showcasing people on the move or "on the town." Like the nightclub or café

Soundie discussed previously, these ferry films do not offer explicit representations of site-based Soundie viewing; rather, they suggest possible viewing dynamics at these exhibition sites. Featuring passengers strolling on deck, viewing the passing skyline, these filmed ferry settings are lively and crowded. *The Man on the Ferry* (1943) by the Liberty Quartette stages a comic premise of an "amateur Casanova" as the captain of the Hoboken Ferry.[24] A *Billboard* review of *Ferry-Boat Serenade* (1941) by Wini Shaw, George Steiner, and his orchestra jokes, "You don't have to get out the crystal ball to guess what the background is."[25]

In *He's a Latin from Staten Island* (1941) by Gus Van, Ray Bloch, and his orchestra, a young Ricardo Montalbán plays the role of a wandering Casanova/musician.[26] Montalbán ambles across the deck, playing his guitar as he attempts to woo a woman who is with another man. Like the other ferry films, *Latin* features musicians entertaining passengers, some of whom even dance. The ferry setting of *Latin*, as a temporary and mobile site of leisure and transit, portrays a casual party ambiance, where men overtly ogle woman and, if the mood strikes, grab and kiss them. Employing an obvious stereotype

FIGURE 7 *Ferry-Boat Serenade*'s (1941) cityscape backdrop provides the illusion of a ferry transit. From Soundies Distributing Corporation of America photographs of the Margaret Herrick Library, Academy of Motion Picture Arts and Sciences.

FIGURE 8 *Man on the Ferry* (1943) stars a captain romancing his passengers on the Hoboken Ferry. From Soundies Distributing Corporation of America photographs of the Margaret Herrick Library, Academy of Motion Picture Arts and Sciences.

in its representation of the "Latin Lover," the short film conveys a socially loose atmosphere, where identity is playful and performative. Drawing upon similar tropes of caricatured ethnicity so rampant in the performance numbers of backstage Hollywood musicals but without the larger motivating framework of a feature-length film, Soundies' use of common ethnic types provides a space that foregrounds identity play without narrative containment. As the song's lyrics suggest, "He wasn't born Ricardo Manuelo Gomez / He got it from the name of a cigar," Montalbán's Casanova figure is touted as mere fabrication, an act of identity tourism sanctioned by the film's lax social space of the ferry and the structure of the musical short.

When situating these representations within Soundies' possible sites of exhibition like the upstairs of a bar by the ferry, such onscreen constructions of both spatial and identity mobility complement the transient atmosphere of their exhibition spaces, an environment where screen consumption fuses with identity play at the fringes of "respectable" social space.[27] With wartime conditions allowing for more fluidity within traditional racial, class, and gender roles, a relaxed and more integrationist social atmosphere emerges in these makeshift spaces, which are further promoted by the presence of popular media like swing music. As historian David Stowe argues, swing, the defining form of popular culture throughout the war (and the music and dance genre featured most heavily in Soundies), is a locus where "the racial and class boundaries of brutally segregated 1930s America were most permeable, for both musicians and their audiences."[28] Like Stowe, Adam Knee claims that swing culture often enacted a "cultural inclusiveness"—"Swing allowed occasion for cross-racial cultural and social interaction on a variety of levels, while also standing as a symbol for . . . American ideals of democracy and opportunity."[29] Soundies and their sites of exhibition could provide such spaces where the integrationist ideals of swing music and culture are at once made visible on the screen and enacted at the exhibition sites while also supporting a spirit of wartime unity and patriotism.

It is fitting then that Driscoll's rare firsthand account of a Soundie exhibition site is a soldier's memoir of a transit locale. The figure of the traveling soldier-as-tourist circulated widely in war-era discourses, journalistic and theatrical alike, including the popular 1944 Broadway musical and famous MGM film *On the Town* (Stanley Donen and Gene Kelly, 1949). Similarly, though less whitewashed, a 1943 *Life* magazine wartime feature on the city of Los Angeles offers an apt description of the soldier on leave: "These uniformed 'tourists' spend quite a bit of money in the city, and almost always have a good time." They "sample the pleasures of Main Street" with "bars, burlesques, cheap movie houses, 'Latin American' dance halls, tattoo parlors, hillbilly bands, and plain ordinary dives for all races."[30] This hodgepodge description of various attractions and amusements for the soldier-tourist could just as well be a description of a Soundies film reel with its various ethnic codings and appeals to musical variety. All of these spaces also constitute viable sites for a Panoram machine. To further this connection between touring soldiers and Soundies, several Soundies films circulated similar images of the traveling soldier, such as *Heaven Help a Sailor* (1941) or *Russian Peasant Dance* (1945), which stages sailors looking at women through binoculars from the back of their boat.[31] The discourses that frame these temporary sites as liminal spaces, featuring brief encounters with various ethnicities (like those in Latin dance halls) and less reputable cultural spaces (tattoo parlors and dives), indicate particular ways that Soundies screen presences could have participated in their sites of consumption, perpetuating fantasies of mobility for the male viewer—or at least this particular version of the white soldier. For African American soldiers or female factory workers, these screen dynamics provided a more imagined mobility for those for whom reprieve from societal constraints afforded by these spaces was perhaps even more transitory.[32]

With the presence of the Panoram screen in transit spaces during the 1940s, the small screen certainly could accentuate this "swing" atmosphere of cultural inclusivity. Adding to this air of both physical and social mobility is the very presence of the moving image itself. Haidee Wasson posits that the increased presence of extratheatrical screens "incorporated the ideals of movement" to audiences during this era. Soundies screen-space dynamics at these transit sites contributed to this emerging culture of moving images for those on the move.[33] However, not all site-specific accounts of Soundie exhibition cultivate this fantasy of mobility, even at transit sites. Some accounts of Soundies in transit waiting rooms suggest the more mundane aspects of these transit sites, where screen-space dynamics evoke relaxation. For example, an account of soldiers viewing a Panoram at a Chicago servicemen's center frames Soundie viewing as a rather benign and wholesome activity, alongside eating free ice cream.[34]

The Panoram's presence at these intermediary sites also foregrounds dreams of postwar domestic consumption replete with new consumer-oriented screen technologies like television and home movie projectors.[35] For example, the Panoram screen at the Servicemen's Lounge at New York's Grand Central Station positions Soundie viewing at a pivotal point between wartime activity and domestic leisure, where the screen offers a serene site of consumption. A 1945 *New York Times* article, "Home from the Wars to a Friendly Town," recounts tales of New York as a haven for the homebound soldier. Modifying the wartime image of New York as the "good-time town, the place where anything can happen—and does happen," the article reframes the city as a respectable and hospitable welcoming center for the returning, war-weary soldier, offering several amenities and services to ease soldiers transitioning back to civilian life.[36] Peppered with anecdotes of young couples getting married and soldiers learning how to put diapers on their newborn babies (a far cry from the accounts of the wartime attractions of the Embarcadero district or Los Angeles' Main Street), the article offers the following description of a Soundie exhibition site: "By midmorning the Service Men's Lounge at Grand Central Station was jammed. At a far corner of the long room, several men were watching the Panoram Soundies, a jukebox gadget that plays music and shows movies at the same time, all for a nickel. At that moment the machine was showing Charlie Spivak's orchestra playing 'Comin' Thru the Rye.'"[37]

According to this account, the placement of the Panoram is not centralized but placed in a "far corner," providing a source of unimposing entertainment for those who might want to watch a film while they wait. Like a domestic console, the Panoram is positioned as ambient, unobtrusive entertainment. A sailor interviewed at the scene, who does not comment on the film, is described as in a relaxing repose: he "stretched his legs and sighed happily." Accompanying this description of respite, an attached photo shows four men in uniform lined up in recliner chairs with a white picket fence enclosing the area. Although the photo caption indicates that this is at the "Pennsylvania station lounge" and not at the Grand Central Station site, the image fits neatly with the article's description of soldiers resting after the travails of war and transitioning into civilian life. While the servicemen wait for their trains to take them home to the promise of their new lives in the suburban enclaves of postwar America, the screen mollifies their transition, turning their act of waiting into a reprieve in front of the Panoram.

What perhaps is most striking about this particular snapshot of a Soundie exhibition space is that the film *Comin' Thru the Rye* (1942), an updated swing version of the Scottish folk song by Soundie regular Charlie Spivak and his orchestra, is mentioned explicitly, allowing for a specific consideration of site-based media viewing. An adaptation of the Robert Burns poem, the song itself became a popular war-era homecoming song due to its folk associations and its lyrics, laden with sexual imagery, suggesting romantic reunions ("If a body meets a body / comin' through the rye").[38] A rupture from Spivak's usual bandstand Soundie, *Comin' Thru the Rye* is an oddly conceived film that presumably is set in rural Scotland, with the band dressed as Scottish farmers and Spivak himself wearing a kilt. In addition to the band playing music on dusty, old instruments outside of a cottage, this ambling Soundie features an assortment of characters: a town drunk, stumbling and searching for his bottle of "rye"; a well-dressed couple out on a Sunday stroll; and a dancing scarecrow (recalling *The Wizard of Oz* [Victor Fleming, 1939]), who becomes animated after getting a hold of the town drunk's rye. Needless to say, the spatial relationship between screen content and exhibition site in this instance does not afford an immediate or direct correlation. However, as Anna McCarthy suggests, by "materializing the unlocalized space of the image within particular spaces, in site-specific ways" certain correspondences emerge between representation and exhibition space.[39] As a film being screened in a space designated for respite from wartime activities, the quaint pastoral setting of the Soundie paired with this Scottish folk song evokes a sense of nostalgic return to home and leisurely peacetime activities. Within the bustling space of Grand Central Station, *Comin' Thru the Rye* mediates the traveling soldiers' homecoming and ushers in the postwar era with a dose of small-screen media viewing.

Whistle while You Work

In addition to transit sites providing Soundies as site-based entertainment for mobile or idling passersby, the Panoram also was utilized at work sites to play prearranged film programs for training and instruction. No longer functioning as coin-operated amusement machines, Panorams are still framed by discourses of screen-space connectivity despite their industrial locales. Featured in factory lunchrooms and restrooms, the Panoram is often positioned as a source of entertainment during scheduled break times and in sanctioned break areas.[40] Given their location in these workspaces, it would seem that the Panoram machine would provide a respite from the doldrums of the job where the screen offers an escapist rupture within the everyday spaces of labor. Certainly, to some extent the films could provide levity to the workday with their popular songs and comedic fare. However, workplace accounts indicate the Panoram's function as not just morale boosting but also instructive, where the screen supplements and extends the space of work-related (and often patriotic) duty. For instance, an account of Chicago-based war plants explains that Panorams were used to both "entertain war workers and also to give educational programs."[41] Directly integrating filmic content into the function of the surrounding exhibition space, the machines would screen "patriotic subjects showing tanks and other machinery in action . . . to inspire workers in war plants with some idea of what the machines of war are doing."[42]

Often accompanying the exhibition of training films at these factory sites, several patriotic Soundies would be played to complete their break-time screening. One fitting example, *Rosie the Riveter* (1943), sung by the vocal trio the Smoothies with harmonica accompaniment from the Cappy Barra Boys, takes place "during the lunch hour in a defense plant's recreation hall so it's topical enough."[43] Not just "topical" and timely, it is also spatially appropriate, as the film's setting is situated neatly within one of its possible viewing spaces. Alternating between scenes of the Smoothies singing in the factory lunchroom with images of Rosie mounting heavy machinery, this Soundie nicely integrates themes of industriousness into the film without being explicitly didactic. Rosie, who is cast as a "hefty, sexy blonde with a pretty smile," also adds sex appeal to the Soundie while maintaining its wartime workplace motif.[44] Considering the possible size of some of these factory recreational areas, it should also be noted that the Panoram machine in some spaces was outfitted with an additional large screen attachment to accommodate "as many as one thousand persons at a time."[45] Alongside the appropriate filmic content, the scale of the screen was similarly patterned to the exhibition site, which would also ensure that as many employees as possible were seeing these films at their "leisure."

Perhaps not surprisingly, the Mills Novelty Company in Chicago, the producer of the Panoram machine, also used the Panoram to promote the war effort to its employees.[46] A *Billboard* photo shows Mills's executives standing in front of the Panoram screen with the patriotic image of a uniformed chorus saluting the Statue of Liberty. The caption reads, "Every employee of Mills three plants bought one or more bonds." As a calculated response to their recent infraction of war production restrictions for continuing the manufacture of Panorams and other amusement devices, Mills attempted to redeem its reputation and construct a positive company image, while the Panoram was recast as an instrument of wartime patriotism (rather than a drain of much-needed aluminum).[47] Using one of their own movie machines as a

FIGURE 9 *Rosie the Riveter* (1943) features the vocal group performing in the break room of a factory during wartime. From Soundies Distributing Corporation of America photographs of the Margaret Herrick Library, Academy of Motion Picture Arts and Sciences.

promotional tool in the domestic war effort at the former site of the Panoram's own production, Mills positions the screen at once as an important fixture in wartime production and also as a symbolic reminder of the screen's expansive potential as a consumer object during peacetime.

Swinging for Uncle Sam

By far the most frequently cited accounts of Soundie exhibition are bond rallies and war-related special events. This does not mean that Panorams were used more in this capacity but that these events proved newsworthy, as the uses of the Panoram in these contexts were more novel and less mundane than a Panoram in the corner of a neighborhood tavern. Exhibition accounts from war bond rallies provide rich sites for exploring the ever-expanding use of site-based film screens during the 1940s, even though they tend to overlook the more unremarkable encounters with the Soundies screen. Further evidencing the import of small screens for public display purposes, patriotic Panorams adapted to these various occasions. Rather than a program of eight Soundies, they would play predesigned programs of newsreels, government PSAs, and, sometimes, a few patriotic Soundies. The Panoram machine also changed in its function as a coin-operated, user-activated machine. Similar to the work sites discussed above, some of these special event sites modified the Panoram to a non-coin-activated machine, repeatedly screening one-reel programs designed for the specific occasion.[48] Although neither a small nor lightweight projector, the Panoram's self-looping rear projector and small glass screen, an all-in-one cabinet on wheels, was amenable to both temporary and semipermanent installations (often remaining in a display locale for months or even years) where it could replay a program continuously and where the heft of its cabinetry situated it as a stable fixture in its environ. Its encased projection system also made it particularly conducive to walk-up viewing without a need to adjust the lighting.

The placement of these movie machines in various public spaces helped cultivate lively environments of "participatory patriotism," resituating the casual viewer as a collective participant in the war effort.[49] Many journalistic discourses centralize the screen's presence at these war events, rendering the Panoram "useful" in these spaces—more of an instrument for mobilizing action than just sideshow entertainment.[50] Referred to as "Machines for Recruiting," one *Billboard* article claims that "many WACS [Women's Auxiliary Corps] and SPARS [U.S. Coast Guard Women's Reserves, whose motto is *semper paratus*] from the Chicago area may have made their decision to 'take the step' as result of appeals, ocular and auditory, by movie machines installed at the Victory Center in Marshall Field store and at the treasury department office in Chicago."[51] In fact, the earliest accounts of Panorams exhibiting films publicly in Chicago were for these war-promotion purposes.[52] Surrounded by large signs encouraging the sale of defense stamps and bonds, a Panoram placed in the lobby area of Chicago's city hall would play as a reward for those who purchased a bond.[53] The following description of the city hall lobby indicates the Panoram's "ideal location" for its recruitment efforts: "Access to the building proper can be made through four main entrances, all converging in the direct center of the building in the main floor lobby, and smack on the spot Soundie and 7th War Loan officials have located the Panoram, fenced in by a counter from which the attendants sell war bonds and stamps."[54] "Fenced in" behind the War Loan representatives, the screen functions as another civic steward, working on behalf of the war effort. Unlike the placement of Panorams at various leisure sites for entertainment or diversion, where its placement in the far corner of a bar seeks to be unobtrusive and integrated into its surroundings, the screen's positioning in such official settings (under heavy signage, behind a counter, and even sometimes with the cabinet "veiled") had an air of stateliness and purpose.[55]

For three years, the Panoram stayed at this centralized installation in the center of Chicago's city hall, generating quite a reaction. Not only did the

Panoram help sell "over $10,000 bonds and stamps" in its first weeks of play; one of the Soundies it played as a reward for purchase, *We'll Slap the Japs Right Into the Laps of the Nazis* (Josef Berne, 1942), was described as "being hummed by workers in the Chicago City Hall" and provided a rallying cry for government workers and passersby.[56] As the title indicates, *We'll Slap the Japs* pulls no punches on its vitriolic delivery. Showing civilians taking up the call to arms, the film celebrates all four branches of the military and their part in the war effort. This racist recruitment poster of a film follows the trajectory of a waiter, a mechanic, a painter, and a businessman as they leave from their day jobs, kiss their loved ones good-bye, and leave for war. The film draws upon collective patriotism by unifying men from diverse backgrounds as it portrays their mobilization to war. From everyday work locales to traversing the high seas, *We'll Slap the Japs*'s forward-moving trajectory and its theme of collective mobilization easily extends into this exhibition space, where it clearly hopes to inspire the same momentum. In particular, the convergence of the four men in the film from their various work sectors nicely echoes the Panoram's central

FIGURE 10 *We'll Slap the Japs Right Into the Laps of the Nazis*'s (1942) four vocalists represent the conjoint effort of each branch of the military. From Soundies Distributing Corporation of America photographs of the Margaret Herrick Library, Academy of Motion Picture Arts and Sciences.

location at the four intersecting pathways of the city hall, where the screen mediates the transition from civilians to soldiers, or, at the very least, patriots.

Later reports from this city hall locale indicate that the site-specific Panoram installation became increasingly more regimented in its screening protocol, with playback being controlled by the attendants. Running preset film programs "at regular intervals," the Panoram would be used to attract large crowds, with extended war-related newsreel content shown from 9 a.m. to 5 p.m. to crowds of one to two hundred.[57] A similar account from an army air show in Detroit describes the use of the Panoram for specialty exhibits: "Machines were specifically equipped to run as controlled, showing chiefly educational and war effort films, with amusement interspersed at will. Coin chutes were blocked for the occasion."[58] Although the primary film content would reinforce the theme of the event, Soundies were used as filler to "hold attention between talks." Situated in noncommercial display contexts, the adaptable Panoram could address both passing crowds or be integrated into larger demonstrations that were both educational and entertaining.

The frequent integration of the screen in these specific programming contexts makes film display a central component to the domestic war effort and in the increasing demand for site-based screen technologies that allowed for film to circulate continuously at a variety of screening sites. For instance, during the Red Cross Drive, Detroit Panoram operator Don Kennedy used Panorams to assist in recruiting nurses at multiple sites; he would screen *Angels of Mercy* (Edward L. Cahn, 1939) "on constant play in important public centers where there is a large amount of traffic."[59] Considered "a terrific and well-deserved plug for the Red Cross," the ten-minute educational film on the life of American Red Cross founder Clara Barton (Sara Haden) features "attractive nurses . . . carrying out various Red Cross duties" and James Newell as a hospitalized soldier.[60] Similar to the recruitment efforts of *We'll Slap the Japs*, *Angels of Mercy*'s repeated viewings work under the assumption that they will directly motivate those watching and propel them to volunteer for the Red Cross. In addition to the four machines Kennedy situated at the "railroad depot, in a large department store and in public buildings," he also planned to rig a machine onto the back of a truck to "carry the message right to the people."[61] Although lugging around such a large machine may seem impractical—with lighter, more portable 16mm projectors widely available—this account again highlights the screen's adaptability to a variety of locales, particularly in this case by setting the screen in motion on the back of a truck, and the usefulness of the Panoram's self-looping projector to provide "constant play."

Department stores were another popular site for utilizing the Panoram to promote war activities.[62] Fusing civic duty with commercial interest, Panoram Soundies would sell war bonds while also promoting themselves as a new novelty media. For instance, the May Company, a large department store in

Denver, used the Panoram to play patriotic Soundies while selling war stamps. Along with the purchase of stamps, the store would hand out promotional cards with a picture of the Panoram on it.[63] With the promise of seeing a "free movie" while purchasing a bond or stamp (along with other department store items), customers were greeted by a "bond girl" and the new Soundies machine. In one instance at the Marshall Field's Victory Center in Chicago, customers could also meet recent Soundies stars such as the Hoosier Hot Shots, the Dinning Sisters, and Nancy Martin.[64] Although the presence of these "aspirational displays" in department stores situates Soundies within the realm of civic duty, their cross-promotional strategies at these consumer sites also reveal the ways the Panoram screens were integrated into their exhibition spaces. As the integration of these screens conflated spaces of commerce with entertainment and patriotism, they further paved the way for future uses of the screen as an automatic, mechanized sales device.[65]

Considering the success of the Panoram as a civic display device in specialized exhibit areas as early as 1942, it comes as little surprise that both the Office of War Information (OWI) and the U.S. Treasury Department produced public-service Soundies specifically for the Panoram machine. During the Fifth War Loan Drive, which ran from June 12 to July 8, 1944, five OWI shorts (*Semper Paratus* [*Coast Guard Song*, 1944], *Caissons Go Rolling Along* [1944], *Anchors Aweigh* [1944], *Marine's Hymn* [1941], and *Keep 'Em Rolling* [1944]) and a thirty-second war loan drive trailer were included in Soundies' newly released reels.[66] The U.S. Treasury Department also released two shorts (*Hands* [1944] and *The Line Is Busy* [1944]) for Soundies during the Sixth War Loan Drive from November 20 to December 16, 1944.[67] These government-produced shorts were inserted into Soundies reels with "no notch . . . so it will immediately follow the preceding 'paid' Soundie as a free play feature."[68] The insertion of patriotic musical shorts into regular Soundies programs, particularly their seamless integration within the reels, blended didactic government content with Soundies' commercial entertainment.[69] As government films emulated Soundies in their single-song format and as Soundies frequently drew upon patriotic themes (including Bette Lynn's *America's Sweetheart* [1943], which is even set at a war bond rally), this further lessened the distinction between Soundies and OWI films.[70] For example, the OWI film *Keep 'Em Rolling* appeared on Soundies Program 1181, couched between Harry Gibson's *Harry the Hipster* (Ben K. Blake, 1944) and the standard *When Irish Eyes Are Smiling* (1941) by Morton Downey, both set in nightclubs.[71] *Keep 'Em Rolling* primarily shows workers manufacturing airplanes while extolling the virtues of wartime restraint and hard work, but its opening sequence includes footage of people dancing in a nightclub to accompany the vocal, "it's lots of fun to dine and dance." Although the film contains a variety of images from war posters (including a caricature of Hitler) to a sing-along segment for the final verse, its placement on the Soundies reel, positioned between two performance-oriented Soundies, tempers the severity of its messaging by resituating it within an entertainment context.

Soundies musical shorts proved an apt film format for the government to adopt and imitate, with roughly 3,500 Panorams placed throughout the United States by 1944, and Soundies regional franchises provided a film distribution network that allowed for the kind of seamless, site-specific entertainment that the government aimed to provide during the war. With their inclusion of more than three thousand Soundies reels during the fall of 1944, these government-produced films ushered their patriotic content into everyday spaces of cafés and bowling alleys without any additional spectacle or fanfare.[72] Even their film content, like the Treasury Department's *Hands* (1944), which illustrates "the importance of hands in daily life, then their significance in war and war production," thematized the everyday and made it meaningful.[73] Although *Hands* was produced for radically different purposes than Soundies commercial bandstand films, a similar patterning and scaling of screen content to their exhibition contexts persists. While *Hands* melds the concerns of wartime production with the fabric of the day to day, the Panoram similarly integrates the small screen into ubiquitous sites of consumption.

Toward a Multiscreen Environment

In 1944, the *Canton Repository* published a dreamy account of a postwar domestic "utopia," replete with robot maids and various automatic gadgets.[74] Included in this futuristic vision of the home are both a television and a movie machine. Even with television suspended in its launch as a consumer technology, the account envisions the home as a multiple-screen environment, a space where film screens and television sets would coexist in the same room. This fantasy of postwar America indexes a soon-to-be-actualized consumer landscape of privatized, small-screen usage. At the time of this account, though, television, as Christopher Anderson explains, only "existed in an inchoate form" as a "projection of social and commercial fantasies."[75] As television manufacturers waited out the war years, small film screens like the Panoram helped sustain and preserve the promise of an expanded culture of moving images and screen circulation. Although the quick rise of television in the late 1940s tends to overshadow the expanding use of portable film technologies, the integration of small, site-based film screens in the 1940s played significant—though often underrecognized—roles in television's entrée into the realm of mass consumption. Expanding television's influences beyond its immediate (and well-acknowledged) connections to radio's broadcast infrastructure, the integration of small screens like Panoram Soundies into commercial and institutional contexts points to intermediary practices and important intersections between 1940s nontheatrical film and early television.[76] The connections between these transitional film and television practices are made explicit when Soundies migrate to television screens by the late 1940s.[77]

Panoram Soundies' diffuse film exhibition sites like cafés and government buildings during the war index a changing cultural landscape where consumers would become further attuned and acclimated to the proliferating presence of small moving-image screens. Whether providing site-specific musical entertainment at nightclubs or patriotic songs for factory workers on break, Soundies' screen interventions established particular modes of and expectations for small-screen viewings just prior to television's mainstream emergence. Rendering small-screen moving images into appropriate or often-functional extensions of their exhibition sites, Soundies helped cultivate an atmosphere of screen-space connectivity, a patterning of moving image to its viewing context. Although Panorams did not migrate directly to domestic viewing sites, their integration into manifold spaces of work, leisure, transit, and commerce maintained and bolstered consumer desire for regular, small-screen encounters.

3

Mobilizing Space

The Panoram Goes to War

The Soundie *Goodbye Mama, I'm off to Yokohama* (1942) presents a popular patriotic song while staging a timely love story. The short opens with a naval officer (Johnny Johnston) and his girlfriend (Marvel Maxwell) parting ways as he leaves for war and she heads for the nursing corps. After he is injured in battle, the soldier wakes in his hospital bed with his girlfriend qua nurse swooning at his bedside. A shorthand version of a clichéd wartime romance, the Soundie's condensed visual storytelling is gestural and relies on heavy dissolves to succinctly ellipse time and space, while the lyrics of the song provide a repeating refrain of its wartime premise. A *Billboard* review critiques the Soundie as a "bad bit" of acting and harshly claims that such theatrics "should have been omitted."[1] *Goodbye Mama*'s particular take on wartime themes may not have made for a riveting short film, but the film's topicality encompasses key aspects of U.S. culture during the war era. As the Soundie quickly traverses a naval ship, a domestic setting, the warfront, and a military hospital, the film enacts the trials and movements of war and the new roles inhabited by U.S. citizens. Its representations of wartime experiences also reveal new spaces and, as this chapter examines, new discourses supporting small-screen encounters during World War II.

The circulation of the Panoram during the 1940s extended far beyond its initial commercial function. As discussed in the prior chapter, Soundies were employed by the OWI and the U.S. Treasury Department in the domestic war effort to sell bonds and recruit participants in the war effort, and the Panoram's

FIGURE 11 *Goodbye Mama, I'm off to Yokohama* (1942) presents a sentimental wartime love story. From Soundies Distributing Corporation of America photographs of the Margaret Herrick Library, Academy of Motion Picture Arts and Sciences.

projection technology allowed for films to be screened at sites like factories and government buildings. As the war effort grew on the U.S. home front, Panorams increasingly migrated from commercial locales to institutional spaces where they were implemented in more official capacities. By 1943, about 1,500 Panorams were located in schools and war plants.[2] Though they were fringe film novelty machines, almost half of all Panorams were repurposed for "war work" during their six-year cultural lives.[3] During this time, the Panoram was used by the U.S. military in training facilities at domestic military bases, veterans' hospitals, government buildings, and sites specifically designed for servicemen during their recreational hours.

The Panoram's migration to military spaces during World War II modified its function as a novelty amusement machine and patterned new ways for interacting with small-screen technologies that would extend well beyond the Panoram's brief cultural life in the 1940s. The Panoram was not the typical military-issue projector like the 16mm JAN, which was the standard equipment for all overseas film operations, designed for maximum portability.[4] With its bulky, and rather deluxe, walnut cabinetry, the Mills's Panoram hardly seems amenable to the makeshift setups required by military protocols. The

Panoram's differentiation from conventional 16mm projectors begs certain questions about what this adapted film jukebox could and in fact did offer in military contexts. Its all-in-one screen-projection unit and automated features provided convenience and efficiency of setup and use. Even though it was not portable in a handheld sense, the Panoram's large cabinet was on casters so it could boast a degree of mobility in that it could be pushed from room to room like a deluxe AV cart. Best for accommodating single or small group viewings, the Panoram's compact, self-operating vending mechanisms enabled modes of film display that were small or even individualized, where screenings could be repeated *ad nauseam* in rooms that did not require darkness or a film projectionist. Seemingly counter to the military's goals of collective instruction and information deployment, the Panoram's features of automation, repetition, and spatial adaptability transformed militarized practices in film projection to an expanding set of small-screen encounters.

Additionally, the Panoram's employ by the U.S. military extended beyond its innovative and user-friendly technological functions to Mills Novelty Company's corporate affiliations with Captain James "Jimmy" Roosevelt, FDR's eldest son, the first producer of Soundies' films as well as the company's first president.[5] Just before the bombing of Pearl Harbor and the United States' entry into World War II, Jimmy Roosevelt stepped down from his position as president of the SDC and reported for duty as a captain in the Marines. Once he was in service, Roosevelt maintained his corporate status as "unsalaried" vice president of the SDC, chairman of the board, and "a heavy stockholder."[6] Although the war imposed production and material restrictions on the manufacturing of amusement and vending machines like music jukeboxes, Mills Novelty Company, manufacturer of "Captain Jimmy's Jukes," applied for priority grants since their machines were already in army camps' recreational areas. By repurposing the Panorams already in circulation around army camps, the U.S. military effectively recast the role of the Panoram as a necessary instrument of war while consequently bolstering consumer-oriented screen technologies within institutional spaces.

Keeping the Soldier Occupied

The presence of movie screens for entertainment at army bases during World War II has been well documented within the context of wider availability and distribution networks for 16mm film during the 1940s.[7] With images of large, makeshift screens set up in mess halls or outdoor amphitheaters, where soldiers, enjoying an evening's entertainment, watch a Capra film or a Mickey Mouse cartoon, popular accounts frame military film exhibitions as familiar and social practices that strive to replicate theatrical film viewing experiences in unlikely, provisional venues. Such nightly screenings of Hollywood fare were a central part of soldiers' experiences on base—"an integral diversion," as Peter Lester explains, "necessary for the maintenance of troop morale."[8] Though vital and significant in its own right, this kind of screen practice represents only one aspect of soldiers' encounters with films during their military service. Like these larger film screenings, Soundie viewing was still organized as a leisure-time activity on base. Soldiers most frequently encountered Panorams in recreational sites like Post Exchanges (PXs) on military bases or servicemen recreation centers located just off base. Situated within or located near the camp, these sites served as liminal spaces where institutional and civilian life melded together, where soldiers sought diversion from work and reminders of home while in service. As microcommunities activating their own social practices and regulations, PXs and military recreation centers offered spaces where soldiers received their mail, bought cigarettes and gum, and drank diluted beer with a 3 percent alcohol content. In these at once official/unofficial places of temporary sojourn, soldiers would be involved in an array of activities that helped keep them occupied and from wandering to less regulated establishments for (undiluted) liquor and prostitution.

According to an anonymous account from a woman who served as an army service club director at Camp Kilmer, New Jersey, during the war, Panorams were installed at "three service clubs, one officer's club and three or four PXs in spite of a regulation forbidding vending machines and forbidding payment for entertainment."[9] Even though Panorams were technically not allowed, club directors regularly ignored commands to remove them and GIs willingly paid money to see Soundies. Since Camp Kilmer was large enough to function like its own "small city," such on-base indiscretions were probably the norm as long as soldiers remained within the parameters of rules governing camp or spaces designed for military recreation.[10] In, appropriately, a former department store converted into a servicemen center in Fort Lauderdale, the Panoram was located on the main floor alongside a dance floor with a few musical instruments, indicating that this was not a space for quiet viewing but for the music and the screen to be enjoyed communally in "a wholesome place of recreation for those men in the armed forces in their off-duty hours."[11] With facilities offering jukeboxes, table tennis, swimming pools, pianos, free ice cream, and cards (but "no gambling"[12]), Panorams were set up in auxiliary facilities where soldiers were engaged in several possible activities and where the screen was a decentralized part of the servicemen's recreational space.

A photo from Lowry Field, a major U.S. Air Force base in Denver, Colorado, shows five soldiers awkwardly crowded in front of a Panoram in a nondescript interior space.[13] They all crane their necks as they gaze up at the Panoram screen.[14] Clearly constructed for publicity purposes, this image is particularly odd not only because of their cramped arrangement but also because the screen is blank, rendering their contorted poses futile. The presence of the dormant screen marks this space not as one for concentrated screen viewing but rather as an atmosphere of camaraderie where the screen itself is secondary. In an environment where open living in functional barracks (including latrines) was the norm, the compressed spatial dynamics of this photo are apropos to army life. The photo also suggests the possible viewing conditions of the Panoram where soldiers would vie for space in front of the screen to hopefully catch a glimpse of some bathing beauty. If sex appeal was one of the main attractions of Soundies on Panorams in recreation areas, the soldier's brief respite from official duties would be dependent on the films in rotation that week. For example, the reel circulating the week this photo was published included the Soundie *When the Roses Bloom Again* (with Buddy Clark and Georgia Carroll, 1942), another sentimental duet of wartime lovers' separation and eventual reunion. However, the film enlivens this ballad with chorus girls wearing little except for roses festooned on their chests. The reel also includes *There'll Be Some Changes Made* (with Ginger Harmon, 1941), which is described as "good on looks but weak on voice" with "a line of fully dressed girls stripping to their bathing outfits in burly style."[15] Amenable to spaces that were well lit, busy, and noisy, the Panoram provided a momentary attraction, but, more likely, the screen's presence was ambient, with soldiers freely circulating and socializing throughout the facilities as Soundies played.[16] As a diversionary and sometimes mundane screen practice, these recreational accounts of the Panoram incorporate commercial entertainment within institutional spaces. Though it was a novelty amusement, the Panoram's placement normalized the presence of the screen for those in service.

Film Is a Weapon

As the Panoram's screen presence became normalized in military contexts, its screen functions increasingly catered to its surrounding contexts. Its shift from an amusement machine to a weapon of war occurs quite literally through the repurposing of its manufactured materials. As a 1942 *Chicago Tribune* article reports, the Mills Novelty Company would no longer produce coin-operated machines like the Panoram during wartime. It states: "The machinery which manufactured the vending robots that told your weight, released a candy bar, handed you a cold drink, or ran off a quick movie while you drank a beer, is now shaping cold steel into projectiles and other war implements which bear an obituary for axis soldiers."[17] Like a vast number of American industries with highly developed manufacturing facilities, Mills Novelty Company is transformed from a manufacturer of automatic vending movie machines to a manufacturer of weapons and war-related equipment. As Raymond Williams states, "New technology is itself a product of a particular social system . . . but . . . contradictory factors . . . may make it possible to use some or all . . . for purposes quite different."[18] Although the Panoram functioned primarily as commercial screen entertainment during moments of leisure, such accounts of material repurposing remind us of the "quite different" possibilities for such machinery. Foregrounding wartime priorities of weapon manufacturing supplanting civilian amusements, the previous account situates entertainment technologies like the Panoram firmly within the discourse of war and signals the shared industrial base of both.

Similarly conflating cinematic materials with defense, *Business Screen Magazine*'s coverage of educational and industrial film's role in militarized settings touts, "film is a weapon" and "pictures are bullets."[19] Stressing the importance of film for military education and training, trade discourse from the war era evidences both the centrality of training films for the military as well as its rampant expansion of its exhibition practices. As Colonel Cohen, executive producer for the Signal Corps Pictorial Center (SCPC), recounts at the war's conclusion in 1946, "What had started out to be a simple training film program had now become a vast, complex medium of information, education, military planning, advanced training and entertainment."[20] Utilizing claims from military personnel to bolster film's status from supplemental to essential—"as important to the men as rations"—these trade accounts move beyond patriotic boosterism to seamlessly meld the interests of the various film industries (encompassing the commercial and industrial) with that of the U.S. military.[21]

Within this milieu, the integration of the Panoram proves particularly apt for meeting the needs of military instruction. One of the primary concerns of relying on films for military training was gauging the efficacy of instruction, particularly when "films can be shown only in darkened projection rooms . . . if the G.I. audience slept through the picture, valuable training time was lost."[22] The Panoram redresses this issue of "considerable dozing" with its rear-screen projection design for viewing in well-lit environments. An ad for the Panoram as an instructional device for the army and navy emphasizes, "darkened room unnecessary."[23] Recasting the Panoram as an instructional tool rather than a coin-operated Soundies' machine, the ad shows a full-page picture of the Panoram projecting an image of an airplane, with its marquee announcing "Educational Sound Films." The ad also claims that these machines have been made available "by special government authorization" and a "push button switch" has replaced their coin operation. This ad clearly illustrates its militaristic film content and emphasizes the Panoram's capacity for projecting training films while it still gestures toward the Panoram's commercial function and versatility by recommending the play of "musical and news shorts" alongside training films.[24]

A 1945 article from the *Washington Post*, lamenting the current state of public education in the United States, noted the "incredible effects of the specialized training given to Army and Navy personnel" by taking "advantage of up-to-date aids: viz. films, records, models."[25] Shifting from conventional film instructional models of darkened classrooms toward an atmosphere conducive to alertness and brightness, the U.S. military's integration of the Panoram evidences their institutional commitment to creating effective, visually immersive learning environments where screens were used purposefully alongside other forms of instruction. For instance, a training center called the "War Room" at the Army Air Force Pilot School at Shaw Field Air Force Base near Sumter, South Carolina, comprised an intelligence library with an adjoining room featuring an eight-by-twelve-foot world map, a six-by-eight-foot relief map, wall panels that were updated daily with pertinent war information from the press, and sandboxes with models of sea and land formations.[26]

Among other visual instructional materials, including a table filled with both View-Masters and stereoscopes, the Panoram was stationed to play a twenty-eight-minute film program on identification and military intelligence subjects that was changed weekly. As seen in the photo, a single soldier stands in front of a Panoram projecting an image of a military airplane. In this didactic image of individualized film viewing of military content befitting of the instructional environ of the "intelligence library," the Panoram evokes a stately presence within the multimedia military library. However, the Panoram itself is still marked by its original commercial function with its rotating banner announcing, "We Proudly Present Panoram Soundies: America's Latest Form of Musical Entertainment." As its programming banner could have been removed (they were designed to be exchangeable to advertise the specific film programs), the Panoram machine offers a residual reminder of its commercial functions and gestures toward other possibilities for small-screen encounters. Although classified military reading materials and popular magazines (*Time*, *Life*, etc.) were available for browsing, the Shaw Field War Room is marked as a place less for reading than for viewing, with flags and insignia covering every wall of the library, including the ceilings. Placed alongside other solo viewing apparatuses in a room festooned with maps and visual aids, the Panoram machine exemplifies the military's approach to immersive visual instruction.

Frequent screen encounters were the norm at Shaw Field, with programming also including a regular Sunday screening of "newsreels and sports features" for groups of two hundred accompanied by a quiz program, where soldiers could win prizes for accurately answering orientation questions.[27] With both small- and large-screen viewing experiences couched within and alongside other orientation activities, the military situates the screen as a necessary wartime technology and seeks to innovate its uses in emergent and varied capacities. For instance, the Panoram was used as part of an outdoor training installation designed to orient soldiers to other cultures.[28] An account describing the training of "a large unit scheduled to go to a South

Pacific island" explains that soldiers "learned about conditions there through the use of a wide variety of teaching aids." The following offers a description of their survival skills training: "A shelter was erected to house a display of the fruit, vegetables, and animals that the prospective resident should know about. Under the same shelter were located two mechanical devices, one resembling a juke-box, called a 'panoram,' to give a showing of sound 16 mm film, and the other similar to a pin-ball machine, an automatic rater, which presented and scored a related quiz."[29]

Comparable to an educational kiosk in a museum space, the Panoram screened films about indigenous fruits, vegetables, and animals of the South Pacific within a simulated hut environ. Rather than some kind of military classroom facility, the seemingly odd site-specific installation of the Panoram machine in a quasi-natural outdoor structure also suggests a trend in educational philosophies, where the film screen is far more than a mere educational supplement.[30] Providing immediate visual instruction at the specific site of hands-on training, the Panoram is central to organizing the hut as a learning space. Though the art-deco walnut cabinetry of the Panoram machine certainly disrupted the look of the South Pacific setting, the screen's images could provide its own island atmospherics while providing the soldiers with necessary survival information. To assess the soldiers' comprehension of the film, a converted pinball machine called an "automatic rater" would quiz the soldiers on the content and give them a score.[31] With the Panoram's placement alongside the rating device, there is an underlying presumption that the Panoram, as an instructional apparatus, disseminates a particular knowledge set that can be gauged instantaneously by the accompanying machine. The dual placement of these repurposed amusement machines in this training setting suggests that they may provide some level of entertainment while providing instruction—a scenario not so different from the implementation of interactive video games into more contemporary military training settings. Like the aforementioned use of the Panoram in the War Room, this outdoor installation also marks this militarized space as an interactive and modern educational site.

In addition to allowing for bright spaces (including daylight) for alert and interactive viewing activities, this kind of mechanized and assessed learning experience evidences the importance of efficiency and effectiveness in militarized instruction. With war-era ads for projectors boasting "more learning in less time,"[32] recurrent accounts from reports conducted by the U.S. military tout the efficacy of film in military training in similar terms of efficiency. Colonel Cohen states, "Any lingering doubts about the value of film, not only in routine training courses, but also in spreading information quickly and in attacking specific morale problems, were completely dissipated."[33] Not only is it presumed that film content in general was easier and faster for soldiers to absorb (certainly more so than reading training manuals or listening to lectures without visuals), but the Panoram machine itself further models these ideals of efficiency and speed with its automatic features, and its short, self-looping film content make the overall instructional screen experience user-friendly and befitting the training goals of the military. Since the Panoram does not require a trained projectionist, the soldier-student can learn directly from the automatic screen without the additional need for an instructor. With the ideals of efficient learning through film becoming a dominant discourse in late-1940s learning environments,[34] the military's mass deployment of and outspoken support for these visual instruction strategies augment the legitimacy of, and market for, instructional screens for postwar classrooms.

Films as Medicine

If films were deemed vital in preparing soldiers to engage in military combat, they also were figured in the equally restorative role of aiding the GI's recovery from the tribulations of battle. In what *Business Screen* refers to as "celluloid therapy," "films fill tremendous needs at the hospitals . . . where battle casualties march the road back to health."[35] From providing instruction on coping with disability ("the fears of the amputee are met by motion pictures") to entertainment for those suffering from "the traumatic boredom of hospital existence," films for recovering veterans "teach new skills or talk of sports or raise a laugh when it is needed most."[36] The film content at hospital screenings is described as ameliorative and instructive by specifically accommodating and adapting to the particular needs of the wounded veterans.

Among these regular hospital screenings, the Panoram's use at a military hospital in Chicago garnered special mention for its military service. On July 14, 1944, the Soundies Distribution Corporation even received a government commendation for "entertaining and rehabilitating the hospitalized veterans" at Gardiner General Hospital in Chicago.[37] In contrast to the aforementioned account of the Panoram's raw materials being used to kill enemy soldiers, the Panoram, it seems, had more benign functions in the war effort as well. Linking rehabilitation with film's ability to entertain, a *Billboard* heading claims that the Panoram "Has Health Value."[38] This account explains that the Panoram was brought to the hospital and played Soundies programs every other Tuesday. Reportedly, screenings were a preferred activity at hospitals, "taking top place even over the 'personal appearances' of stars of stage and screen."[39]

These Panoram programs were tailored specifically to avoid associations with wartime trauma and official military duties. Retaining their prior associations as novelty amusement machines, Panorams only played Soundies, and anything having to do with the military was "eliminated from the reels."[40] Such Soundies programs comprised musical shorts, like "top band

and girl acts," providing "entertainment for wounded servicemen" in this institutional setting.[41] Other popular Soundies genres for hospitalized veterans mentioned are "comedy, western and hillbilly" musical shorts.[42] "Aside from the entertainment value" and "boost they give to the morale," Soundies are described as being "therapeutic" in that the musical content of their films acts as a kind of physical therapy. The films "unconsciously and automatically" caused the patients to wiggle their fingers and toes to the music, "thereby getting much needed exercise."[43] According to *Billboard*'s enthusiastic account, soldiers responded to Soundies with "whoops and yells . . . stamping and the whistling," which the hospital staff took as "an indication that the boys are doing fine."[44]

In addition to the films themselves being seen as therapeutic through their entertainment value for the individual soldier, the circulation of films, their exhibition, and their technological integration in military hospital environments are also figured in medical discourse that positions film as central to wartime recovery, rehabilitation, and transition. For instance, the structure of a Soundies program in veteran hospitals tended to be of a shorter duration (about thirty minutes) so that the same program can be repeated throughout all the wards. This notion of increased film circulation put the Panoram operators on a rotation comparable to medical staff that allows for maximum distribution of services. In order for these film programs to circulate throughout an entire hospital, the projection equipment had to be portable: "Wherever possible . . . the use of portable equipment carts . . . is encouraged to facilitate in-the-ward film showings."[45] This emphasis on the portability of the projection technology directly compliments medical discourse of patient accessibility and mobility.[46]

The wheeled Panoram satisfies the need for mobile film projection while also encouraging further mobility from the patients: "Some of the boys . . . go from one ward to another right along with the unit, seeing the films over and over again."[47] In addition to the Panoram being adaptive to the hospital environment—with its automatic projection and ease of program repetition with its self-looping mechanism—the emphasis on the Panoram's mobility seems to directly extend from the screen's possible rehabilitative functions. According to *Billboard*, the Panoram is "wheeled from room to room since many of the men are unable to get out of bed to the main auditorium or some assembly point."[48] Here the film machine not only provides good entertainment; its mobility reframes the Panoram as an assistive medical device, where small, individualized film screens accommodate those not able to participate in collective, auditorium-style viewings. The article's accompanying photo, captioned "Movie Machine proves great Help to Wounded Veterans," also documents a GI in his hospital bed with three uniformed servicemen at his side. The Panoram machine plays in the background, with only one man vaguely looking toward the screen, which also indicates that these screens were becoming commonplace in the busy hospital environment.

The Panoram's attributes announce its modernity through mechanized patterns of automation and mobility, while the film content, with its purported therapeutic effects, is readily integrated into the institutional viewing context. Seen as an adaptable component to a range of medical activities, one account of a Panoram viewing in a military hospital explains that "treatment can be continued while the show is going on: backs can be rubbed, temperatures taken, medications administered thru the entire program while the boys comfortably enjoy the movies from their beds or wheel chairs."[49] These details offer an unexpected and lively portrait of film exhibition, where screen viewing occurs and is situated alongside a host of other therapies. In these militarized, medical surrounds, the discourses of film and its technologies are repeatedly interwoven with the hospital's own therapeutic endeavors. From adaptable film programs purportedly aiding veterans in their healing to the Panoram's design protocols allowing for increased accessibility to film viewing, these accounts of institutional Panorams help mobilize the screen into postwar, civilian practices. Similar to the way many civilians were called to action by the Panoram at war rallies during the war's inception, the Panoram's placement at the veterans' hospital effectively bookends the soldiers' wartime service.

From Service to Sales

The U.S. military's use of the Panoram positioned small-screen technologies into expansive spaces and practices, both institutional and otherwise, for military personnel during the war. By the war's end, the soldier's familiarity with these small-screen technologies would prove amenable to their reentry into postwar society. With government incentive programs like the GI Bill designed to assist their reconversion to civilian life, the returning veteran (especially the white male) was met with ample opportunities to participate in the recovering postwar economy.[50] Recognizing a valuable business opportunity, SDC announced a franchise opportunity designed exclusively for veterans seeking employment upon their return from service.[51] The SDC proposed offering rent-to-own discounts for vets who were interested in owning and operating Panorams. In addition to offering fiscal incentives, the SDC also planned to offer veterans a "serviceman school" where vets could learn "standard operating policy" for a Soundies franchise. The SDC proposed teaching the operators about the machines through training films which would be played, naturally, on the Panoram.[52]

The SDC's veteran plan maps a direct and clear transition from soldier to salesman, where the Panoram is still used as a training device for veterans who are familiar with this mode of filmic instruction while coaching them on the possibilities of the Panoram as "a powerful advertising medium." Recognizing a rich opportunity to fill the "idle time" between Soundies on the Panoram with advertising films and slides, the general manager for the SDC anticipated that a "constant flow of commercial films and announcements . . . will not only provide an important, new source of revenue to operators, but will serve to increase the cash collections from movie machines."[53] Similar to the military's use of Panorams to fill idle time for soldiers at recreation centers or hospitals with moving images and sounds, the industry envisioned the postwar Panoram providing a "constant flow" of commercial images. While evoking what would become the future magazine format for advertising on U.S. television, it differs from Soundies' prewar commercial model, where the Panoram screen only flashed lights while awaiting the next customer to drop a dime into the machine. Patterning the military's protocols of efficient, automatic playback, the lag time in awaiting coin operation is made more efficient in these aggressive marketing plans and offers a new modality for screens being in perpetual play. Although no new Panoram machines were manufactured after the war—ultimately rendering these veteran business opportunities moot—the Panoram's varied military exhibitions helped cultivate new ways of thinking about small-screen exhibition practices, their flow of images, and the potential functions for self-contained projection units.

In a series of Mills's projector ads that ran in *Business Screen* from 1943 to 1946, the marketing of the Panoram and their revamped model of the push-button Sono-Vision touts their convergence with military affairs while using its military functions as a catalyst for further postwar opportunities. With both the U.S. Navy and U.S. Army always topping the list of users featured in their ads, Mills's ads for the Panoram and Sono-Vision frequently feature military subjects on their screen displays. For example, a Sono-Vision ad from 1945 shows servicemen loading military cargo onto a plane.[54] Although the image clearly marks the projector as a utilitarian machine for military training, the language within the ad mingles wartime service with sales. The ad reads, "to train and sell!"[55] With emphasis on the machine being "time-saving," "mobile," "self-contained," and requiring "no darkened room," the ad clearly addresses the aforementioned training protocols of the military while also looking toward peacetime by making mention of "your postwar sales and training plans." Building their commercial integrity on the institutional legitimization of the U.S. military, Mills Novelty charts a seamless transition between the machine's functions for training and sales. The ad beckons the current serviceman as it defines and shapes the soon-to-be salesman in the postwar market. While planting this seed for commercial enterprise, the ad also acknowledges the current production constraints on the "release of critical materials." Once these materials are available, which "we sincerely hope, will be soon," Mills urges the buyer to place their order since supplies "for the first 12 months will be limited."[56] Although the claims are tempered, the ad focuses on the future availability of the machine rather than its present-day function, ultimately serving as little more than a wartime placeholder in the projector market.

Although subsequent marketing efforts remove the self-contained projectors from their military training capacities soon after the war, residual aspects of their military discourse continue to circulate around the promotion of these projectors through 1946. A surreal Sono-vision ad boasting "three-dimensional selling" depicts a projector encased in a transparent globe with a free-floating ear and an eye hovering in the background.[57] The projector's screen displays a nondescript image of a man doing a demonstration, but the language of the ad is decidedly militaristic: "You enlist each of the three dimensions in your sales task force." In addition to this notion of recruitment, the ad calls the projector the "most persuasive sales and advertising weapons you have ever used."[58] Recalling the military's integration of film technologies as essential armaments, this ad now situates the projector as a "weapon" of consumer culture, mobilizing sales through the power of the automatic screen.

Panoram production folded by 1947, but Mills was still pushing its repurposed Panoram-style machines for retail displays in stores and businesses.[59] However unsuccessful this push may have been, their marketing initiatives prove revelatory of expanding postwar desires for mobilizing screens in retail contexts. Drawing upon soldiers' manifold screen encounters during their military service, GIs, now returning to the civilian workforce with not just exposure to but also specific training in this kind of screen technology, could identify with this notion of the mobilized moving-image screen. Armed and equipped with more strategies for incorporating moving-image technologies into their everyday lives, the returning soldiers are then rendered the target demographic for buying into this tech-savvy dream of a postwar America.[60] Having been trained, entertained, and sustained by film screens during military service, the mobile private emerges from military service adept in shaping a consumer culture where moving-image screens, ranging from televisions to home projectors, take precedence as the foregone conclusion of wartime.

The Mobilization of the Moving Image

From these various iterations of the Panoram's circulation beyond its initial commercial capacities to institutional environs, the enduring protocols that frame the Panoram's implementation throughout these military contexts repeatedly underscores the importance of automation, screen integration, and mobility. By retaining its commercial function as an automatic film-vending technology, the Panoram's individual, small-screen viewing is repeatedly marked by notions of user control (at the push of a button) and programming repetition with its self-looping projector. By placing the automatic film machine into institutional military spaces, these individualized and user-friendly screen encounters transcended their prewar novelty and commercial functions, positioning the screen as integral to a range of military training practices and helping to expand institutional screening spaces.

As an amusement machine in servicemen's recreational centers, as a therapeutic machine in veteran hospitals, and as instructional devices at military training sites, the military's functions for the Panoram maps broader desires for both screen technologies and moving-image content that can be scaled to and integrated with its surroundings. From the positioning of films as weapons of war to therapeutic remedies, the diverse discourse of military film exhibition frames site-specific screens like the Panoram as always functional to a particular viewing context. By rendering these screens as ordinary, utilitarian fixtures in often-bright multipurpose environs (from hospital wards to outdoor training facilities), the military's innovative implementation of cinematic technologies into the daily lives of its users made small film screens not just automatic but also natural and ubiquitous in their placement in the broader cultural landscape.

Rather than the war putting a halt to the development and expansion of moving-image technologies with its production and material restrictions (as is often recounted in the histories of U.S. television, for example), the military's uptake and bolstering of film technologies evidence innovative screen adoption, adaptation, and expansion. The U.S. military's specific mobilization of the Panoram repositions the screen as a vital solution to wartime constraints and a viable tool for the GI's postwar economic prosperity. The military's adoption of the automatic, small-screen Panoram reframed the display of film from movie viewings in darkened rooms to individualized and integrative small-screen engagements. As the Panoram represents just one of the many film and moving-image screen technologies employed by the U.S. military during World War II, such institutional appropriations of consumer-oriented screen technologies reveal emerging screen protocols that extend well beyond the practices of war. In their training of the mobile private in automatic and integrated film technologies, the U.S. military helped usher in a postwar consumer culture, where soldiers and screens find their way home from the war.

Part II

Short Forms and Enduring Formations

4

Up Close and Personal

The Shifting Aesthetics of the Jukebox Short

A group of wholesome-looking teens lounge in a college dormitory. With a school pendant hanging on the wall, attractive young women sitting in chairs casually readings books, and friends relaxing on a couch nearby, this college scene provides the backdrop for a Mel-Tones' Soundie, a rendition of *Lullaby of Broadway* (1945). Featuring smooth vocal harmonies, light instrumentation, and, most importantly, tightly framed close-ups of smiling, friendly vocalists, *Lullaby*'s quaint staging of a music performance—particularly for a musical short—is striking in its simplicity; there is no spectacle, no dancing, no band, not even a performance venue. As opposed to the theatrics of a Hollywood musical or the featured musicianship of big-band orchestras so common in the late 1930s and early 1940s shorts, *Lullaby* instead evokes a saccharine simplicity in both its song style and its static staging of the young singing quintet. Although such college-themed Soundies comprise a small fraction of Soundies, *Lullaby*'s mundane musical representations illustrate key aesthetic changes in Soundies during the mid-1940s, a style developed around the visualization of personal song delivery and an emphasis on commonplace settings as sites for musical performance.

With music recordings constituting the source material for their films, Soundies' aesthetics and representational strategies were informed heavily by current music trends and the availability of touring musicians. But the visual representations found in Soundies are not just a direct reflection of the recorded music. Even though the various producers of Soundies were not always innovative in their visual treatment of bands and often employed boilerplate backdrops and setups, especially with their limited budgets and production turnaround time, they did far more than just document musical performances. Soundies producers introduced and developed their own visual techniques that provided new ways for experiencing music on and for the small screen. Positioned at the intersection of the music and film industries, Soundies evidence emerging trends in both recorded music and film, and their formal qualities highlight key changes at the intersections of popular media practices during the 1940s. As the reliance on music recordings began to usurp the role of live performances on the radio throughout the 1930s and 1940s, trends in media consumption increasingly became oriented around consumer playback technologies like the long-established phonograph and its coin-operated offshoot, the jukebox, which numbered around five hundred thousand by 1940.[1] These changes in decentralized media practices also include moving images with the increased use of small-gauge film projectors in a range of educational, institutional, and domestic spaces. The proliferation of these user-friendly media technologies opened new consumer spaces where both moving images and music could be encountered and informed the kinds of media that would circulate there. In their short and scaled-down representations, Soundies producers developed and cultivated a new film-music aesthetic based on these new modes of media interactions that were becoming increasingly dispersed and integrated into everyday spaces.

In addition to changes in popular media practices, a major factor in the stylistic development of Soundies during the 1940s was the American Federation of Musicians (AFM) recording ban. With wartime budgetary and material restrictions being imposed on Mills Novelty's manufacture of new Panorams soon after their initial launch in December 1940, the burgeoning SDC was already facing limitations in their proposed plans for development and expansion. Adding to their uphill battles, the announcement of the AFM recording ban provided yet another hurdle for the producers of Soundies. From August 1, 1942, until November 1943, union musicians caused an all-out halt in the music industry by refusing to make new recordings until union demands were met.[2] Hollywood was exempt from the ban, but Panoram Soundies—because of their similarities to and associations with the then lucrative jukebox industry—were not. To compensate for the shortage of both new music recordings and available film stock due to wartime manufacturing restrictions, the SDC found ways to circumvent the ban on union musicians. Incorporating strategies similar to those of the recorded music industry, the SDC made films featuring recordings from vocalists, a cappella groups, and nonunion performers, many of whom were African American. They also stockpiled footage of musical performances from older and lesser-known films.

Prior to the AFM ban, early Soundies borrowed from the formal conventions of 1930s Hollywood musical short subjects with their emphasis on jazz-oriented bandstand performances like Warner's jazz shorts. Due in part to these restrictions in the recording industry, the SDC began to cultivate their own style of juke-films that incorporated a variety of music styles and entertainment scenarios. Soundies document the end of the big-band era and witness the emergence of other commercial music genres like spirituals, country western, and rhythm and blues, styles that highlight vocalists and small bands with pared-down instrumentation and fewer highbrow associations. Historian Adam Green claims that BMI, which supported a variety of black music styles, contributed directly to the rise of black music during this era by making a deal with jukebox operators.[3] Unlike ASCAP and its more limited Broadway and orchestral fare, BMI catered to the niche markets that were being cultivated at jukebox locales across the United States. Bolstered by the wartime mood for patriotism, simple ballads, and Americana, these changing popular musical styles provided new listening experiences not often found on major radio networks or in Hollywood at this time. Consequently, these shifts in the circulation and availability of popular music styles directly influenced the music recorded for Soundies, which increasingly aligned itself with and borrowed from the programming selections from jukeboxes.

In filming smaller bands and vocalists, Soundies producers began to develop a screen aesthetic based less upon musicianship and theatrical performances and more on the personalization of musical experiences, a smaller scale of music-screen representation befitting the pared-down styles of music while also correlating to the often-intimate scale of spaces where Soundies would be viewed. Rather than the expected setting of a big-band performance venue, Soundies increasingly were set in domestic interiors, cafés, or quaint spaces like gardens and parks. With popular music now being visualized through condensed camera work and commonplace settings, Soundies provided new ways to integrate both film and music into the surround and constituted a pivotal moment in the imaging of popular music for the small screen that anticipated musical programming on postwar television. They helped reimagine the form and possibilities for circulating popular music and other forms of short media across media platforms.

"Slick, Static, and Devoid of Surprise": Soundies' Staid Musical Aesthetic

In November 1942, *Los Angeles Times* film columnist Philip Scheuer lamented the declining quality of Hollywood's musical films: "The fact is that appeal to the ear has replaced appeal to the eye . . . visually and artistically the camera has ceased to exist."[4] Unlike the visual spectacles of 1920s and early-1930s musicals like those of Berkeley, who "created showy, rhythmic patterns out of music," or the "truly cinematic" Lubitsch musicals, the columnist sardonically condemns the "practical" musical aesthetic and claims that "even a Hollywood steeped in shortages and restrictions can evolve a better kind of musical than she is giving us at present": "They simply point their mikes and cameras at a stage and let 'em roll. It's always a stage (in a theater, a night club, a honky tonk, a skating rink, a fashion show, a what not) or a band stand. That's where folks put on a show, ain't it? And never mind cutting away either: If she's a singer, let's see her mouth and movements; if he's a slide trombonist, let's watch him blow! Maybe it ain't art—but it's real!"[5] The reviewer's critique points to key tensions in representing music on film. First, it calls attention to the often-perceived divide between sound and image, with the reviewer claiming here that music has sadly become more dominant than the visual. Second, the reviewer outlines two possible modes for representing music on the screen, either conceptually or through performance. Expressing a desire for film that's more classical than realist, this account of filmed musical trends aptly captures the changing musical aesthetic of the late 1930s and early 1940s Hollywood features and shorts, dominated by static shots of bandstands performing a few musical numbers.

The tensions surrounding the representation and integration of popular music on film was not new to this era or to Soundies, as the advent of sound on film in the 1920s fueled similar debates about how music could best be used on the screen. Like Soundies, filmed popular music from the late 1920s and throughout the 1930s often circulated in the form of stand-alone shorts featuring staged performances of songs or vaudeville comedy sketches.[6] Even as feature-length musicals were gaining popularity in the late 1920s, Vitaphone Varieties and their mode of presentational and performance-oriented shorts circulated widely—the difference being that these short films were exhibited alongside other feature films, lending the reception of these shorts to a broader theatrical context.[7] Featuring many of the same big-band orchestras who would go on to film Soundies (Artie Shaw, Cab Calloway, Jimmie Lunceford), Warner's big-band shorts from the late 1930s certainly provided a viable format from which early Soundies would borrow. Offering three sequential shorts per reel, these roughly nine-minute films primarily featured static bandstands with a specific emphasis on instrumentation. A typical Warner's short starts with a shot of the entire bandstand and then introduces the bandleader. From there, the cameras structure themselves around the orchestration by either focusing on a soloist or a particular band section. Occasionally, canted low-angle shots indicate changes in tempo, and the split screens would compress entire band sections into the screen in opposing medium shots, as if to stage band sections against each other. In *Symphony of Swing* (1939), a Warners-Vitaphone short featuring Artie Shaw and his orchestra, several of these split-screen techniques are used as well as superimposition of soloists. Providing an illustrative composite of big-band orchestration, the film highlights specific instruments, as if to instruct the audience how to listen as much as to entertain them with its music.

Similar in scope to Warner's musical shorts from the 1930s, Soundies, particularly during their first year of production, extended this tradition of bandstand films but offered a more stripped-down product with fewer camera setups. Jimmy Roosevelt's Globe Productions produced the first eight Soundies in July 1940, and they include three films featuring Lorraine Page's orchestra. Although most of these films include dancing, the main emphasis is on the band onstage. By featuring exclusively big-band orchestral arrangements, the SDC wanted to claim ties to Hollywood and bolster the "quality" of their films while sharpening their distinction from peep-show films on coin-operated machines. An early review of Soundies in *Time Magazine* claims they are "less like the peep shows of the penny arcades than it is like the cinema's onetime musical shorts."[8] However, SDC also sought to maintain a difficult balancing act in not wanting to be seen as competition to Hollywood features, a stance taken by many in the 16mm nontheatrical field at this time.[9] Roosevelt even claimed that Soundies would give "tavern-hounds . . . a taste for full-length pictures" and "stimulate attendance at the picture houses," thereby framing Soundies as promotional advertisements for Hollywood musical features.[10]

Though not as elaborately produced as the Warner's shorts, this first reel of Soundies replicates the style of older bandstand films by showcasing performances in nightclubs replete with choruses, orchestras, and audience members. *Row, Row, Row* (1940), for example, features singer Joy Hodges singing about a Romeo ("Row-me-oh!") wooing his lover. As Hodges glides from the stage floor to tables throughout the nightclub, she progressively builds upon the chorus of "row, row, row," with each delivery becoming more sultry and breathy. Even with Hodges's sultry performance and the film's added visual gag of oarsmen rowing Hodges off the stage, early reviews express disdain for this style of staged musical performance. Coverage from a Soundies premiere party in *Look* claims that Soundies are "on the monotonous side" but "they will probably get by on their novelty," referring to their exhibition on the Panoram.[11] Reviewers from both *Variety* and *Motion Picture Herald* claim that, even with lots of dancing and occasional sex appeal, they "fail to maintain sustained interest,"[12] and *Time* magazine calls 1940s Soundies "tepid."[13] What is clear from these early accounts is that public tastes found this kind of filmed musical entertainment to be an already-dated practice in need of development. From the outset, Soundies producers recognized the need to expand and update the types of films that would play on the Panoram. With the initial Soundies launch primarily consisting of "musical selections played by name orchestras," early accounts indicated production plans "to broaden out into straight vocalists, variety, crossfire comics, and even three-minute comedy shorts, with a thread of a plot."[14]

Throughout 1941, Soundies' first full year of production and distribution, the films are similar in scope and production to the early test films. Using nightclub sets and big orchestras, the production quality remained comparable to mediocre Hollywood fare. In fact, three 1941 Soundies feature songs (*Pete the Piper*; *A Knife, a Fork and a Spoon*; and *Broadway Caballero*) from James Roosevelt's feature *Pot o' Gold*, a 1941 musical starring Jimmy Stewart and Paulette Goddard, and use set pieces from Roosevelt's Globe studio. Although they employ different musicians and do not use actual excerpts from the feature, they credit the film in the opening titles. Additionally, cast members from *Pot o' Gold* and other actors involved with Globe Productions often appeared in early Soundies, furthering the continuity between Soundies shorts and features. When SDC president Jimmy Roosevelt had to resign just two weeks after the company's lavish New York premiere to take his post in the U.S. Marines, sources were quick to clarify that Roosevelt would remain closely affiliated with SDC as a stockholder and a director.[15] Such connections to Hollywood (and Washington) VIPs were instrumental in positioning Soundies and Mills as frontrunners in the "nickel movies" race.[16]

Within one year's time, however, Soundies started to rebrand themselves as their own kind of juke-film. Responding to the first wave of lukewarm reviews and lack of interest beyond its novelty phase, the SDC recognized the need to align with other coin-operated amusements, particularly the more traditional and omnipresent jukebox, with which they often vied for attention in various public spaces. In a detailed account from producer/director Jack Barry from *Billboard* in early 1942, he clearly demarcates Soundies viewing practices from theatrical film and further claims that Soundies are a "new medium" requiring a break from Hollywood's classical style: "It has been necessary to develop new techniques which contradict certain long-established motion picture practices. We have had to tailor our productions with the fact in mind that our customers don't give the screen the prolonged concentration they give the theater screen; therefore certain types of intricate treatment are out. Certain lighting effects and camera techniques which might be acceptable for the theater screen couldn't be used. We had to place emphasis, also, on music which is peppy and bright and eliminate slow, draggy numbers."[17] Rather than actors being "oblivious of an audience," Barry contends that actors in Soundies are treated best by "close-up camera treatment." He continues, "Elaborate settings for long shots and intricate routines are just as much out of place as they would be in the intimate night club, where the accent must be on intimate delivery . . . Split-second treatments and up-to-the-minute music are musts." In addition, Barry twice highlights the importance of tempo with respect to the music selections, claiming the need to eliminate "slow, draggy numbers." With the presumed distracted viewing of Soundies, Barry also places emphasis on sound over the moving image, which would also become a truism in early television being referred to as "radio with pictures."[18]

With his emphasis on direct address, close-ups, and quickly paced edits and songs, Barry proposes a style of short filmmaking organized around screen size and viewing and listening practices. Panorams, he suggests, invite camera techniques that are simple and focused with the smaller scale of the screen in mind. The framing of the image to the size of the screen may seem obvious or even intuitive from a contemporary perspective, but these production practices had to be developed through trial and error and with the increased understanding of new screen practices, as was also the case with early television's often uneven representations. Because of wartime restrictions as well as the pending AFM recording ban, much of what Barry envisioned for a successful Soundies reel would not be fully realized, but his commentary marks a clear shift in the style of musical films and in their changing modes of reception.

The Ban of the Band

Jack Barry's desired treatment of musical subjects most directly manifests on the actual Panoram screen with an increased emphasis on singers, often shot in close-up in direct address to the audience and with less focus on the other members of the band. *Hi Diddle Diddle* (dir. Andrew Stone, 1943), a war-era screwball comedy, offers a rare glimpse of two musical shorts playing on a Panoram machine and nicely—though in an unintentional parody—captures the stylistic shifts in the juke-film aesthetic. When the scene begins, the Panoram is positioned as a background source of diegetic music in a small tavern. Playing a nonvocal orchestral short, the Panoram is all but ignored except by cabaret singer Leslie Quayle (June Havoc), who, upon entering the tavern, jokingly comments, "Remind me to get one of those for my bathroom." Even in a passing comedic aside, Quayle acknowledges the Panoram as a new kind of screen technology and as particularly suited for small spaces (even for a private bathroom). After the instrumental film ends, a man puts a dime into the Panoram and then a livelier, Latin-themed song, "The Man with the Big Sombrero," begins to play. The Soundie knockoff features the singer Quayle and nicely emulates the Soundie's style, replete with innuendo and ethnic flare. The actual Quayle, sitting at a table in the tavern, quickly quips, "Say, she's pretty good." The scene then focuses on the film within the film for a verse, until the tavern Quayle stands up, begins to dance, and joins her screen-self in a duet.[19] "The Man with a Big Sombrero" illustrates many of the formal qualities outlined by producer Jack Barry: upbeat music, close-up shots, direct addresses to the audience, and intimate staging and delivery. In addition, its use of Mexican costuming and song matches well with Soundies' frequent appeals to the "exotic" with their use of ethnic music and themes.

Hi Diddle Diddle's playful rendition of Soundies illustrates the shifting schema of musical shorts from bandstands to solo vocal numbers and provides another good example of the recurring trope of screen-space connection found frequently in accounts and representations of Soundies' exhibition practices. The presence of a Panoram in a Hollywood feature from 1943 also offers a timely commentary upon the surmounting tensions among live musicians and the increased reliance on musical recordings and playback technologies within the media industries. As Tim Anderson argues, this was a not a minor resistance to technological change by union musicians; the 1940s constitutes a pivotal moment in the reorganization of the "techno-cultural assemblage," where artists and executives alike across the media industries engaged in the "struggle over the terms, forms, and goals of popular musical production in the United States."[20] With singer Quayle's own participation in the filmed performance, "Sombrero" conveniently reconciles this tension between live performer and recorded music in a harmonious resolution and interplay. In actuality, this was far from the case.

When Petrillo's AFM recording ban initially went into effect in August 1942, record companies had already braced themselves for the shortage by stockpiling recordings and releasing back catalogs. The SDC, who had distributed roughly five hundred films at that point (almost a third of the total number of Soundies that would be produced), felt confident they could weather these temporary restrictions and adopted similar strategies. Since no new Panorams were being manufactured due to wartime restrictions and the existent machines had a high turnover in locations, they claimed to not worry about exhausting their supply.[21] Within a few months, however, their attitudes changed. By January 1943, according to *Billboard*, the recording ban had "taxed the producers' ingenuity to the limit" requiring them to experiment in their production of short musical films: "Unable to use musicians, they are forced to buy old musical tracks . . . or concentrate on vocals only. This condition has made the use of old musical shorts very popular."[22]

Another account explains how SDC's publicist-turned-producer/director, William Forrest Crouch, also employed musical talent that was not covered by the ban (like harmonica and banjo players) and comedic novelty acts and vocalists, in addition to repurposing old film shorts.[23] These resourceful, if not desperate, tactics had many enduring consequences like the removal of the bandstand from the musical short. Additionally, the augmented use of vocalists, nonunion musicians, and instrumentalists from lesser-known music genres like western, R&B, and hillbilly all provided more musical variety as well as a new kind of screen presence that included African Americans. Some black musicians, of course, belonged to the AFM and were consequently restricted by the ban, but there were several black artists recording in "race music" genres who were provided with expanded opportunities during the ban. Of particular note, the flourishing of independent record labels like Capitol and Decca and their legitimation of African American music would aid in an increased black presence on the Panoram screen that would far exceed Hollywood's representations at the time.[24]

During the ban, the short musical form diverges from Hollywood-derived bandstand films and takes on multiple forms, including dance numbers, comedy, and variety acts, with less emphasis on musical performance itself and a greater alignment with trends in the recorded music industry, particularly the cultivation of niche music markets. That is not to say that bandstand films disappeared entirely. With several Soundie reissues from 1940 to 1941 and clips circulating from lesser-known 1930s musicals and shorts, vestiges of this older style of musical film still circulated but in a different context and alongside a greater variety of musical shorts.

In unintended ways, the production limitations of the ban aided in the realization of Jack Barry's aforementioned filmmaking practices. With Soundies' representations moving toward personality-oriented performances for this new medium, particularly with their emphasis on vocalists, such techniques increasingly became standard and necessary during the ban to circumvent the use of union musicians. *Caravan*, a Mills Brothers' Soundie released in October 1942 (two months after the start of the ban), most directly evidences the increased reliance on vocalists and how their talents could be utilized during the musicians' strike. As the Mills Brothers' signature sound consists of their a capella vocal arrangements, *Caravan* stages their voices as stand-ins for an actual band by simulating trumpet sounds and other instruments, for example.

Offering a direct commentary on the current AFM strike, the premise of this Soundie is centered on a barnyard dance where one of the dancers complains that the band "done stood us up." One of the Mills brothers responds in this (rather atypical) opening rhyming dialogue sequence: "No jive? And no jumping? / Well, I guess this calls for something." The Mills Brothers then proceed to sing an instrumental number while the barnyard dance commences. This rustic, black-cast Soundie features the skillful Mills Brothers as well as a few outstanding dance performances (incorporating styles that evoke early forms of break dancing) and divides its focus between song delivery and

FIGURE 12 The Mills Brothers watch a dancer in this production still from *Caravan* (1942). From Soundies Distributing Corporation of America photographs of the Margaret Herrick Library, Academy of Motion Picture Arts and Sciences.

dance. Shots once reserved for bandstand close-ups now feature dancers, the vocalists, and a few gags for comedic effect.[25]

Clearly recognizing the timeliness of this Soundie, the *Billboard* review of *Caravan* describes it as "a new kind of movie machine short: a program without the use of musical instruments. This is used to test the possibility of employing nonmusical acts, due to the recording ban laid down by the American Federation of Musicians."[26] Other vocal groups like the Song Spinners, the Escorts and Betty, and comedic vocal acts like Rufe Davis and the Hoosier Hot Shots were also utilized during the ban.[27] Playing upon the novelty of the voice providing orchestral replacement, Rufe Davis's Soundies *I'm the Sound Effects Man* and *Mama Don't Allow It* (1942) centralize his vocal talents for musical impressions.[28] *Mama Don't Allow It* shows Rufe performing live on a radio soundstage with several close-ups of his clownish faces while he mimics various musical instruments. Like the Mills Brothers' *Caravan*, *Mama Don't Allow It* similarly provides a premise for the lack of a band performance. As Davis repeatedly sings that "mama don't allow" music to be played, his vocal talents become necessary in supplying the banned/band instrumentation. Davis's vocal performance is intercut with scenes of two children listening and tap dancing to his broadcast at home. These cutaways emphasize the domestic space of the radio broadcast, while the Soundie provides a depiction not just of song delivery but also of its circulation and reception.

In visualizing and locating the consumption of popular music as a domestic, privatized practice for young audiences, the film doubly displaces the performance of live music: first through Davis's own vocal remediation of banned musical instruments and also through the context of the radio broadcast. Even though *Mama Don't Allow It* still provides room for live performance through the presence of Rufe Davis at the radio station, it clearly is playing upon current tensions within the music industry all while circumventing the constraints of the recording ban through its own filmed production of a nonunion vocalist. By broadening the circulation of recorded popular music through their films (and in their film representations), the SDC further positions its practices within a changing media environment that emphasizes a pared-down musical aesthetic and smaller but more diffuse reception contexts like the home audience.

The frequent employ of vocal talents, particularly these literal substitutions for the missing instruments, acknowledge the industry's perceived lack in available music recordings that had been dominated by the aesthetics of big-band arrangements since the mid-1930s, and such stand-in performances were not always well received. One *Billboard* reviewer, claiming that music was "sorely needed," showed disdain for this practice, calling the Mills Brothers' *Caravan* ". . . less than successful" and the talents of Rufe Davis "freakish."[29] The reliance on vocal talents, though, soon became more standardized and surmounted the status of just gimmick or cheap substitution. During and immediately following the ban, trades sources focus on the rising popularity of the singer as a noteworthy rupture in the popular music landscape and frequently cite the AFM ban as a determining factor. A *Billboard* survey of GI favorites from 1944 notes, "Of the 13 top platters chosen by the fighting forces, nine of them feature vocalist above the bands, if they aren't 100 per cent singer features," and adds, "the Petrillo ban is probably responsible to some extent for this overwhelming popularity for the vocal efforts as against the full band jobs."[30]

Of course, multiple factors influence popular music trends and, as music historian Peter Townsend in *Pearl Harbor Jazz* notes, the rise of the vocalist during this era should not be solely attributed to the recording ban, as singers were already gaining prominence and increasingly were featured in big-band recordings.[31] A 1943 article in *Billboard* claims that "America" wants its music simple with "preferences for light-hearted lyrics" from straight vocalists, especially during wartime.[32] Given this pervasive patriotic spirit, sentimental crooners and popular screen stars like Bing Crosby and Frank Sinatra began to top and consequently dominate the charts during the ban. As Soundies producers had limited financial resources, big-name acts like Crosby were rarely featured in Soundies. In fact, Crosby's only appearance in a Soundie was during the ban, and it was footage taken from *I Surrender Dear* (dir. Mack Sennet, 1931). Crosby's performance appears in the Soundie *Musical Movie Memories* (1943), which also includes footage from a comedic number by Bob Hope from 1932.

A typical Soundies reel during the ban might feature as many as three vocal groups by lesser-known acts (like the Song Spinners and the Smoothies), two musical dance acts (one usually black-cast), a comedy song (often hillbilly), a big-band Soundie reissue, and old film excerpts like the aforementioned *Musical Movie Memories*. This kind of programming variety did more than just compensate for the lack of available bands; it participated in the expansion of nonunion music styles—encompassing everything from spirituals, blues, and hillbilly to western music—and a greater circulation of black talent on the screen. As Tim Anderson asserts, "Variety acts as a principle for modern media economies," and this aesthetic shift is central to the reshaping of the popular music industry at this time.[33] Soundies made these heterogeneous musical styles visible and available by circulating images of black performers to places where black voices were heard (like on the jukebox or radio) but seldom seen. During the two years of the ban, the number of black-cast Soundies doubled in production with novelty numbers also increasing.[34] While the upper echelon of popular white recording artists seldom was found on the Panoram, black musicians Louis Jordan and the Mills Brothers, both topping *Billboard* charts in 1943, were prolific in Soundies during the ban.

The SDC's increased exposure of nonunion black musicians during the AFM ban dovetailed with changing practices in the recording industry as well as the proliferation of jukeboxes. As the recording ban allowed for independent record companies to promote nonunion musicians and thereby increase their sales, "these changes," Townsend explains, "favored country or folk music over the Broadway-Hollywood idiom of popular song that operated under the old system."[35] More so, BMI, countering a proposed effort from ASCAP to charge jukebox operators new licensing fees, struck a deal with the coin-machine industry in 1940, which resulted in their "friendly relationship" with jukebox owners.[36] The steady supply of BMI music, which heavily relied on small music publishers recording R&B and county and western genres, playing in jukeboxes across the country also helped shape this turn from the "Broadway-Hollywood idiom" to "folk" and other varied music genres. With almost half a million jukeboxes located in public places in the 1940s, jukebox operator purchases accounted for 40 percent of the recorded music market.[37] Their impact on the kinds of popular music that circulated in everyday spaces across the United States cannot be overlooked. Several accounts from

Billboard indicate that the jukebox was the preferred medium for music delivery among GIs and teens alike, and it had strong associations with white, working-class consumers.[38] Trade accounts further indicate that the stripped-down music styles of country and Americana were more conducive to repeated play in taverns and in spaces better suited to sitting and drinking than dancing, ultimately making the purchase of these genres more profitable for jukebox operators than the dance genres of big band and swing.[39]

The coupling of these conditions in the music industry and the jukebox trade had an immense influence on Soundies' own expansion of popular music styles and their shift from bandstand shorts to juke-films. Soundies' visual interpretations of nonbandstand music also quite literally added new faces to the already-changing sounds of American popular music. By providing moving images to these emerging American music genres, Soundies' already small-screen aesthetics became further concentrated around smaller bands with simple, straightforward performance styles. No longer performing in nightclubs or on bandstands, musicians were removed from their stages to environs that evoke various aspects of Americana and the home (rustic settings, campfires, frontiers, and cabins). For example, the Emerson Mountaineers, also known as Tom Emerson's Hillbillies, were featured in sixteen Soundies, many of which were released during the ban because of their nontraditional instrumentation like the accordion and the ocarina. Located in a cabin setting, *Seven Years with the Wrong Woman* (1943) shows the sextet performing a "lugubrious" song about love gone awry.[40] Mainly focusing on their forlorn faces, the film showcases the various members of the band as they relay their tales of heartache couched in corny jokes ("They say love is blind / but search 'til you find / a face you can stand everyday"). They are staged with their instruments, but the Soundie primarily offers close-ups of faces, preferring emotionality to musicianship. The band members also sing to each other as much as to the audience directly, minimizing the performance of the music itself and emphasizing their storytelling. Unlike earlier bandstand Soundies that recreate the feel of live musical performances, these Soundies foreground mood and personality more than musicianship or showmanship and at times even attempt to tell a story.

Rather than presenting a showy spectacle that evokes the experience of a nightclub, these juke-films are directed toward personalized and direct engagement with their viewers. This new mode of visual-music engagement not only reflects changes in and availability of popular music genres; Soundies' cultivation of a small-screen aesthetic of familiarity and closeness also highlights what Paddy Scannell calls the "individualizing power of modern communication systems."[41] Claiming that 1940s popular crooners evoke a style of "sincerity" that can only be made possible through their mediations in recording and broadcast technologies, Scannell characterizes this change from the "extraordinary" public voice of the concert hall to the more "ordinary voice" on a recording as the displacement of "public performative values . . . by private performative values that privileged the particular and the personal."[42] Coupling this audio-sincerity with the filmic close-up,[43] Soundies like *Seven Years* visualize a domestic mode of address that resonates more with the broadcast formats of radio and presage early television aesthetics.

With their featured vocalists, pared-down songs and music styles, and the downsizing of bands in general, Soundies developed new modes of personalized small-screen engagement. When James Petrillo lifted the AFM recording ban on Soundies in late October 1943 and big-band music could come back into the picture, the face of popular music on film, the very way it was imaged, had altered dramatically.[44] Although more instruments returned to Soundies after the ban, they were no longer featured and became upstaged by close-ups of dancers, vocalists, and the occasional small bandleader. This is not to say that the AFM ban or Soundies were the sole cause of this emerging trend in popular music and its representational practices. The ongoing changes in the formal attributes of the Soundies musical short, however, illuminate important interstices and convergences across popular media industries at this time. With Soundies performers later emerging as popular 1950s television personalities like Nat King Cole and Lawrence Welk, their films reimagined musicianship on and for the small screen as personal and direct in its delivery and ordinary in its settings—an aesthetic that helped shape the visual economy of popular music for the small screen while also making recorded music intrinsic to small-screen formats and spaces.[45]

The Jukebox Film and Shifting Screen Expectations

Soundies' cultivation of a juke-film aesthetic changed how people encountered and anticipated encountering recorded popular music.[46] Within the fourteen months of the recording ban, Soundies producers, out of desperate resourcefulness, not only weathered the ban but also honed their craft in picturing music for the small screen. Favorable accounts of Soundies on the Panoram surfaced throughout the mid-1940s, indicating a sustained level of interest and popularity in the juke-film beyond the AFM ban. According to one *Billboard* report, the Armory Post Restaurant in Springfield, Massachusetts, experienced a 15 percent increase in business due to a recent installment of several Panorams.[47] With jukeboxes "running a poor second" to the preferred Panorams, patrons "played the machines constantly, taking advantage of the relaxing benefits of enjoying music and movie[s] with their meal." Highlighting the more ambient experience of "relaxing" to Soundies films, "numerous armory employees professed that they mistook the machines for 'television sets.'"

This correlation between small-screen technologies, relaxed viewing experiences, and short, mood-evoking programs recurs throughout popular trade discourse and speaks favorably to the ongoing proliferation of Soundies on small, domestic screens. Even with wartime material shortages continually slowing the production of Soundies and Panorams after the ban, trade accounts portend a promising future for Soundies in the postwar market, particularly in the burgeoning television market.[48] As early as 1944, Soundies, it was hoped, would provide an ideal visual model for new modes viewing of short media on the small screen. One *Billboard* article explicitly frames the formal attributes of the Soundie as perfect for television screens and overtly recognizes Soundies' favorable small-screen aesthetics. As "productions stick to close-ups so necessary for the small screen on juke box movies," the Soundie "uses practically the same technique as is now used for television . . . talent is concentrated in [a] small area, therefore making action suitable for television screens."[49] With a reported stockpile of 1,500 short subjects at that time, Soundies can be "instantly used for video" with "all current and future reels being made with the new field in view."[50]

An intermediary between Hollywood films and television both aesthetically and technologically, Soundies were among the first films to make their way onto the television screen. By the summer of 1950, after the SDC ceased production, Soundies (whose catalog was now owned by Official Television, an adjunct of Official Films) were leased to six television stations nationwide under a one-year contract: WCBS-TV New York, three NBC stations (WNBQ Chicago, WNBK Cleveland, and WNBW Washington), KTTV Los Angeles, and KRON San Francisco. By November, Official sold the entire Soundies package of what they called *Music Hall Varieties* to three more stations (WNAC-TV Boston, WFIL-TV Philadelphia, and WBTV Charlotte) and additional half-packages to WJAR-TV Providence, KPRC-TV Houston, GMQ Havana, and XEW Mexico City, resulting in a profitable $400,000 deal for Official.[51] With the stipulation of a "maximum showing of any one film . . . four times a year," Soundies could provide these stations with up to five hours of programming a week.[52]

Used primarily as brief musical filler during the early 1950s, Soundies also appeared in a few television-deejay shows where they were used as visual records.[53] Even as early television programmers borrowed and adapted programming models and broadcast structures from radio, they also recognized Soundies as viable visual content for television screens, a visual format with an equally strong aural component. Although television broadcasters would not come to rely heavily on Hollywood films until the end of the 1950s, both their imagined and occasional use of Soundies during television's formative years helped expand television from primarily a live broadcast medium with event-oriented programming to a repository for short film. More so, these mentions of Soundies as a viable (if not lasting) content for television suggests that their juke-film format could circulate beyond the Panoram and that, perhaps, popular music had a place on television and other future small screens.

The synchronicities and overlap between Soundies' demise by 1947 and early television's rise to prominence point less to Soundies' failures (as its business was on shaky ground since its inception) than to the larger trends in media in which Soundies partook, an environ organized by the increased circulation of short media on user-oriented technologies. From its outset, Soundies promotional materials envisioned particular modes of short-media use and engagement. The SDC defined Soundies by their brief duration; they play "for a period of a few seconds less than three minutes."[54] Emphasizing their duration in microterms of minutes and seconds, the less-than-three-minute Soundies are contrasted with the length of features ("an hour or two") and other shorts ("fifteen minutes"). Accompanying the length of films are implications about their patterns of reception. Unlike feature-length films "created with the intention of being seen only once," it claims, "Soundies must be so good, so rich in fast and concentrated action . . . that the same persons may want to see the very film fifty or more times!"[55] Defined not only by their brevity, Soundies also suggests an intensified, repetitive viewing experience (fifty times, no less) by the same individual.

These assertions by the SDC anticipated particular modes of short-media engagement based on repetition. Initially, Soundies were deemed as failures for not encouraging repeated viewings. Rather than entertainment that urges repetition, a reviewer from the first Soundies premiere notes a time lag: "Despite it all, however, 2 ½ minutes seems too long for most of the subjects . . . Or mebbe it's in those slow spots you're supposed to sip your beer."[56] Several early reviewers shared this skepticism of Soundies as repeatable amusement. Framing Soundies as a visual counter to the jukebox, trade reviews predicted that individuals would not "repeatedly view like they repeatedly listen."[57] Linking repetition with music-based media, these reviews, both from 1940, presume that visual media cannot elicit that kind of reception practice. Whereas visual novelty has a brief shelf life, "popular songs privilege repetition and regularity" and, according to Rick Altman, "align linguistic and musical systems to take advantage of multiple simultaneous closure cues."[58] As Soundies shifted toward a juke-film aesthetic in the mid-1940s, they developed a more apt visual counterpart to the jukebox, which consequently encouraged more musical modes of engagement that relied upon repetition and maximum profitability.

The juke-films reliance on mood, personality, and simple-song delivery further aligned the Panoram with jukebox practices like self-selection, the ability for the consumer to pinpoint and play a specific media short. As self-selection is a key component to the jukebox's success, this should seem a fitting function for Soundie playback on the Panoram, and yet it is never fully actualized. Although the Panoram was individually activated by inserting a dime, the Panoram's continuous film loop made selection a bit of a grab bag, and the Panoram's lack of a self-selecting mechanism is framed as a major flaw from its inception. Accounts from the Panoram's premiere in 1940 are quick to point out, "There's no selector. You take what comes next,"[59] and others ask, "Why no selector?"[60] Making the Panoram's lack of self-selectivity appear outmoded, early reviews of the Panoram are placed alongside such jukebox innovations as dial-in and remote-control machines, which tailor to individuals at tables and booths and begin to privatize the act of consumer selection.[61] Anticipating a postwar resurgence of the Panoram and Soundies market, *Billboard* reports that a "selective movie machine definitely is in the works for the post-war market," indicating how central individual selection was thought to be should the Panoram remain viable.[62] Another report from 1944 similarly claims that Soundies ". . . hope ultimately to perfect a selective mechanism which permits customers to choose their own subjects as they do with juke box records, instead of having to see the reel in unchanged sequence as they do now."[63]

Although the Panoram never fulfills this expectation, the rhetoric of self-selection persists throughout the SDC's six-year circulation. A misleading headline, boasting "Soundies Subjects May Now be Selected," describes Soundies' updated cataloging system, which allows distributors to choose their own reels of eight shorts, which, claims the article, will better serve "Negro locations especially."[64] Sidestepping actual technological innovation, the ability for Soundies distributors to more carefully select and cater to the tastes of their patronage suggests the same desire for more localized (though not totally individualized) viewing practices. It also dovetails with the broadening of independently recorded music markets during the AFM ban, allowing for black artists and regionally specific music to circulate on jukeboxes and on more niche-oriented radio stations.

Couched in the languages of self-selection and repetition, these consumer-oriented discourses position Soundies within the then popular and profitable jukebox vernacular and provide a clear sense of an emerging media practice reliant on individual operation and catering to personal taste preferences. Sometimes framed as an object of contention and even a potential public menace, these user-controlled media technologies inspired debates around these protocols in popular media consumption. An article in *Variety* coins the term "jerk-box" to address the noise complaints resulting from the jukebox's musical presence.[65] Similarly, the opening scene of 1946 noir classic *Blue Dahlia* (George Marshall) features an altercation between two men over the music coming from a jukebox at a bar. The jukebox is playing an upbeat swing number, a number more suitable for group dancing than for men slouching over drinks at the bar. Referring to the jukebox, a man at the bar complains, "Give that thing a rest, will ya?" His friend, intervening, says, "Pipe down. It's his nickel," but the man persists, "That thing gives me a headache!" The scene lays out both sides of the jukebox conflict: the choice of the individual consumer to spend his nickel and select his own musical entertainment and the perceived disruption of these user-controlled media in public consumer spaces.

Revelatory of short media's increasing circulation, the discourse of selection exhibits the desire for media playback at the hands of the individual consumers with complete control of their entertainment (despite both the jukebox's and the Panoram's limited range of options) but at odds with increasingly media-saturated environments.[66] Although this tension between user-controlled technologies and spaces might seem to be resolved in the domestic sphere, where individual tastes do not have to contend with the collective public mood, similar debates persisted in how families organized themselves around domestic television viewing in the 1950s and continue to be addressed through ongoing developments in personalized technologies like headphones and personal screens. By developing these small-screen modes of personal address through their films and their coin-operated mechanisms, the SDC's enduring legacy of the juke-film is not just stylistic; Soundies' short-form media and their small-screen engagement maps a lineage in contemporary media culture geared toward ever-personalized media selections and repetitive screen interactions.

5

"A Swing Half Breed"

Soundies' Hybrid Identities and Raced Attractions

Of the 1,850 Soundies produced from 1940 to 1946, 247 (16 percent) feature black artists and were marketed as Negro films in Soundies Distribution catalogs.[1] In addition, several other Soundies—though not explicitly considered black films—incorporated black dance performances and overt appropriations of black cultural forms, making the number of Soundies to incorporate black talent disproportionately higher than mainstream Hollywood filmmaking during this era. Though Soundies are overlooked in most U.S. film histories because of their nontheatrical status as low-budget 16mm films, Soundies garner some mention in histories of African American film representation, particularly those focusing on histories of jazz on film, due to their inclusion of prominent black musicians and performers like Nat King Cole, Count Basie, Cab Calloway, and Louis Armstrong.[2] Although the documentation of these preeminent musicians is significant, Soundies' broad deployment of racial and ethnic stereotypes complicates the redeeming musical value of these films.

Already largely underrepresented in Hollywood films, black musicians often suffered from misrepresentation when their image was fashioned for the screen. For example, a Louis Armstrong Soundie entitled *Shine* (1942) prominently showcases the artistry of Armstrong on his trumpet while pairing him with a host of derogatory images like shoe-shining and eye-rolling, slack-jawed comedic dancing. The film further literalizes the lyrics to *Shine* by featuring a set piece of a very large black shoe centered high on the stage, dangling over Armstrong's head. By surrounding Armstrong with images associated with black labor, *Shine*, a song ostensibly about Armstrong's dapper décor and a film intended to display his remarkable musical talent, reverts to familiar, demeaning images of blackness.[3] Part of what makes Soundies so visually uneven is their strategy for placing image with musical performance. As scholar Amy Herzog explains, Soundies illustrate the "impossible embodiment" of visualizing the abstractions of music in often quite literal visual signs (such as the aforementioned shoe in *Shine*), often resulting in excessive and even contradictory modes of sound and image representations.[4] This tendency to at once show the music being performed and visually illustrate the content of the songs, all within Soundies' limited production resources, lends itself to an odd assortment of film representations, particularly when considering Soundies' frequent depictions of raced identities.

Soundies such as *Shine* evidence the complex politics of black filmed musical representations during this era. Their visualization of popular music allowed for an augmented black screen presence and, at their best, allowed for new images of black performers to circulate to audiences through the United States, particularly given the venues like bars, taverns, and restaurants where Soundies would be shown. The logics of identity construction that frame these diverse and contradictory representations evince the contested and contradictory identity politics of the war era. With America entering into World War II, questions of American character and national identity circulated prominently in intellectual and popular spheres within and alongside broader wartime sentiments of increased U.S. patriotism and unity. "In battling against totalitarian enemies," historian Philip Gleason explains, "it was understandable . . . that Americans should exalt the principle of diversity."[5] Within Soundies' representations, this articulation of pluralistic American identities figures prominently through overtly patriotic Soundies but, more often, and at times more subtly, through their programming formats. Featuring not just popular black musical genres but Hawaiian, Latin, and Irish songs as well, Soundies proudly and strategically showcased variety in their program releases, creating a mix of musical genres and cultural representations.

As musical shorts, Soundies provide a rich terrain to explore these varied identities on the screen. Unlike feature-length musicals that are bound to the trajectory of narrative, Soundies privilege performance in and of itself without diegetic containment. Free from possible narrative constrictions that might demand certain representational types, Soundies are motivated by the logics of music, visually interpreting popular songs and lyrics. Within this realm of musical performance, an amalgam of cultural forms (like dances, costumes, and lyrics) enacts the very processes of racial and ethnic identity production. The visualization of swing music on the screen, for instance, allowed for popular forms of black expression to be made available to mainstream white America. The same could be said for Latin-inspired Soundies, like the rhumba or the mambo. At times, Soundies' identity constructions are visualized quite literally within the films through tropes of identity morphing, while others are visualized more subtly through the theatricality and performativity implicit in Soundies' performance-oriented films. As Soundies formally provide a privileged forum for identity construction through the musical short, their diffuse exhibition contexts broaden the circulation of racial identities and ethnic formations to potentially diverse audiences, creating new kinds of integrated screen encounters.

Through their evocations of American unity and inclusivity, Hawaiian and Latin Soundies frame cultural differences as marketable commodities, rendering these ethnic forms as appealing and highly appropriable to white audiences. Soundies' logics of difference vary when it comes to their representations of African Americans, as black Soundies were sometimes integrated and other times made explicitly for black audiences. This array of black representations and their often complex negotiations of African American identity politics during the 1940s are evident across ten Soundies featuring Dorothy Dandridge, an emerging actress at the time. Dandridge is sometimes a featured star and other times comic relief; her multiple roles and modes of performance in Soundies, which will be discussed later in this chapter, often contradict the pervasive portrayals of integration and equality presented in Soundies evoking multicultural themes.

Constructions of Ethnicity: The American Mash-Up

Capitalizing on popular music and film trends, Soundies would draw on certain ethnic iconographies to add variety to their programming content. For example, Soundies Program 1223 included a Chinese song with "an oriental motif," two western songs, a Latin dance, a hula, and a "boogie" with "sepia femmes."[6] Frequent Hawaiian themes allowed for Soundies to feature bikini-clad hula girls, and Latin Soundies provided danceable rhythms and often comedic, Carmen Miranda–esque characters. The range of musical styles and genres featured in a Soundies program even extends to the representational strategies within individual films. In fact, if there is any commonality within the disparate body of Soundies' films, it is their frequent blending of multiple forms of cultural expression and music. The popularity of the rhumba spurred multiple mash-up Soundies, including *Rhumba New York* (1943), *Rhumba Swing* (1946), *Rhumba Rebop* (1946), *Rhumboogie* (1943), and *Hula Rumba* (1946).

Within the context of Soundies' programming variety, these performances of ethnic differences suggest a broader embrace of cultural pluralism in the

United States, at least through popular entertainment. These representations of differences, though acknowledged and even at times lavishly performed, are framed and contained under the pretense of a unified American patriotism, a melting-pot mentality that seeks to engage with cultural differences only to erase or to assimilate them. As Gleason explains, popular notions of cultural unification and inclusion "... had a powerful, but somewhat paradoxical, effect on thinking about intergroup relations, ethnocultural affairs, and national identity. The substance of its message, and its practical effect, was strongly assimilationist in tendency. . . . yet the message was couched in the language of pluralism and diversity."[7] Between the Good Neighbor Policy's rhetoric of pursuing Latin American countries as friendly World War II allies and valuable trade markets and the popularized GI fantasy for brown-skinned island women, both Latin American and Hawaiian representations, for instance, provided nonthreatening and appealing constructions of cultural differences.[8]

In *Hula Rumba* (1946), a Soundie fusing Latin-inspired rhythms with Hawaiian dancing, the dancers are featured in hula skirts but are transformed

FIGURE 13 Hula dancers pose in the mash-up Soundie *Hula Rumba* (1946). From Soundies Distributing Corporation of America photographs of the Margaret Herrick Library, Academy of Motion Picture Arts and Sciences.

repeatedly via wipes into "Mexicans" with sombreros and serapes. As the Hawaiian / Latin American dancers are played by white performers, such white role-play simplifies and idealizes the process of U.S. cultural assimilation and identity appropriation. As part of the gimmick of an ethnically coded song, not only do performers don outfits to signify some act of identity tourism, but also, as a moment of visual interest or a way to literalize the lyrics of the song, the very act of transformation is shown, highlighting the performance of shifting identity. This cultural exchange occurs three times in *Hula Rumba*, making these acts of identity transformation the primary visual component in an otherwise straightforward performance-oriented Soundie. With the fluidity of their coupling in this particular Soundie, promoting a blurred exoticism, both the Latin and Hawaiian cultural forms are constructed as readily interchangeable and easily appropriated by dominant white culture.

Identity-passing performances in Soundies commonly feature whites posing as the other, privileging whiteness as the norm and the other as a fantasy type.[9] The Soundie *My Shawl* (1942) by the Borrah Minevitch Harmonica Rascals playfully foregrounds the act of white identity tourism. In the film's brief introduction, radio announcer Don Wilson explains that the performance features "the exotic Chiquita and a chorus of Cuban beauties, most of whom were born in Brooklyn." He then remarks, "We will now take you to El Jive-Oh Cabaret in . . . (laughs) Havana." A self-acknowledged nightclub rendition of Cuba, the film features chorus girls dancing with large shawls swinging around them only to reveal their lack of clothing while the male musicians look on from the side of the stage. Playfully performing Cuban identity and locale, *My Shawl* slides between staging Cuban cultural forms while asserting an irrepressibly U.S. (specifically Brooklyn) presence. Presenting an imagined construction of Cuba that is safely controlled and maintained, *My Shawl*'s cheeky aside about Brooklyn girls playing Cuban dancers ostensibly refers to the popularity of Latin dance forms being appropriated by mainstream U.S. culture.[10] The popular circulation of this joke of Latin passing, especially with New Yorkers who are considered more privy to multicultural exposure, makes manifest, and even literalizes, the Good Neighbor Policy's cultural exchange between the United States and Latin America. By foregrounding the white appropriation of these cultural forms (and turning it into a joke) as opposed to a mutual cultural exchange, such representations foreground white U.S. privilege, a flexibility with self-making, and an ease in traversing cultural barriers without limitations.

Another Latin-themed Soundie, *He's a Latin from Staten Island* (1941), again uses the logics of cultural pluralism to frame ethnic difference.[11] Starring a young Ricardo Montalbán as a stereotypical Latin gigolo, *He's a Latin* features Montalbán serenading women as they ride on the Staten Island Ferry through the New York Harbor.[12] In the final shot of the film, a stodgy white man pulls a blonde woman from the arms of Montalbán, stealing a quick kiss from the woman. The man hands Montalbán his guitar as he escorts the woman away from him. As a minor transgression, the stolen kiss frames Montalbán as a stereotypical "Latin Lover" driven by his sexual attraction to white women as well as an entertainer figure whose function is to amuse white female audiences. Unlike the taboo of miscegenation elicited by black male sexuality, the "Latin Lover" is framed as less threatening to whiteness, and, in this instance, the transgression is even made humorous.[13]

Although Montalbán is coded as ethnic, the title of the film reminds us that Montalbán is not completely foreign. The film tempers Montalbán's differences through his association with Staten Island, thereby further containing the romantic embrace. Montalbán's emerging screen persona similarly evokes his ethnic ambiguity. During his early career, Montalbán, like other minority actors of this era, was cast in a variety of roles; he played an American Indian in various westerns, a Japanese Kabuki actor in *Sayonara* (1957), and a Caribbean man in the Broadway musical *Jamaica* (1957), where he starred opposite Lena Horne in an all-black cast. Even in his other Soundie appearances, he sometimes appeared as the Latin "Ricardo" but also as Irish in *It's a Great Day for the Irish* (1941).[14] As a flexible figure of race and ethnicity, Montalbán fits nicely into Soundies' schema of fluid representational logics. His constructed identity in *He's a Latin* suggests a broader fascination with Latin American cultures, while the Soundie tempers the extent to which these two cultures can intermingle.

Soundies' representations of American diversity illustrate the contradictions embedded in both cultural pluralism and assimilation through their positioning of identity mash-ups. Soundies' performances of hybrid constructions further reify the myth of American self-making. As Michael Rogin posits, the recurring trope of "blacking-up" on film shows "a culture that mythicizes self-making . . . blackface fetish acquires power by being shown to be put on" and evidences "white power over black to personal mobility and self-expression."[15] Rather than ostensibly asserting difference, Soundies' performances of identity construction paradoxically erase difference in favor of a unified American ideology of the self-made man. Although only a few Soundies feature actual blackface, such cultural appropriations abound in Soundies' performances of on-screen identities.[16] In the midst of their blending ethnic forms like Irish, Latin, and Hawaiian music and dance, these hybrid Soundies trouble the status of cultural difference and, further, beg the question of whether blackness is just one among multiple markers of difference that can be appropriated easily by white U.S. culture.[17]

Swing Aesthetics and Black Musicality on Film

The patriotic and culturally unifying rhetoric of World War II often presented blaring contradictions when it came to dealing with issues of African American equality. While discourses pronouncing cultural diversity in terms of Latin or Irish ethnic inclusion circulated widely, the ongoing injustices in the practices of racial segregation, including the U.S. military, perpetuated institutionalized racism.[18] Arthur Knight characterizes the racial attitudes of the World War II era as exhibiting a "profound dis-ease about the place of African Americans in the putatively egalitarian and anti-racist nation."[19] Although clear racial tensions were surmounting, especially with race riots in Los Angeles, Harlem, Chicago, and Detroit in 1943, the rhetoric of integration remained largely contained to discourses of ethnic immigrant assimilation and not racial equality.

When racial issues surfaced during the war, the United States considered African American demands for civil rights as, in Knight's words, "dangerously disruptive of a patriotic national atmosphere even as, in increasing numbers, white Americans found themselves entertained by African Americans, and especially African American musicians."[20] In lieu of this contradiction, the augmented presence and circulation of African American performers in Soundies provides a dynamic site for interrogating the burgeoning racial politics of the era. Music historian David Stowe argues that swing, the most popular style of jazz during the war era, becomes a locus where "the racial and class boundaries of brutally segregated 1930s America were most permeable, for both musicians and their audiences" and that the contradictions between the "American ideals of racial toleration and the experiences of African-Americans both in the military and as civilians" were "posed more starkly and played out more vividly" within swing culture.[21] More so than in the patriotic political discourses of the 1930s and 1940s, then, it is in these popular cultural forms where burgeoning racial identities are more fully engaged and where we see the politics of African American integration on display.[22]

Similar to Stowe, Adam Knee claims that swing aesthetics enacted "cultural inclusiveness": "Swing allowed occasion for cross-racial cultural and social interaction on a variety of levels, while also standing as a symbol for . . . American ideals of democracy and opportunity."[23] A consideration of swing culture as an instrument of social change through its popularization of integrationist politics extends as well to big-band Soundies, a site where swing music and culture are enacted and made visible. For example, *Let Me Off Uptown* (1942), a Gene Krupa Soundie, features African American trumpeter Roy Eldridge and couples him with white vocalist Anita O'Day.[24] They take center stage together to share in two brief interchanges of dialogue. The film also features two African American dancers jitterbugging. The female dancer is light-skinned and the male dancer is very dark, echoing the O'Day and Eldridge pairing and furthering the integrationist dynamic of the film. Though many big bands were often integrated in recordings and radio performances (where musicians could not be seen together), the visualization of an integrated band was an uncommon performance practice during this era, and it often was met with condemnation and even violence.[25]

Even with the film's significant display of integration, *Let Me Off Uptown* cannot be framed as wholly progressive as it still exhibits some of the contradictory racial politics of the era. Eldridge, the star of Krupa's otherwise all-white band, literally is hailed by his bandmates who enthusiastically bow toward him in reverence during his trumpet solo. This lavish display of affection for the only African American in their band situates Eldridge as exceptional while treading upon notions of an implied innate black musicality so often constructed around black entertainers of this era. Further, the song's lyrics describe a white foray to Harlem: "If it's pleasure you're about / And you feel like steppin' out / All you've got to shout is / Let me off uptown." With background cutouts indicating classic Harlem spots ("rib joints, juke joint[s], hep joints"), the film fetishizes black culture (including Eldridge) as a valued commodity for eager white audiences. It also could be argued that the use of black dance accompaniment, which we see in many white big-band Soundies, figures as a marginalizing presence, a mere raced side spectacle.[26] Similar to the aforementioned constructions and appropriations of ethnic diversity, *Let Me Off Uptown*'s display of integrationist politics is somewhat tempered through the ways it manages to fetishize black culture through its particular strategies of visualizing an integrated band.

Soundies' swing films complement emerging trends in black musicals during the war years. In 1943, Hollywood produced two all-black-cast musicals favoring this new swing aesthetic: *Cabin in the Sky* (1943), with its underworld jazz sequence, and the revue musical *Stormy Weather* (1943). Constituting a marked shift from the pastoral style of all-black-cast musicals like *Hallelujah* (1929) and *The Green Pastures* (1936), both films, according to Arthur Knight, try to "make sense of *new* black music," to carve out a space for new modes of black representation.[27] Such depictions of swing feature more showy and performative jazz club numbers, very similar to the big-band swing performances found in Soundies. Like Stowe's take on swing culture, Arthur Knight claims that this new black performance aesthetic exhibits "a subversive cultural politics of style," one "commanding recognition."[28] Soundies featuring swing-era greats like Cab Calloway and Fats Waller, for instance, both of whom were highly engaging showmen, often exhibit degrees of subversion with their off-color double entendres. Rather than merely providing demure musical accompaniment, their personas are lavish, boisterous, and commanding, and they were considered A-list entertainment in Soundies program reviews.

To claim that all films incorporating aspects of swing culture are inherently radical or subversive is of course problematic and oversimplified. Some film scholars have found 1940s representations mere perpetuations of former black film stereotypes, just with different clothing.[29] Donald Bogle characterizes black representation in the 1940s as endemic of the "Negro Entertainer Syndrome" in its cultivation of "the myth that Negroes were naturally rhythmic and natural-born entertainers,"[30] a legacy that persists and extends into our current cultural milieu. The suggestion of a naturalized black musicality certainly can be seen as regressive and limiting to black cultural representation, but, as Thomas Cripps argues in *Slow Fade to Black*, such representations of innovative black cultural forms can also revive staid musical genres and representations, bringing new forms of representations to the screen and new opportunities for black artists.[31]

Soundies may offer few exceptions to the black entertainer stereotype, if taken in its strictest sense; in fact, they seem to be capitalizing on this representational trend of the black nightclub performer. However, as the dazzling spectacle of the entertainer figure provides a stark contrast to the pervasive image of the black servant in the 1930s, representations of glamour and authoritative showmanship in the films of Cab Calloway or Duke Ellington should not be dismissed solely as stereotype or taken lightly because of their musical performance context. Perhaps, like Arthur Knight suggests, we rather should ask what is at stake in these images of African Americans "just singing and dancing,"[32] in providing entertainment for white Americans while giving more ample representations to African Americans artists, and further ask to what extent these images participate in the contradictory representations of unified diversity during the war. If, as both Arthur Knight and David Stowe suggest, theatrical films of this era, which only feature select scenes of black musicality, can still evidence the integrationist politics of swing culture with potentially subversive styles of showmanship, then Soundies, short films explicitly focused on providing images of black musicianship, provide a privileged site for interrogating these dynamics of raced identities during the 1940s.

Even Cowgirls Get the Blues: Dorothy Dandridge's Crossover Constructions

Although any number of Soundies could illustrate these various mobilizations of black identities, the ones featuring Dorothy Dandridge, whose film career was launched through her work in Soundies, provide an array of identity representations, even while operating within the logics of the black entertainer. In these early Soundies, Dandridge at once evidences racial mobility and integrationist politics while still contending with the limiting conditions of a segregated entertainment milieu reliant on common black stereotypes.

The following analyses consider several Soundies to show how racial dynamics circulate through and across multiple films, evidencing the contradictory attitudes toward American identity politics during this era.[33] Appearing in all-black-cast Soundies, Dandridge is posited as a racial exception, often as a featured singer backed by a cast of somewhat darker-skinned chorus girls; in more integrated Soundies featuring white musicians, she is clearly marked as black and placed into more marginalizing roles of servant or primitive. For example, *Billboard* reviews of her Soundies repeatedly refer to Dandridge as "that cute negro singer and dancer,"[34] racially coding her for white audiences. Dandridge's ability to cross over to white audiences paradoxically is contingent on her being marked racially, not as a stigma, but, like Roy Eldridge, as a desirable commodity. In some of Dandridge's Soundies, though, intended for both black and white audiences, Dandridge is presented as a racially ambiguous figure working across both black and white cultures.

Dandridge's legacy as a black film star often is framed by discourses involving her untimely death and Hollywood's inability to fully cultivate a black female star in the 1950s.[35] Considered the real-life embodiment of the on-screen stereotype of the "tragic mulatto,"[36] Dandridge's star persona consequently becomes reduced and limited to this specific framework. As a sympathetic and a sexually desirable figure to white and black audiences alike, Dandridge's popularity in Soundies certainly evidences this prevailing film practice of privileging lighter-skinned black women. Press photos in African American newspapers boasted Soundies featuring "glamorous brownskin beauties lovely to look at and lovely to hear,"[37] and the casting of lighter-skinned women was standard practice in Soundies.[38] As former Soundies dancer Jackie Lewis Parton explains, "The browner girls and the darker girls weren't able to get the jobs . . . because they wanted all fair girls."[39]

Dandridge's popularity in Soundies affirms these raced casting practices, but her roles in Soundies also engage with her lighter skin color in ways that exceed and complicate tragic mulatto discourses. As a flexible figure with cross-racial appeal, Dandridge's roles in Soundies often enact innovative identity formations. One of the primary ways Soundies mobilize Dandridge as a figure of racial integration is by situating her in the act of identity transformation, either through literal character morphing within her Soundies or through her lavish costuming and highly performative roles. Enacting the self-making mythos of American individualism so prominent in representations of ethnicity during this era (like *Hula Rumba*, for instance), Dandridge's Soundies indicate similar enactments of identity play, where her racial difference is at once pronounced but also shown to be an unstable and more fluid construction.

Dandridge performed in ten Soundies between 1941 and 1942: *Swing for Your Supper* (1941), *Jungle Jig* (1941), *Yes, Indeed!* (1941), *Lazybones* (1941),

FIGURE 14 Dorothy Dandridge meets the preacher at the pulpit in *Yes, Indeed!* (1941), a Soundie staged at a black church. From Soundies Distributing Corporation of America photographs of the Margaret Herrick Library, Academy of Motion Picture Arts and Sciences.

Easy Street (1941), *A Zoot Suit* (1942), *Congo Clambake* (1942), *Blackbird Fantasy* (1942), *Cow Cow Boogie* (1942), and *Paper Doll* (1942). In her earliest Soundies, Dandridge appears as a vivacious young singer and emerging talent. Often staged in all-black contexts like a church (*Yes, Indeed!*) or a Harlem dress shop (*Zoot Suit*), Dandridge emerges as a figure of black mobility and vitality, exuding promise for her own career and for black communities at large.[40] In *Swing for Your Supper*, her very first Soundie, Dandridge is the featured star, singing at a lively "rent" party, where admission is "twenty-five" if "you come in and jive." Wearing a tight-fitting but still wholesome-looking sweater, she sings about how she was raised on "rhythm-a-tic" in order to earn a living. She proclaims optimistically, "Right now I'm flying high, I'm gonna reach my goal. Swingin' for my supper, they put rhythm in my soul." The lyrics of the song at once construct Dandridge as a black entertainer figure as well as a self-made artist striving to make a living, much like those hosting the rent party. However, she is distanced from the other black entertainers in the film, both by her featured, lighter-skinned appearance and her positioning as outsider to the rest of the party. During the dance sequence, Dandridge looks on at the swing dancers, who are darker and at times made to seem comical with close-ups of exaggerated faces and costumes. With her contrasting skin tone as well as being the only person given voice in the film, she is not framed as just another black entertainer. As the dancers provide the spectacle of the film and fulfill the conventional roles of black entertainers, the light-skinned Dandridge emerges as a symbol of black mobility and racial exceptionalism. *Swing for Your Supper*'s theme of overcoming financial hardships through Dandridge's industrious ability to entertain touches upon socioeconomic realities for African Americans during the war, even if it is couched in lively, musical expression.[41] *Swing* poses the problem of racial and economic discrimination and offers the light-skinned Dandridge as a solution: the self-made, highly entertaining mulatto.

Such assertions of African American hardship also appear in Dandridge's black-cast Soundies, *Easy Street* and *Zoot Suit*, and, again, Dandridge is posed as a figure who is able to overcome her economic status. Rather than presenting the image of Dandridge as the hardworking mulatto, these two Soundies express the desire for escape from economic hardship and present images of Dandridge as a fantasy of leisure and prosperity. In both Soundies, Dandridge is the featured singer and is dressed to the nines. In *Easy Street*, Dandridge saunters along the street in a gown with a feather boa, crooning that if she "could live on easy street" then she "wouldn't want a job today." As the lyrics indicate that such a life of leisure is an improbable dream, the film enacts this fantasy by having Dandridge ride off in a carriage, presumably leaving the old neighborhood street corners behind her. Similar to her star treatment in *Swing*, the light-skinned Dandridge is contrasted with darker-skinned actors in the film, and Dandridge again is posited as a figure able to rise above the economic limitations of racial discrimination, at least partly because of her skin color.

A Zoot Suit (with a Reet Pleat) also focuses on black upward mobility, and it is perhaps the first Soundie featuring Dandridge that was intended for both black and white audiences. Having been made popular in various recordings by the Benny Goodman Orchestra, the Andrews Sisters, and Paul Whiteman, the song *A Zoot Suit* already was circulating to predominately white

FIGURE 15 Dandridge sings with the band at a lively rent party in *Swing for Your Supper* (1941). From Soundies Distributing Corporation of America photographs of the Margaret Herrick Library, Academy of Motion Picture Arts and Sciences.

audiences on the radio and jukeboxes. When translating this popular song to film, though, Dandridge and Paul White (who appeared in two other Soundies) give voice and image to it. The production choice to add black talent to a song about zoot suit fashions not only lends to greater crossover appeal for black audiences but also indicates the increased popularity of black images of swing culture with white audiences. With the music provided by Ted Fio Rito's Orchestra (while not showing this all-white band), *Zoot Suit* features both Dandridge and Paul White shopping for new clothes for their Sunday date. In their respective dressing rooms, they both make very specific demands for their new duds. White sings, "I want a zoot suit with a reet pleat / And a drape shape, and a stuff cuff / To look sharp enough to see my Sunday gal," to which Dandridge counters, "I want a brown gown with a zop top / And a hip slip, and a laced waist / In the sharpest taste to see my Sunday man." The parallel arrangement of this Soundie, cross cutting from his/her dress shops, keeps the mood lively and the tone fast, creating a musical makeover montage. After they respectively try on their new outfits and dance in front of the dressing room mirrors, the film concludes with the two being brought together on the street where they show off their new duds.

FIGURE 16 Dorothy Dandridge and Paul White model their new fashions in *A Zoot Suit* (1942). From Soundies Distributing Corporation of America photographs of the Margaret Herrick Library, Academy of Motion Picture Arts and Sciences.

This Soundie's overall tone is light and playful, but its fashion statements are not frivolous or coincidental. With wartime restrictions on fabric, the zoot suit became a lavish and un-American style, a subversive fashion statement associated with not only being unpatriotic but also with disenfranchised Latino and African American youth subcultures. Associations with this outlandish style of dress expressed a counterculture politics of opposition, particularly with the appropriately named "zoot suit riots" occurring the following summer of 1943.[42] Newspaper accounts suggest that Soundies were resoundingly popular with black communities,[43] and *Zoot Suit* is significant in circulating images of black leisure and conspicuous consumption. Like *Easy Street,* it expresses the desire to overcome economic disenfranchisement through the figures of Dandridge and White. More specifically, this Soundie enacts this desired transformation through an actual change of dress. As part of Soundies' larger schema of identity constructions, *Zoot Suit*'s emphasis on style and clothing presents images of African Americans that beg to be seen, commented upon, and noticed, not as expressions of cultural assimilation or racial uplift but as acts of lavish defiance. The songs translation from white to black also gives new meaning to the lyrics. For example, the lyrics "I wanta look keen so my dream will say, 'You don't look like the same beau' / So keen that she'll scream, 'Here comes my walkin' rainbow'" take on a radical inflection with White's slippery delivery of "the same beau" as "sambo," suggesting a radical reimaging of traditional black stereotypes.

Although *Zoot Suit* may have carried countercultural significance, particularly for black audiences, White's comedic performance style still evokes demeaning black stereotypes, with moments of eye rolling and over-the-top mugging for the camera. He creates a particular contrast to Dandridge in the film, both in his skin tone and his performance style. Whereas Dandridge is perky and precise with her movements, White is rubbery and even buffoonish at times. Such vestiges of this older black performance style suggest an expected mode of behavior for white audiences. In another Soundie featuring White, *The Walls Keep Talking* (1942), he plays an even more demeaning role of a frightened buffoon in a haunted house. In *Zoot Suit*, the presence of Dandridge ultimately redeems or, at the very least, counterbalances White, and overall the film conveys images of black exuberance and possibility through a performed politics of style.

Lazybones (1942), an integrated Soundie starring Hoagy Carmichael, seems geared for predominately white audiences. Playing the role of a servant, Dandridge here is paired with Peter Ray, and they perform a comedic dance routine. Carmichael, in typical fashion, is seated at the piano with two women in evening gowns at his side. Their interest, though, is in watching Dandridge and Ray. As Carmichael sings "Lazybones, sitting in the sun, how you gonna get your day's work done?", Dandridge assists Ray, who is balancing a tray on his head, while occasionally throwing in a few tempered dance moves. If the connection as to whether Ray represents the titular Lazybones is a bit indirect at first, it all becomes clear at the conclusion of the piece when Ray finally slides the tray onto the piano, leans up against it, and yawns widely. More so than a brief dance interlude, as is often the case with African American dancers in Soundies featuring white musicians, Ray and Dandridge's balancing act / dance routine is the main focus of the film, and they are even credited during the opening sequence. Dandridge's depiction as a dancing servant clearly positions her as a marginalized performer—a safe source of white entertainment. Within this context, it's difficult to argue that Dandridge wholly exceeds the limits of black stereotypes. However, her presence is neither overtly buffoonish nor meekly servile. Conscientious and careful, Dandridge is focused on Ray's tray not spilling. Dandridge even directs Ray and chastises him for his antics by stomping her foot and clapping to get his attention. Similar to her elevated status in *Swing* and *Zoot Suit*, she is positioned as superior to Ray who has to perform the far more demeaning role of Lazybones.

Dandridge's precarious positioning is complicated further by Hoagy Carmichael, who is at once another entertainer as well as a spectator to the servant's antics. Carmichael provides the narration through his song, which often is in direct address to Lazybones with statements like "you'll never get your corn meal made." Performing a song about idyllic plantation life, Carmichael at once sings about black subjects while also appropriating blackness through his adopted vocal stylings, even performing a subtle, if unconscious, minstrelsy.[44] Similarly, in the orientalist Soundie *Hong Kong Blues* (1942),[45]

FIGURE 17 Poised at the piano, Hoagy Carmichael indulges in an orientalist fantasy in *Hong Kong Blues* (1942). From Soundies Distributing Corporation of America photographs of the Margaret Herrick Library, Academy of Motion Picture Arts and Sciences.

Carmichael "tells the story of a colored man" and even portrays him in the song's narration: "That's why he said, 'I need someone to love me.'" Throughout the song, Carmichael slides seamlessly between these roles, sympathetically singing about a black man's arrest in Hong Kong while also evoking him. When he describes the man "bobbing a piano just to raise the price for a ticket to the land of the free," Carmichael plays with extra flourish as if to reenact his movements. According to Krin Gabbard, "Carmichael ended up playing parts that could just as easily have been played by blacks."[46] Considering his roles in films like the piano player Cricket in *To Have and Have Not* (1944), Carmichael's performance in *Lazybones* is "very much like Hollywood's black servants and companions,"[47] an entertainer who has little to do with the narrative of the film. The primary exception to Carmichael's positioning as a black entertainer in this film is the placement of two white women in evening gowns at his side. Clearly they are in a privileged position, being entertained by both Carmichael and the black dancers, but they also function to provide eye candy for Soundie spectators. In terms of racial and gender hierarchies, Carmichael should have dominant status. However, the women's interactions with Carmichael, intended to be flirty, come off as strained and awkward and only temper the representation of his masculinity. For instance, Carmichael slaps away one of the women's hands as she reaches for his cigarette, as if refusing her advances.

The coupling of Dandridge and Carmichael in this Soundie, both figures evoking liminal if not ambiguous racial constructions, reveals the complex dialectic of "racechange."[48] "Not simply mimetic," Susan Gubar explains, "racechange is an extravagant aesthetic construction that functions self-reflexively to comment on representation in general, racial representation in particular."[49] While neither actor performs racechange overtly, Dandridge's embodiment of the tragic mulatto and Carmichael's performance of black musicality and restrained masculinity forge an uneasy construction of racial identities that threaten to unsettle this short comedic film about black male inferiority. Nor do Dandridge's and Carmichael's racechange performances destabilize the inequalities in these representations. As Gubar explains, there is never an easy trading or exchange of racial categories because of the existent power dynamics in U.S. culture's privileging of whiteness while devaluing blackness.[50] Therefore the politics of racechange are always asymmetrical, and the prevailing racial logics of *Lazybones* are consequently maintained and untroubled.

As racechange performances point to the instability of the racial dynamics that fuel and perpetuate these cultural representations, Dandridge's roles reveal the possibility of racechange through the challenging of fixed stereotypes and troubling easy racial categorizations. However, the framing of her gender within these films limits some of these possible moments of transgression.

For instance, in the Mills Brothers' Soundie *Paper Doll*, Dorothy Dandridge is constructed as the object of black male desire. Unlike her featured status as a singer in other all-black-cast Soundies, here she appears as a dancing doll come to life after being cut out of a magazine to dance for one adoring Mills brother who "would rather have a paper doll to call his own than a real-life, fickle-minded girl." In miniature form, Dandridge is thoroughly objectified through this performance as she is constructed solely as a fantasy figure. More coveted as a love object than the life-sized women who accompany the other Mills brothers, Dandridge is rendered a marketable commodity, here contained by her gender as much as her race.[51] Keeping within Soundies' larger schema of identity transformations, the animation of the Dandridge doll, as the culminating gimmick of the short film, mobilizes her representation, indicating that the light-skinned Dandridge is the preferred representation of a black female and, in turn, the image that is able to cross over quite literally from one medium to another and to circulate broadly into mainstream popular culture.

Even more so than *Paper Doll*, *Congo Clambake* and *Jungle Jig* sexualize Dandridge through their overt use of primitive stereotypes and thereby most easily are dismissed for their blatant racism. Although both Soundies star Dandridge as a dancing native, they differ radically in the framing of her performance. *Congo Clambake*, a nonvocal jazz number by Stan Kenton and his orchestra, features the premise of an illustrated lecture on "Boogiejiva, Africa," of which Dandridge appears within the film as a scantily clad "native" dancing to jive music.[52] Overtly racist in its depictions of Africa, this Soundie even integrates found-film footage of Africans with lip plates to make the wartime joke that "even in Africa, a slip of the lip may sink a ship." After a few clips of the filmed native dancers framed by shots of the female lecturer, the Soundie focuses on Dandridge, who emerges from out of the "jungle" dancing provocatively. Through its illustrated lecture premise, this Soundie clearly positions blacks as primitive objects of white study as well as the target of a few quick laughs. Its representation of a nontheatrical film lecture also resonates with possible racist viewing practices at actual Soundie exhibition venues. Even though Dandridge is given featured status as a dancer and evokes modernist jazz stylings in her movements more so than the primitivism of the other male dancers, *Congo Clambake* thoroughly secures Dandridge as a sexualized, exotic object of white male fantasy. This is furthered by Stan Kenton's musical track, supplying a white interpretation of jungle rhythms not so different from the lecturer's comments within the film.

Jungle Jig features Dorothy Dandridge in similar jungle garb, and yet the context for this Soundie, a "Harlem Night Club" with Cee Pee Johnson and his orchestra, makes the evoked primitivism less of a joke for white audiences and more of a stylistic choice for black performers and musicians.[53]

FIGURE 18 Festooned in sequins and feathers, Dandridge performs a primitive role in *Jungle Jig* (1941). From Soundies Distributing Corporation of America photographs of the Margaret Herrick Library, Academy of Motion Picture Arts and Sciences.

Throughout the song, allusions to Africa blend with jazz themes from lyrics like "when the tom toms beat it out / all the cats jump up and shout." Like *Clambake*, Dandridge is clad in feathers, but this time they are festooned with sequins as well. Although the short film's utilization of African imagery could be seen as reductive and offensive like in *Congo Clambake*, the performances in this all-black setting are modern and lack the African nativism—particularly the demeaning framing of the performance as a travelogue given by a white lecturer. Unlike her role as a dancer in *Clambake*, Dandridge is given a voice and offers a commanding performance. Clearly playing a sequined spectacle within this contemporary Harlem club setting, Dandridge's performance fuses African and jazz themes. Within this all-black entertainment setting, there is no pretense of *Clambake*'s ethnographic positioning but rather a mythos of self-making out of constructed cultural forms.

Perhaps these acts of identity play and appropriation are most apparent in *Cow Cow Boogie*, a Soundie featuring Dandridge as a black cowgirl. Western themes and music are popular among Soundies genres, but *Cow Cow Boogie* is the only black cowboy Soundie.[54] Not a complete anomaly, the figure of the singing black cowboy (or, in this case, cowgirl) circulated in popular film representations at this time. During the late 1930s specifically, a brief film trend of all-black-cast Westerns starring Herb Jeffries were produced for predominately black audiences, including *Harlem on the Prairie* (1937), *Two-Gun Man from Harlem* (1938), *The Bronze Buckaroo* (1939), and *Harlem Rides the Range* (1939). These formulaic westerns include musical numbers usually sung by the cowboy hero. Jeffries, who is far lighter than his darker-skinned cowboy compatriots, was often paired with a darker supporting cast, particularly his buffoonish sidekick, Dusty Bottoms (Lucius Brooks). This color-coded casting was pervasive in all-black-cast films of this era, and *Cow Cow Boogie* proves no exception. Maintaining the same color coding, *Cow Cow Boogie* pairs a light-skinned Dandridge with a darker comedic sidekick. Set in an old-west saloon with an all-black cast of cowboy patrons and dancing chorus girls, Dandridge, like Jeffries, is situated as the star of this film. In this instance, however, rather than a cowboy hero, Dandridge substitutes as the singing cowgirl.

Similar to the black singing cowboy films, *Cow Cow* draws upon certain utopian impulses: the idealized American frontier as well as an all-black world free of racial prejudice. By positing this all-black world in a mythic American West, the Soundie constructs a conjoined utopian setting that is rife with contradictions. As the myth of the American West is predicated upon the ideals of an unfettered white masculinity, a colonialist expansionism justified by logics of manifest destiny,[55] rendering this world black and the cowboy hero female certainly unsettles this white masculine mythos. This contradiction in representational codes is prevalent in Soundie racial logics in general, where unifying appeals to American self-making jut up against assertions of ethnic and racial identity. Dandridge as a black cowgirl exposes these racial logics through her implicit racechange performance, posing the question of what it means to make cowboys and cowgirls black, to recode (or recolor) aspects of the American mythos.

Cow Cow Boogie's representational motifs of a black old west and the song's subject matter of a black cowboy hero point to possibilities of African American identity transformations in significant ways. Within the song's lyrics, the construction of the black cowboy hero is arranged in and through contrasting terms. Dandridge sings of a singing cowboy who blends elements of the American West with a "touch" of Harlem: "Way down in Santa Fe, I met a cowboy riding the range one day. . . . I heard him singin' the most peculiar cowboy song. It was a ditty he learned in the city. . . . get along, get hip little doggie . . . Singin' his cowboy song, he's just too much. He's got a knocked out Western accent with a Harlem touch . . . he was raised on the local weed. He's what you'd call a swing half breed." As a "swing half breed," the cowboy figure is epitomized by his hybridity, his seemingly odd blend of two cultural traditions. Similar to *Jungle Jig*'s self-conscious merging of African and Harlem themes, *Cow Cow Boogie* even foregrounds hybridity as a theme. Such hybrid constructions, Stuart Hall claims, are central to the formation of black popular culture. He states, "Always these forms are the product of partial synchronization, of engagement across cultural boundaries, of the confluence of more than one cultural tradition, of the negotiations of dominant and subordinate positions, of the subterranean strategies of recoding and transcoding, of critical signification, of signifying."[56] The figure of the black cowboy as it is constructed in *Cow Cow Boogie* as a black cultural form not only exemplifies this "engagement across cultural boundaries," but the figure's very mention brings to the surface the question of any "pure form" in U.S. popular culture. Troubling the essentialisms of simple stereotypes, such hybrid identity formations, Homi Bhabha has argued, often emerge at sites of cultural formation and resistance: It is "borderline work" that "innovates and interrupts the performance of the present."[57] This instance of cultural appropriation and adaption—and even of an implied racechange performance—provides an avenue for challenging white masculine ideals and offering new forms of representation and identity formations.

Dandridge's performance furthers the possibility for a resistant decoding of the film. Not nearly as straightforward as a simple Soundie performance might suggest, Dandridge's cowgirl persona is playful, engaging with and inflecting the song's lyrics in understated ways. In Donald Bogle's biography on Dandridge, he contends that aspects of her performance rely on subtle commentary and asides. For example, Bogle claims Dandridge is addressing a segment of the black entertainment community with her familiar "weed pun" in singing, "He was raised on local weed." As Bogle clarifies, "Tumbleweed it was not."[58] Such signifying pervades her entire performance. As she winks at different times to the camera in direct address, Dandridge repeatedly shares her joke with potential audiences while she adds particular emphasis to the lyrics like "swing half breed" and the "peculiar" cowboy talk. Through her performance, Dandridge reflexively comments upon the complexity of asserting a nonwhite, and even a nonmasculine, American identity.

These possible moments of transgression, however, are contained through the gendered constructions in the film. As Robyn Wiegman states, "Race as a category of difference is not a structure that parallels gender relations, but one that intersects and confirms them—a structure intrinsic to the patriarchal economy of U.S. culture."[59] Within the confines of these doubly displaced utopias of an all-black old west, the racial and gender identity transgressions are contained to some degree. Rather than erasing color difference, the all-black cast recreates racial hierarchies through a light-skinned Dandridge juxtaposing the stereotypical darker buffoon, and Dandridge's leading role as the singing cowgirl is managed by an audience of ogling black cowboys. Further, as Richard Dyer suggests, the nonrepresentational elements of musical film like the rhythmic choreography of the dance routine, the melody of the song, and the abundance of female bodies on display can evoke a utopian sensibility of pure entertainment.[60] These aspects of the musical assist in erasing the racial tension implicit in the song lyrics by delighting in the moving female form and Dandridge's engaging persona specifically. Additionally, rather than providing a visual representation of the black cowboy hero constructed in the song's lyrics who could possibly assert an even more complex nonwhite masculine presence, the Soundie emphasizes more typical figures of entertainment: dancers and comedians. In a curious tension, the film image evades the difficult task of representing a potentially multidimensional cultural figure, while the song and performance search for such possibilities. Ultimately, *Cow Cow Boogie*, as a nonnarrative short, interrogates the politics of representation, particularly of black female representations. It asks, What does it mean to perform blackness in film through an iconography marked by whiteness and masculinity, to embody burgeoning social possibilities while having to work within the readily available roles that are marked by oppressive politics of both race and gender?

Through her often-hybrid personas (the upwardly mobile mulatto, the black cowgirl, and even the burlesque native), Dandridge's Soundies evoke the transgressive potential of racechange and hybrid identity performances. With the breadth and range of her various Soundie roles (a servant, the paper doll, the churchgoer), all circulating within two years, Dandridge's emerging star persona embodies and articulates the contested racial logics of the early 1940s. While at times succumbing to the existent limitations of black film stereotypes and maintaining the image of "that cute negro singer and dancer,"[61] Dandridge's borderline constructions of identity within the context of the performance-oriented musical short also provide possibilities for a transformative identity politics during the 1940s while wrestling with larger discursive ambiguities in articulating new American identities at this time.

Although Soundies featuring the musicianship of big-band greats like Count Basie, Duke Ellington, and Cab Calloway often are touted as more historically significant to the histories of jazz on screen, the representational motifs and identity politics found among the vast range of Soundies, as the prior examples have shown, extend well beyond straightforward documentation of black musicianship. In these representations—moments where musical genres are embodied through and in tandem with identity constructions—the importance of Soundies within the politics of 1940s racial representations takes on new inflections. The fact that so many Soundies centralize themes of identity itself, where representations of race, gender, and ethnicity are the very subject of these short musical films, indicates broader cultural concerns with issues of identity formation, particularly with defining a unified American self. Within this field of identity representations, Soundies introduced and more broadly circulated black identities into mainstream culture. This circulation, of course, is double-edged, providing ample opportunities for black self-expression and artistic innovation while also couching such depictions within and alongside conventional and demeaning representations of blackness.

Perhaps more so than black-cast Soundies, Soundies enacting white fantasies of black cultural appropriation evidence the uncomplicated ease of white-passing and further point to the asymmetrical politics of racechange. Whereas performances of black-passing and identity formation can enact moments of transgression, as some of Dandridge's performances have shown, white appropriation of black cultural forms often is normalized in this entertainment milieu. Two Soundies featuring imitative musical parodies, Glen Miller and the Modernaires' *Jukebox Saturday Night* (1944) and Day, Dawn and Dusk's *Rigoletto* (1945) throw into relief the instabilities of racial passing and identity play.

Jukebox Saturday Night consists of typical Soundies fare where performers are showcased in a crowded club setting, evoking similar spaces to where viewers would supposedly watch the Panoram or engage with other jukebox technologies. With dancers on the floor and a jukebox in the far background, the Modernaires are seated at a table front and center. Singing about their favorite music, they function more like a live jukebox by quoting moments from popular songs. During a shift in the song's melody, the tenor of the Modernaires does his best impression of the acclaimed black vocal group the Ink Spots in a crooning falsetto. Rather than directly quoting the Ink Spots' classic "If I Didn't Care," he sings a parodic "If I Didn't Know." The live singers-as-jukebox set up the premise for the brief parody, and the moment certainly speaks to the shifting terrain for the circulation of recorded popular music.

In terms of identity performance, it also exemplifies a subtle minstrelsy, or easy borrowing, of black cultural forms by white artists for white audiences. This is especially clear when the singer imitates the baritone speaking voice of one of the Ink Spots: "Now, you listen to me here, honey child, if I didn't know all of them little things I'm ah s'posed to know, then I wouldn't be one of the Ink Spots." Showcasing the singer's vocal range and skillful impersonation, the parody is not intended as overtly derisive but as an amusing anomaly. His adoption of black vernacular, though, blurs the line between homage and mocking. As Eric Lott (borrowing from Raymond Williams) explains of minstrel performances, such cross-racial borrowings are indicative of a "peculiarly American structure of racial feeling" in which a "dialectical flickering of racial insult and racial envy" coexist.[62] Capturing the intimate and inextricable relations between self and other in American identity politics, this "cross-racial desire" is "less a sign of absolute white power and control than of panic, anxiety, terror and pleasure."[63] The Modernaires' borrowing of the Ink Spots clearly suggests their popularity among white audiences, and, more so, the ease of the white artist's appropriation suggests the uneven power dynamics of white racechange and the consequent normalcy of the white theft of black popular culture.

Conversely, black vaudeville trio Day, Dawn and Dusk's *Rigoletto* displays black appropriation and transformation of white culture, but here the appropriation is framed by overt consternation. Based on their popular stage routine, *Rigoletto* portrays a dialogue between a jazz singer and piano player who want to "swing" and "syncopate" the classics and a fervent Verdi (in powdered whiteface) who strives to preserve his classical composition:

> VERDI: Please, don't swing my melody!
> SINGER: We hate to tantalize you, but we mean to modernize you.
> V: Let my *Rigoletto* be.
> S: We want to syncopate it, even though we know you hate it.
> V: Tell me why you pick on me?
> S: Because you're out of fashion. Syncopation is our passion.
> V: I'm as mad as a man can be.
> S: So what!?!

Ostensibly staged as a debate between modern and traditional, young and old, the dialectics of racial conflict, couched in the vernacular of swing culture, cannot go ignored.[64] The singer and piano player, dressed in zoot suits, stand on behalf of change with little concern about Verdi's protest as they continually sing over his lyrics and interrupt his lines. By the song's conclusion, the jazz singers ultimately convince Verdi to "compromise and harmonize" his song. The bringing together of two oppositional cultural forms of jazz and opera epitomizes the Soundies' musical mash-up trope, where cross-cultural formations and adaptations are often the subject of the film.

Like other Soundies, *Rigoletto*'s visualization and performance of the musical mash-up amplifies the identity politics at play. With a black Verdi performing with an overly powdered whiteface and wig, *Rigoletto* portrays a racechange figure who undergoes a transformation of attitude toward jazz and presumably toward black presences in popular culture. In allowing his Rigoletto to "swing," whiteface Verdi embodies the more revolutionary potential of racechange performances, where black fantasies of resistance and change can be enacted and visualized. Even though the all-black performers may temper this racialized conflict with their tidy resolution to "harmonize" through musical expression, *Rigoletto*'s staging of a black adaptation of popular musical forms as a site of struggle suggests black resistance to white authority while showcasing African American artists intervening in and contributing to dominant culture. As Day, Dawn and Dusk were particularly popular with white audiences,[65] the display of these somewhat covert expressions of resistance indicates the potential for Soundies to circulate new and even revolutionary images of black identities into mainstream culture.

In their translation of popular songs to moving images,[66] Soundies construct identities through performances that visualize and embody diverse musical genres and lively lyrical content. Although their films at times recycle conventional representations of black stereotypes, their musical scenarios also propel new kinds of identity constructions and racial dynamics both on and off the screen. As Soundies' meanings are coshaped and activated by their screen apparatus and viewing contexts, Soundies' constructions and representations of racial identity similarly intertwine with their technological practices and exhibition spaces. Their documentation of black artists and musicians in the 1940s is significant, but, when further coupled with Soundies' broader context of circulation, these representations of racial integration and cultural diversity on the screen extend to broader screening dynamics. According to Alice Maurice's *Cinema and Its Shadow*, it is during moments of cinematic "transition and technological vulnerability" that race as a filmed subject is foregrounded, entwined to, and reflexive of the technological protocols of cinema.[67] Coupled with the Panoram's jukebox mechanisms and integration into everyday spaces, Soundies' racialized rhetorics express integrationist politics on and off the screen.

Given Soundies' diffuse circulation at leisure spaces across the United States, their on-screen displays of racechange constructions could have accentuated the already-lax social mores at nightclubs and furthered integrationist tendencies. Whereas the recorded music industry allowed for black voices to be heard and circulate more widely to black and white audiences during this time—especially through the cultivation of localized jukebox markets—the SDC similarly elevated black visibility through its variety formatting precisely by modeling jukebox programming and distribution strategies. For instance, the SDC's recommended placement of various filmed musical genres alongside one another on a Soundies reel for greater consumer selection inadvertently could promote an atmosphere of diversity and inclusion. Conversely, a Panoram operator wary of an integrated film program could have blocked Soundies designated as "Negro" in their distribution catalogs entirely from particular exhibition spaces. Because of these possible variances in their distribution and exhibition practices, the circulation of Soundies exposes both the possibilities and limitations of American self-making during the 1940s while emphasizing the commercial viability of visualizing popular music for the screen through constructions of race and ethnicity.

6

Postwar Screens

Soundies on Television and the Rehash of the Film Jukebox

A 1965 *Billboard* article entitled "Cine Juke Box: Just a Novelty?" questions the future success of the Scopitone machine as it expands its distribution from France and Germany to the United States.[1] As the coin-machine industry speculated upon the staying power of this film jukebox, the article recalls the "panaram [*sic*]"—the first generation "cine juke box"—and its brief lifespan during the 1940s. Despite the media industry's acknowledged awareness of the short-lived success of Soundies, the reemergence of the film jukebox during the 1960s evidences the music and media industries' continued pull to capitalize on similar small-screen enticements. By the mid-1960s, the idea of a film jukebox in the media landscape seemed more amenable in everyday locales than it did in the 1940s, when a small moving-image screen was viewed as an intrusive novelty and potential competitor with Hollywood movies. Further, media practices that were emergent and inchoate during Soundies' initial run, like the notions of individualized screen viewing and user self-selection of media content, could resonate with a generation accustomed to daily encounters with television. As postwar screen viewing shifted toward domestic television, the circulation and delivery of small-screen commodities cultivated a new generation of media consumers during the 1950s. With television ownership increasing from 9 percent in 1950 to 90 percent by 1960, "Americans," as Gary Cross explains, "quickly adapted to their privatized visual entertainment."[2] Accompanying the growth of more privatized modes of media consumption, popular media industries began identifying distinct market segments, particularly the burgeoning teen market, which was the largest age group in America by the early 1960s.[3] According to Lizabeth Cohen, these segmented consumer markets wanted "more opportunity to express their separate identities through their choices as consumers."[4] With such selective, small-screen consumers, a culture only anticipated by 1940s Soundies, the film jukebox perhaps, if marketed correctly, could now flourish.

After the SDC's demise in 1946, Soundies were no longer being produced and Panorams were no longer being manufactured, but they did not disappear from the cultural landscape altogether. They both continued to circulate in discourses surrounding musical film shorts and film jukeboxes in the 1950s, 1960s, and beyond. Whereas a static view of Soundies' history would emphasize its dominant phase as an ephemeral 1940s film practice and technological oddity, Soundies' residual histories position their relevance in a myriad of media practices involving the circulation of short-form media on small-screen technologies.[5] The first section of this chapter considers the circulation of Soundies films after the initial demise of the SDC in 1946 and follows their migration onto domestic film and television screens. Soundies' remediation on early 1950s television carries forward the arguments about the emerging aesthetics of the short musical form on the small screen as well as the perceived portability and adaptability of the musical-short format to fledging television programming structures and domestic viewing contexts.

The second strand of this chapter charts the Panoram's afterlife through its various technological adaptations, from photographer's assistant to peep-show viewing device. The Panoram's various incarnations in and migrations to these contexts illuminate particular continuities between small-screen technologies and their viewing practices—namely, media consumption that foregrounds issues of brevity and the immediacy of screen interactions. The economy of the short film in these contexts also extends to the value placed upon the media object. Particularly, with movie machines' adaptations to peep-show devices, the relationship between short-film viewing and the consumption of film as economic exchange is made overt with each brief screen interaction becoming a separate commodity.

The final section evaluates the reemergence of the coin-operated music-movie machine during the 1960s. In the resurfacing of the film jukebox, the Scopitone, an important relationship between short film and television aesthetics emerges that articulates resonances between and among small-screen media practices. As Soundies' screen atmospherics paved the way for the television screen in the late 1940s, the Scopitone's rehash of Soundies borrows in turn from the popular aesthetics of 1960s television with its use of color film and appeals to youthfulness. With its adaptations of the Panoram's playback technology like individual film selection and self-loading film cartridges, the Scopitone more fully realizes long-standing consumer fantasies for individualized, small-screen media.

Last Call: The Postwar Demise of Soundies Films

After six years of wartime production restrictions, it would seem that the end of World War II would provide a boon for the SDC. Offering business incentives for war veterans who discovered Soundies while on leave or at military PXs and recreation centers,[6] the SDC finally hoped to hit its stride by 1946. Instead, the business quickly went under, and Soundies Films, Inc., the final incarnation of the company name, halted film production in early 1947.[7] A result of poor business practices and the novelty of film jukeboxes wearing thin, the image of a Panoram playing a Soundie in a neighborhood bar or nightclub faded quickly from the cultural landscape. Within a year, Soundies were framed as a failed public screen practice. In 1948, the *Cleveland Plain Dealer* reported that Soundies had "flopped" and even was surmising that television, which was replacing Panorams in taverns, would most likely suffer the same fate.[8] In Michigan, where Soundies "lost much of their popularity here in the past 18 months," actions were taken to prevent movie screenings in bars because film was considered a "fire hazard" and the "dimming of lights" was seen as "objectionable."[9] At the same time, another screen practice, television, became "acceptable" in the same spaces. While Soundies were considered a "threat to the restaurant-tavern market television receivers" in 1940, television had replaced the Panoram screen by the end of the decade.[10] Such accounts make clear that Soundies became a defunct form of public amusement in taverns and bars during the late 1940s and that television, though not guaranteed a success yet, quickly was replacing film as the preferred medium for smaller screens in these venues.

The demise of the SDC does not mean Soundies disappeared completely. Rather than playing on the Panoram, however, they circulated in domestic spaces to private film collectors and on some early television programs. As early as 1942, Soundies were being licensed to various film rental agencies. In 1945, Castle Films, a longtime distributor of small-gauge film shorts (since 1918), purchased 101 Soundies.[11] Castle primarily was a direct-mail film distributor, though they also sold short reels at local department stores, drug stores, and camera shops.[12] Castle catered to the burgeoning home market throughout the 1930s and 1940s as well as institutional settings like schools, libraries, and civic organizations. Their catalogs included short subjects like cartoons, sports, comedy, newsreels, and sometimes hastily cropped excerpts from old features. Soundies were a good fit with Castle's selection of shorts and expanded their catalogue of music-related films. Entitled "Castle's Music Albums," Soundies were distributed as three-film reels (roughly nine minutes) that would be linked by music genre or some loose representational theme like "College and Carnival Rhythm" or "Jazz and Jitters." Castle continued to sell Soundies "Music Albums" until 1953.[13] In 1947, Official Films took over the entire Soundies library of 1,850 films and similarly repackaged the films into themed reels.[14] In 1947 and 1948, Blackhawk Films also purchased Soundies in order to amass enough of a library to sell reels for private consumption.[15] Classified ads sold collections of Soundies for "only $2.50" per reel and claimed they were "ideal to add variety to your home shows."[16]

The repackaging of Soundies by these various film distributors is significant for a few reasons: it showed that Soundies were a viable media commodity without the Panoram machine, it brought Soundie consumption to the home as well as a myriad of nontheatrical exhibition contexts (classrooms, community centers, etc.), and it evidences the flexibility of short films as commodities. No longer on endless looping reels or activated by the drop of a coin, the Castle Music Album adapted the Soundie short into an even smaller unit whose playback was now in the hands of individual consumers. Not just a new way for media industries to capitalize and reinvigorate their old film products, the smaller packaging and more diffuse circulation of Soundies in the late 1940s also further privatized and segmented media consumption practices. Similar to the distribution of the 45-record singles in augmenting the diversification of popular music genres in the 1950s, the repackaging of Soundies for the home market expanded the distribution of media content featuring African Americans and made it available for purchase by individual film consumers and collectors.[17]

Television: A New Home for Soundies

The migration of Soundies to private film collections was by no means their sole entrée to the domestic viewing realm. By the late 1940s, the potential promise for Soundies' circulation beyond the Panoram screen resided in the new medium of television. Soundies' afterlife on television (lasting roughly from 1948 to 1951) charts an even more ephemeral trajectory than their initial six-year run on Panoram machines. Soundies' remediation onto early broadcast television, though brief, played a significant role in imagining and shaping programming for the new small screen. They were used in a variety of early television formats, including disc jockey programs and as programming filler during station downtimes. Even as late as 1960, when Soundies had long departed from television broadcasts, comedian Jerry Lewis derisively called television "Instant Soundies."[18] Lewis's loose comparison between the popular screen aesthetics of 1960s television with Soundies illustrates their enduring legacy in shaping midcentury television aesthetics and programming content.

As early as 1944, Soundies were seen as adaptable to the emerging medium of television. Because of their short length, Soundies promised to provide entertaining filler for early television's erratic time slots. As discussed in chapter 4, the visual style of Soundies was seen as a perfect match for television because, as one *Billboard* article explains, "most of the productions stick to close-ups so necessary for the small screen" and Soundies already used "practically the same technique as is now used for television."[19] Though entering the home in different media formats, Soundies' emergence on domestic projectors and television screens should not be seen as wholly separate or incidental practices but constitutive of significant movements in postwar screen culture. This begs certain questions as to why Soundies, though fading from their public circulation, specifically coalesced with proliferating, small private-screen practices. What made Soundies, among the range of film formats and genres available, particularly conducive to home screen viewing? Why did their particular form prove to be so adaptable and apropos to emerging practices in screen viewing? The Soundies catalog from Official Films / Television certainly made Soundies an available and affordable programming option, and their three-minute duration provided brief segments of entertainment. A flexible programming commodity, Soundies could be paired or grouped into blocks of varying times. Alongside other short films produced cheaply and independently by small film companies during the late 1940s, Soundies had no connections to major Hollywood studios, which were slow to become involved in early telefilm production and distribution.[20] Further, Soundies had the advantage of being filmed originally with the scale of small-screen viewing in mind, aiding in their visibility on the particularly small screens of late-1940s television sets.

In addition to their cost, scale, and adaptability to different programming formats, Soundies' often-intimate modes of direct address also worked well in the domestic realm, a space well acquainted with and accustomed to the personal address of radio. As early television borrowed and shared radio's established networks, broadcast structures, and programs, the audio component of this emerging screen media further made it compatible with the hybrid audiovisual aspects of Soundies. As Michel Chion states, television was a form of "illustrated radio."[21] As such, the circulation of Soundies on late-1940s television screens reveals the extent to which television was thought to be radio with pictures, best suited for providing visuals to accompany music. Although Soundies oftentimes were used as filler between shows and commercials, they soon were adopted as viable programming content through the televised disc jockey show.

Between 1948 and 1950, Soundies, it seemed, found their new home on television with disc jockey programs—shows designed around the play of popular music. With Soundies providing the visual component needed to accompany songs in short, discreet programming segments, early television producers considered Soundies perfectly amenable to the new medium. A few experiments with disc jockey shows emerged in the late 1940s, including television shows featuring already-famous radio personalities Al Jarvis (*The Al Jarvis Show, Make Believe Ballroom*) and Paul Brenner (*Requestfully Yours*). "Using pic Soundies instead of his usual wax wares," one early review of the *Al Jarvis Show* predicts, "Jarvis's step into tele may well be the start of a video trend."[22] Similarly, a description of Soundies being played on *Requestfully Yours* illustrates how Soundies quite literally supplanted the record: "With exclusive Eastern rights to Soundies . . . WATV is now programming a video version of Paul Brenner's *Requestfully Yours* show once a week . . . Brenner is shown putting a needle to a platter, with a view then dissolving to a Soundy [*sic*]."[23] According to *Variety*, this dissolve technique "has drawn an unusual reaction . . . As a result many viewers are under the impression that Brenner gets both sound pictures from the wax recording."[24] Anecdotes emphasizing the slow dissolve between the record and the Soundie and the confused viewers interested in the "television type record" are repeated throughout the trade presses. The remediation of Soundies as televised records nicely illustrates television's role as "illustrated" radio. For early television producers, Soundies help mediate and quite literally visualize the radio-to-television transition for their broadcast audiences through Soundies' particular musical short form.

By 1950, several television stations followed the programming trend of video deejay shows and continued to align radio and television, using Soundies as the intermediary audiovisual programming form. In a detailed review of these new shows, *Billboard* refers to television as "The New Home for Disc Jockeys,"[25] and a *Newsweek* article entitled "Picture Jockeys" states, "What records were to radio, short-shorts movies will be to TV . . . as brief fillers, as mood programming—in short, in any way that a disk jockey uses records. And as the disk jockey interpolates commercials between each record, so, the stations hope, will the picture jockey between Soundies."[26] Although Soundies proved newsworthy during this brief video jockey boom, reactions to their recirculation were mixed. For instance, one reviewer offers that the "idea of using Soundies is swell in theory, but n.s.h. in practice. Trouble is pic sound tracks are old and full of woes which only serve to detract from Jarvis' sock work as an emcee and annoys the viewers."[27] Similarly, the *Times-Picayune* (New Orleans) warned, "Big trouble, of course, is that a lot of the popular songs featured on these short films may be sadly dated, by now."[28]

Even as Soundies were proving a profitable acquisition for Official Television by early 1950,[29] whose "library is the only one enabling a TV station to program a visual disk jockey show," they were being rendered obsolete.[30] According to a review of multiple disc jockey shows in the summer of 1950, Soundies were unable to sustain enough interest on their own and had to be supplemented with other forms of visual music content like live performances, dancers, and even abstract visualizations (e.g., the sound-generated visuals used on *The Whirligig Show*).[31] As early television is considered to be a mostly live medium in the late 1940s and early 1950s, Soundies' filmed content may have presented another disconnect in the otherwise live feel of the deejay program.[32] The emphasis further shifted from the filmed musical content to the deejay who could plug in a variety of programming materials, including live music and guests.[33] One reviewer surmises, "Soundies, slides, art work are not enough while records are playing."[34] As much as Soundies circulate in journalistic discourses in this early television programming context, they are not recognized as stand-alone television content.

The not-so-successful rehash of the 1940s Soundie on television may echo its failed trajectory during its initial run on the Panoram jukebox, but its circulation on early television gave way to other forms of short-form musicals on television. One direct spinoff of Soundies is the little-recognized Snader Telescriptions, a collection of more than one thousand music shorts filmed between 1951 and 1953.[35] Though often loosely referred to as "Soundies" in trade reviews, these shorts were filmed live, without lip syncing, and were similarly utilized in television deejay shows and as station filler.[36] Other than their liveness, their look and musical aesthetic are interchangeable with standard, performance-based Soundies. Throughout the 1950s, "Soundie" was used as a generic label for a variety of musical programming content on television like these musical telescriptions and helped smooth the transition of remediating radio programming onto television.

Extending from the aforementioned deejay shows with their shifting emphases on television personalities, several popular and often long-running musical variety shows employed Soundies' small-screen performance aesthetics and even featured former Soundies stars, including *The Lawrence Welk Show* (broadcast locally from 1951 to 1955 and then nationally from 1955 to 1971), *The Liberace Show* (1952–1969), and *The Nat King Cole Show* (1956).[37] The popular *Your Hit Parade* (1950–1959), a carryover program from radio, featured a top-ten countdown of the most requested songs of the week and similarly captured both the look and feel of a Soundies reel with its intimate screen aesthetics, their range of song styles, and sound-stage lip-synching scenarios. From cowboy ranches to domestic interiors, these quickly pieced together soundstage scenes visualize and recreate versions of popular music similar to Soundies, which often used lesser-known artists to perform standards. Unlike the frenetic shooting styles of 1980s music videos on MTV or even the youthful exuberance of rock films like *A Hard Day's Night* (1964), these televised short musical formats from the 1950s relied upon staid and straightforward performances and music styles that catered to maturing domestic audiences.

The emerging popularity of rock 'n' roll in the mid-1950s eventually challenged this tradition of screen music and instead made way for more youth-oriented formats. The long-running television show *American Bandstand* (1952–1989), for example, nicely illustrates this evolution in television formatting and its remediation of music shorts.[38] *Bandstand* originally aired as a deejay show featuring filmed musical shorts like Snader Telescriptions, but it switched its formatting to become a youth-oriented dance show by 1956. Accompanying the changes in music styles and target audiences, the visual format of the televised music short moved from debonair performers crooning on soundstages to bobbysoxers dancing in front of roving cameras and teen idols lip-synching to swooning crowds. Even with such dramatic changes in format with their emerging emphasis on youthful performances, *Bandstand*-style programming nonetheless speaks to the persistence of filmed popular music on television and its appeal as both an audio and visual domestic medium.

The Panoram Peep Show

Three years after Soundies Films released their last films for the Panoram, the *Times-Picayune* reported, "You will never see any of those machines around these days."[39] Though the films enjoyed an almost immediate afterlife on home screens in the early 1950s, the Panoram—at least in its original form—seemed to disappear from its initial exhibition sites. Even during the 1940s, the Panoram appeared in the back ads of *Billboard*, selling for a fraction of its suggested cost to coin operators and retailers. Framed as either an insufficient viewing experience with its small screen or, conversely, unable to meld into its environs as seamlessly as the standard music jukebox, the Panoram constantly struggled to carve out a defined niche as a film jukebox. From the Panoram's inception, coin operators had pointed out the machine's flaws or areas for improvement such as its lack of film selectivity. Within a year of the Panoram's release, operators began modifying and tailoring the machine. The two major modifications included big-screen attachments and running the music from neighboring jukeboxes through Panoram speakers so the presence of two sound-producing machines would not overlap one another.[40] Both of these popular adaptations to the Panoram addressed the particular needs of their exhibition spaces, either by broadening the viewing range to accommodate larger spaces and bigger audiences—as was the case in wartime factories—or by streamlining the speakers for better sound conditions. These early technical modifications ultimately were meant to enhance the Panoram's function as a musical movie jukebox and/or to recreate more traditional, theatrical viewing conditions for the films. Subsequent adaptations of the Panoram would prove otherwise and point to a revived interest in small screens for individualized interaction.

One of the earliest (and oddest) adaptations of the Panoram for something other than coin-operated film playback is their placement in professional photography studios, particularly for children's portraits. Used as "a first-rate attention-getter,"[41] the Panoram would screen kid-friendly films, "usually one of the Disney animal variety" (an accompanying photo shows Bambi on the screen).[42] The camera would either be attached to the side of the Panoram or the "machine's coin box is removed to accommodate a small camera."[43] According to these accounts, the machines proved a profitable novelty for photographers and enabled them to capture "extremely natural portraits" of children engrossed in a movie.[44] Similar to television screens in medical waiting rooms and bank lines, or attached to chairs at dentists' offices, this example of the modified Panoram integrates screens in spaces for mundane functions and not purely for entertainment.[45] The adapted Panoram becomes an instrumental screen at a place of business even utilizing theatrical entertainment, in this case Disney films, for functional purposes in a place of business.

The notion of a Panoram functioning as an independent film projector not explicitly bound to Soundies' musical content resituates the machine in a larger tradition of film viewing machines, including early cinema technologies and a long tradition of peep-show devices. *Penny Arcade* (1942), an early Soundie with Lucille Bremmer, shows a couple meandering through an arcade, playing with various attractions like a fortune-telling machine and a punching-bag game. As they look through old Mutoscopes, they watch film clips from *Fatty and Mabel Adrift* (1915), a Billy Franey silent short, and a repurposed Soundie called *The French Canadian Can-Can* (1941) with Fifi D'Orsay. In addition to placing *Can-Can* alongside other older film shorts, *Penny Arcade* nicely conveys the continuities between early cinema-viewing formats and the one in which the Soundie *Penny Arcade* would be shown. As Soundies on the Panoram quickly slipped into obsolescence during the postwar era, several Panoram machines were adapted into Solovue peek machines. This adaptation included covering their screens and attaching binocular-style viewing apparatuses to the former screen area.[46] Reminiscent of late-nineteenth-century amusement machines like the Mutoscope or Kinetoscope, this adaptation of the Panoram harkens a return to early cinema's arcades and amusement attractions rather than a technological innovation or evolution of the machine. Appropriately enough, these modified Panoram machines migrated to arcades, were given larger coin slots (for quarters rather than dimes), and showed films ranging in degrees of illicit content from burlesque striptease to pornography.

For example, a *Seattle Times* article from 1944 links Soundies to the initial days of U.S. cinema production when noting that Soundies producer William

Forest Crouch rented Edison's old studio in the Bronx. Likening Soundies' fast production schedule to Edison's own early productions, the article states, "So speedily are the films turned out that performers often see themselves on the juke-box screen only a few days after they have completed the production."[47] Illustrating the quick turnaround, an accompanying photo then shows Soundie performers watching themselves on the Panoram at a nearby restaurant during their lunch break. Similarly, a 1946 *Billboard* article commemorating the twentieth anniversary of talkies reflects upon the history of film machines, in which the Panoram is situated as a revival of the earliest arcade film machines. Highlighting the tumultuous coin-machine industry and its subsidiary status to theatrical film, the article opines that the "coin machine phase of the movie industry, however, probably will not get more than a brief passing mention at any of the functions sponsored by Warner Bros."[48] Placing the evolution of movie machines within the larger contours of American film history, both accounts situate the Soundie and the Panoram as marginal media practices located within the nontheatrical tradition of coin-operated movies. Even though these accounts explicitly call attention to a larger, more varied history in cinematic projection, they reinforce a dominant tradition of theatrical film screening that needs nuancing, especially with regard to contemporary, multifaceted screening practices, where big-screen viewing has become one among many viewing options.

In addition to these associations with cheap and efficient film production and exhibition practices, the Panoram is further distanced from the legitimacy of Hollywood through repeated inferences to the criminality of the coin-machine business. An article in the *San Diego Union* from 1950 frames James Roosevelt's involvement with Panoram Soundies (by then a defunct business) as a scandal because of the "corruption and gangsterism" of coin-machine companies like Mills Novelty Company, the Panoram's manufacturer.[49] Aligning the Panoram with disreputable business practices, the report claims that the Panorams were used against regulation at service and officer's clubs, which forbade vending machines and "payment for entertainment" during the war.

The Panoram's already-degraded status as a coin-operated technology—a reputation it never successfully surmounted despite various attempts by Roosevelt to link Soundies with mainstream Hollywood—is only exacerbated as it moves explicitly into the peep-show business. Earliest accounts of the Panoram being converted to a "Solovue-Peep movie machine" appear during 1947, when Soundies Film, Inc. release a few 16mm films for arcades.[50] Though no particulars about the content of these films are given, the emphasis on "peep" and "peek" machines for individual viewing implies that the film content is no longer tame, musical fare. Additional classified ads from specific arcades seek these adapted Panoram machines with no mention of Soundies films.[51] What is clear from these trade sources is that as soon as Soundies ceased production in 1947, coin operators quickly adapted the machines for arcades as their last potential avenue for profit. In her analysis of Panorams as peep-show machines, Amy Herzog explains the "de-evolution" of the Panoram as a biological metaphor of "parasitic inhabitation": "The Panoram itself became a discarded shell, a fossil left behind by a fickle media industry, a cast-off technology the pornographic trade subsequently scavenged and reanimated for its own illicit purposes."[52] Countering narratives of technological evolution or progression, Herzog aptly highlights the repurposing of the Panoram as a "cast-off" technology. However, the Panoram's residual elements and subsequent adaptations support a larger technological narrative than just devolution. Rather than framing the peep show as an odd deviation or mutation from the Panoram's exhibition practices,[53] the Panoram's peep-show biography in fact highlights broader media that persist into mainstream media practices such as a desire for more personal modes of screen viewing and the enduring fascination with short attractions as portable, nontheatrical entertainment.

In 1950, Panoram peep shows attracted national attention during a lawsuit against San Francisco arcade owners. In a bit of political muckraking against Jimmy Roosevelt, who was running for California governor at the time and hoping to legalize slot machine gambling, newspaper coverage of the trial focused on Roosevelt's relationship to Soundies and the Panoram business venture, particularly the Mills Brothers. Containing descriptions of the testimony and the films in question, the article clearly emphasizes the Panoram as the primary film technology for peep-show viewing. In the police sergeant's testimony, he states, "It is a rebuilt type of the machine that Jimmy Roosevelt built."[54] More than a hundred of these converted machines could be found along San Francisco's Market Street, with only sixteen of those converted to quarter slots for color film. The report also clarifies that these Panoram machines are still labeled as playing Soundies but adds that "none of them had sound working." Although no physical descriptions of the machines are given, this account indicates that these Panorams are the converted, Solovue models "viewed by one spectator at a time." Some of the exhibition conditions are noted, such as the machines being "marked 'for art students only' and 'no minors allowed,'" though "several minors and no indefinable art students" were seen viewing these films. According to the trial reports, the films show "'posturing blondes and brunettes in the nude' and deal even more frankly with erogenous aspects" with their "only purpose . . . to excite the passions of a person who looks at it." Similar accounts of Panorams as peep-show machines continued to circulate throughout the 1960s and into the early 1970s, including a 1960 newspaper reference to 251 "pornographic" Panorams in Seattle "cabarets."[55]

Similar to musical shorts being labeled "Soundies" on 1950s and 1960s television, the Panoram name persisted as the generic label for peep-show movie machines, with even the pinup films sometimes referred to as "Panoram

Loops."[56] Not until 8mm machines came into greater circulation in the 1960s and early 1970s did the 16mm Panoram fade from the peep-show exhibition circuit. Around this time, private booths were added to the converted Panorams, further removing the consumer from the public arcade atmosphere.[57] As a marginal and marginalized residual media practice, the adaptation of the Panoram purely as an exhibition format divorced from Soundies points to significant continuities between exhibition format, technology, and media content. Many of the reasons Panorams proved to be successful and profitable as peep-show devices extend from their initial function as self-contained, portable film projectors. Already designed to be coin operated, they immediately were amenable to forms of arcade commerce and, in some cases, already on location. Further, the duration of the short form is similarly conducive to its implementation as a vending commodity. With its associations to early cinema attractions extending through its peep-show afterlife, the Panoram's media cycle evidences a marriage of short-form content and small-screen viewings, a particular kind of everyday media practice that foregrounds brevity, immediacy, and short media as discreet commodity objects, not so different from, say, the viewing of pornographic shorts on the internet or the purchase of separate media files on iTunes.

La Soundies: The Return of the Cinema-Jukebox

This particular marriage of short, popular music movies with coin-operated viewing machines resurfaces during the 1960s. An explicit revival of the Panoram Soundies phenomenon, the French Scopitone replicated Soundies both in form and screen format. The Scopitone machine and Scopitone films, which first gained popularity in France and Germany in the early 1960s, promised to be the next big thing in the United States by the mid-1960s. Early U.S. trade accounts claim that the Scopitone would "revive an amusement machine originally introduced in the early 40s"[58] and link it directly to "Soundies of two decades ago," which the "old-timers" would remember.[59] Strikingly similar to the Panoram, there were some differences; the Scopitone used color film and allowed for the individual selection of films from a rotating carousel, redressing a major shortcoming of the Panoram. During their height in popularity in 1966, there were five thousand Scopitone machines in Europe and three thousand in the United States.[60] With competing models including the Cinematic, Cinejukebox, and Color-Sonics, Scopitones were the most successful of these revived movie machines and became the more generic term for this kind of film practice.[61] Ultimately, like Soundies, Scopitones' film jukeboxes would prove another short-lived business venture, but their circulation underscores important trends in the midcentury media landscape in its continued convergence of popular music, the moving image, and the everyday screen.

In her well-known essay "Notes on 'Camp'" (1964), Susan Sontag includes Scopitones among her many examples (including "stag movies seen without lust" and "old Flash Gordon comics") of the camp aesthetic.[62] The inclusion of the Scopitone on Sontag's "camp" list nicely captures the playful, pop-oriented mood of their films, as well as the B-level stars that often appeared in them. Capitalizing on youthquake culture and the emerging pop-rock market, Scopitones are full of sex appeal and go-go dancers, sometimes creating odd juxtapositions when paired with more downbeat songs like Dick and Dee Dee's "Where Did All the Good Times Go" or Brook Benton's "Mother Nature, Father Time" (1965). In addition to their exuberant tone, Scopitone producers were eager to market their films as the next generation of Soundies, with a clear demarcation in their visual treatment of music. Jay Lovins, president of Hollywood Film Associates and producer of Scopitones, stated, "The old concept of a singer, well-photographed, but merely standing or walking slowly on a sound stage will not motivate consistent business for the coin machines."[63] Instead, the films are "exceptionally vivid" in color, include a variety of locales, and employ editing that is "jet-paced."[64] The go-go aesthetic and upbeat appeals to youthful mobility in Scopitone films clearly draw upon the mood and tone of 1960s pop music while employing the visual strategies of 1960s television advertising, including their use of color, their evocations of sex appeal, their frequent use of jet-set locales, and, of course, their short duration.[65] For instance, several Scopitone films are set poolside (often with throngs of bikini-clad go-go dancers), in Las Vegas, or even on airplane tarmacs, suggesting a party atmosphere and an upwardly mobile lifestyle.

The Scopitone's implementation of popular 1960s televisual advertising tropes is significant in considering that television was not only the dominant media during this era but the dominant pastime as well. According to Lawrence Samuels, "Americans would spend more time watching television than pursuing any other past time in 1961."[66] Whereas the Soundie did not have to compete directly with television at the time of its initial circulation (though it certainly was thought to be a driving force in Soundies' demise by 1947), the Scopitone had to define itself well within the age of television. Frequent descriptions of the Scopitone refer to it as a "TV set" on top of a jukebox.[67] Some models even mount the screen on a much narrower neck, further making the screen appear boxy and television-like, somewhat separate from the body of the machine. Rather than seeing the television as a competing screen presence in public places, Scopitone producers replicated the aesthetics of television (particularly its advertisements) and framed the current screen-friendly culture as an opportunity to expand viewing practices, where they could "rack up coins from today's TV-trained generation!"[68] With the flow of media content working in both directions, Scopitone producers assert that television and Scopitones could mutually benefit one another. Believing that television stations will "prove a market for these three-minute color musical movies," Scopitone distributor David Rosen also claimed that "many of the popular film titles have been getting exposure on television—enhancing their appeal for coin-operated play."[69] One report suggests that Scopitone films, like Soundies in 1950, can play on "TV jockey" shows, making "short video tape segments that might be to television what records are to radio,"[70] while others see television shows like *American Bandstand* as venues for producing cheap music videos that could in turn circulate on Scopitones: "Dick Clark films promise to be some of the more inexpensive products because the films can be shot while the group is taping for TV."[71]

With television having proven successful with its adaptation of musical shorts on variety and teen dance shows, what then is to be gained from the circulation of short musical films in public vending machines during the age of, and in competition with, the television? As the other adaptations of jukebox movie machines have similarly suggested, the return of the Scopitone clearly is motivated by the business interests of the coin-machine industry, identifying opportunities and spaces for people to spend their time spending money, similar to the jukebox. As an ad for Color-Sonics blatantly announces, the "new dimension to the sound of music" is "money."[72] Beyond the coin-machine industry's economic interest in a pay-for-play technology, the appeal of the Scopitone is its ability to more specifically cater to its viewers and enhance the atmospherics of its potential viewing sites. A Color-Sonics ad makes this connection explicit in describing desired locales: "Wherever spirited people gather to wait for the next plane or show—or spend hour after hour enjoying themselves" like "cocktail lounges, theatres, hotels, bars and grills, terminals, coffee shops, discoteques, key clubs, arcades."[73] One Scopitone distributor claims they are a "big location item . . . you need a resort or some type of location where there is a flow of people. It is the type of equipment in which you have to have people moving by."[74] In addition to emphasizing the "flow of people" around the machine, the Scopitone—as "strictly a big town item"—adds a cosmopolitan air to their intended sites.[75] As in early Panoram promotional materials, the Scopitone is imbued with a sense of distinction with its placement in "luxury spaces where juke boxes have never been admitted"[76] and "class sites that previously rejected placement of a jukebox."[77]

One promotional photo from a pub located at the historic Palmer House in Chicago, considered "one of the top cinema jukebox locations in the country,"[78] features Scopitone star Joi Lansing standing in front of the machine with her own image displayed on the screen behind her. In the Scopitone's initial introduction to the United States, a *Life* magazine article similarly positions French pop star and yé-yé girl Sylvie in front of the machine and explains, "Her face even shows up on a new kind of jukebox. She is standing in front of a Scopitone, a splendid machine which plays a record of Sylvie singing and simultaneously shows a three-minute film of her."[79] Although an inaccurate description of how the Scopitone works (the sound is not on a separate record but on the film's magnetic soundtrack), it emphasizes a common motif in movie-machine promotional materials that can be found in Soundies' newspaper coverage in the early 1940s as well. As a promotional technique, a star standing by his or her own image is not so novel, but, in the case of the film jukebox, the image and literal embodiment of the star interacting within the space of exhibition is significant in suggesting the screen's intended function in space. It at once reinforces the class distinctions that both the Scopitone and Soundies hoped to promote as being something more sophisticated and chic than an ordinary jukebox while emphasizing the visuality of this "new" screen technology, which enables musical performances to be personified.

In actuality, the Scopitones' success in aligning their viewing contexts with choice consumers is debatable (like the Scopitone machine located at Sid King's Crazy Horse Bar, a club in Denver "famous for its Exotic Dancers"[80]), as is their ability to capitalize on youthful exuberance, since their musical performers often were out of step with the developments of a more radical 1960s counterculture expressed through the rising popularity of psychedelic music.[81] Although Scopitone producers and distributors are quick to point out their "'youthful' film emphasis,"[82] the overall aesthetics are ultimately a bit contrived and exaggerated (hence Sontag's camp designation). The films try to capitalize on a freewheeling youth market, but Scopitone's branding of an exuberant, jet-paced lifestyle often seems to cater to a more mature demographic. Their blend of a youth-oriented aesthetic and a rat-pack style of entertainment is best realized with both Nancy and Frank Sinatra Jr. starring in Scopitones. Nancy Sinatra's famous *Boots* (1966) features a throng of go-go dancers wearing minisweaterdresses and boots, at once youthful and risqué. Frank Sinatra Jr.'s cover of the Cole Porter classic "Love for Sale" embodies the generational shift in aesthetic from Soundies-era crooner to emotive pop star. Set poolside, *Love for Sale* (1965) features Sinatra accompanied by a small chorus of bikini-wearing girls. The film opens with a cheeky gag of Sinatra wearing a comedic mustache, flippers, and a life preserver around his waist. He then sheds his costume to more appropriate swimwear. The lyrics of the song suggest that the vocalist is the love-commodity, but the film is ambiguous as Sinatra gestures toward the women to imply he is marketing them as well.

The borderline-risqué content of Scopitones (undulating bodies, up-skirt shots, etc.) is similar to Soundies' own reliance on chorus girls and leering leg pans. An early review in *Variety* describes a Scopitone pilot reel as a "wiggly femme" film, one that would be "a boon to indoor girl-watchers."[83] This tactic suggests not just using sex to sell music—though this is certainly a key part of it—but also an ongoing pairing of sexualized content with this type of 16mm film format. With representations ranging from the playful and flirty to the illicit and pornographic, the persistent linkage of short film forms with coin-activated media delivery systems foregrounds not just the commoditization of media transactions in general, the "love for sale" at the drop of a coin or the push of a button, but also the itemizing and packaging of shorts as an ideal, individualized media commodity.

In the Scopitone's updates of the film jukebox, it switched to color film and a magnetic soundtrack (in some models it was still optical), and, most importantly, the Scopitone at last redressed a long-standing critique of the Panoram—self-selection. In contrast to the 1940s Panoram playing a looping reel of eight short films in succession, Scopitone films were loaded on individual cartridges and stored on "revolving drum magazines" or "carousels" within the body of the machine.[84] This modification enabled Scopitones to be played by selection at the push of a button on the display console, with consumers choosing specific music shorts like a traditional jukebox. Whereas the Panoram programming order was predetermined by the placement on a film loop, the Scopitone reconfigured viewing patterns where people could watch the same film repeatedly or in any chosen order. Depending on the model of film jukebox, the "revolving drum" would hold approximately thirty-six films, which also augmented the range of films available for viewing and offered consumers the illusion of a greater sense of variety and choice.[85] The Scopitone's new mode of selection and playback also revealed a few drawbacks. Some reports indicate that customers would have to wait for films to reload after play: "After one film finishes, a new selection can start within five minutes."[86] The waiting time between three-minute films surely slowed the pace of viewing and the repetition of play. Similar to the Panoram's flashing colored lights, Scopitone manufacturers redressed this lag time by keeping the screen illuminated and maintaining its visual presence through a "color kaleidoscope effect" or even "color slide advertising" on the screen during the interim.[87]

A 1966 Scopitone ad called "Carousel of Stars" portrays this new mode of film selection through its depiction of recording artists (Debbie Reynolds, Barbara McNair, and James Darren, for example) in individual, circular head shots swept across a whimsical bar of music notes.[88] While not making reference to or explaining the inner workings of the revolving carousel within the machine, the ad aptly visualizes the stars as separate entities, and their encircled heads suggest their own film reels. In addition to promoting the recording artists—a rather formulaic technique—the ad contains a full-length photo of the Scopitone machine in the bottom corner of the page. At once featuring the machine itself while not explicitly addressing its technological components or innovations, "Carousel" sells the faces of stars by replicating the carousel mechanism of the machine, an emphasis on the delivery of an image or a single personality, while their separate circles reinforce the compartmentalized film cartridge.[89] The ad reframes film as a personality-oriented commodity for individuals and articulates the way each film becomes its own self-contained consumer object.

The Scopitone's implementation of 16mm (and some 8mm) film cartridges similarly highlights the film commodity as a separate media object. Early ads and trade reviews boast how the automatic, continuous loop cartridge "lets you [the exhibitor] drop in a film cartridge as easily as a record."[90] Emphasizing the cartridge as a new film delivery system, the ad boasts that "26 film cartridges produced at Paramount studios in Hollywood" are available to offer "a full theatre of entertainment with the same kind of stars who made the jukebox yesterday's favorite American entertainment."[91] The intermedial comparisons between films and music jukeboxes come as little surprise, but the additional comparisons between film cartridges and records suggest new attitudes toward the promotion and circulation of short film commodities akin to the record single in popular music distribution.[92] Refiguring how films are transported, perceived, and delivered as consumer objects, the Scopitone's self-contained film shorts point to the next phase in the distribution of film for individual viewing through singular cartridges rather than film reels of eight. For example, Tel-A-Sign, the U.S. manufacturer and distributor of Scopitone machines, reported working on a "home model" of the machine that would be "8mm, cartridge-film fed,"[93] suggesting an early predecessor to further film playback formats like film "cassette machines" and eventually VCRs with videotapes.[94]

The Scopitone faded from the media landscape within a few years after their initial push in the United States, but the return of the film jukebox during the 1960s continued the promotion of small screens circulating short media. The Scopitone's cartridge that enabled the specific selection of film shorts helped realize and strengthen the consumer discourses that initially undergirded Soundies' 1940s screening practices. Similar to other coin-operated technologies, the film jukebox helped cultivate a significant mode of consumerism by promoting the desire to watch and listen to short media while on the go, waiting, drinking a cup of coffee, or having a meal and helped shape a larger culture of on-demand media playback. Midcentury modifications like Solovue attachments and self-selection only strengthened these possibilities. Poised between 1950s Hollywood's shifting industrial structures, the rise and predominance of television as a domestic screen practice, and the rampant growth of teen music markets, the persistent presence of short visual media forms with small, increasingly personalized screens reveal a mediascape where transmedia practices and formats become the locus for ubiquitous media integration.

Conclusion

Short and Sweet

Rescaling Screen Culture

Thomas Schatz characterizes the 1940s as a "Boom and Bust" decade for U.S. cinema, particularly for the Hollywood industry.[1] Bolstered by the support of the U.S. government during the war but then stymied by the Paramount Decree in 1948, Hollywood endured the tumult of the 1940s but not without undergoing major structural changes. Although the SDC's corporate history follows a similar trajectory (though with a much more modest boom period), I am hesitant to characterize the end of the 1940s as a bust for film culture in general. As the rapid growth and continued integration of screen practices like Soundies reveal, the 1940s evidenced an expansion of moving images in the United States. What might be seen as bad business for Hollywood, particularly with the dismantling of its exhibition arm, actually evinces a media culture not as much in demise as in transition. With the proliferation of 16mm moving-image technologies and screening spaces beyond the purview of Hollywood, the 1940s can be understood as an era that altered the scale of moving images and their pathways for circulation. Rather than relegate the history of U.S. screen culture only to the dominant industries of theatrical film and domestic television, interstitial media practices like Soundies help reimagine how screen media could become an everyday encounter.

Such examples of media diffusion into daily life abound in Soundies' own representations. For example, *Take the A-Train* (Delta Rhythm Boys, 1942), a Soundie version of the jazz standard about venturing uptown to Harlem for a night on Sugar Hill, opens on a crowded subway platform where the conductor provides the lead vocals. The film shows the vocal quartet board the train with their dates and then cuts to the 145th Street and Lenox Avenue street sign. Upon entering an all-black club, the Delta Rhythm Boys sit at a table and watch dancers already in the middle of their floor show. Like other Soundies, *A-Train* engages directly with the lyrical content of the song and visually illustrates the journey uptown by using a subway platform as its main performance setting. This black-cast Soundie displays themes of black cultural expression, which only are crystallized by the film's overt marking of space through its Harlem locale. With its coupling of all-black performers, music, and iconography, *A-Train* provides a rich text for the analysis of popular culture in the 1940s, but it also indexes particular discourses central to the cultural work that Soundies and their emerging screen presences can perform. As the Delta Rhythm Boys traverse spaces, lip syncing all the while, their music-images circulate from the subway platform to the jazz club (which also features its own black performers). At once showcasing black mobility as well as the mobilization of black entertainment, *A-Train* effectively puts the act of musical exhibition into motion, particularly with the aid of the train. Aptly illustrative of this book's approach to Soundies, *A-Train* triangulates multiple spaces, music and dance performances, and the technological mediations of the train to engage the dynamics of media circulation and a culture in transition.

The film concludes with a return to the crowded subway platform where the singers, inadvertently blocking the doors to the arriving train, get mowed over by a crowd flooding out of the train, and the sounds of their bustling briefly swell as the musical soundtrack fades. As the performers are pushed out of the way to make room for the influx of passengers, this final moment situates the music as both barely acknowledged and fully absorbed into its environ. Throughout this book, I have suggested a similar range of dynamics that the presence of Soundies brought to its various sites of exhibition—musical attractions, relaxing diversions, participatory and patriotic sing-alongs, aspirational presentations of identity mobility, therapeutic relief, and annoying atmospheric distractions. Ultimately, though, like the concluding moment of *A-Train,* Soundies screening practices bespeak the daily integration and absorption of media across ubiquitous sites, rendering music and moving images as both ordinary and integral to their environs.

Underlying and unifying the various aspects of Soundies history that this book has examined are the shifting scales of media culture during the 1940s. As Nick Couldry and Anna McCarthy note, studies of media and the spaces they both represent and occupy draw attention to the complexities of "scale-effects," where the micropractices at specific media sites intersect with macro issues of media distribution, circulation, and consumption.[2] Soundies and their site-specific practices throw into relief these entanglements of media-scale. Signifying the diffusion of film-viewing sites accompanied by the proliferation of small-screen technologies, Soundies draw attention to three primary shifts in media scale: the more intimate visual scale of Soundies' film representations to accommodate small-screen viewing, the scaling of film duration and format to render the media object into a discrete and efficient unit for individual consumption, and the scaling of Soundies' spatial representations to situate the screen within its environs. These shifts in scale suggest a downsizing of media (shorter forms, smaller screens) while equally supporting an expansion of media spaces, content, and screening practices.

Soundies' enactment of these shifts is by no means unique. As part of the expanded use of 16mm film projectors in a variety of screen contexts during the 1930s and 1940s, the circulation of Soundies on small screens provides early iterations of broader marketing trends in postwar screen culture and of our own fragmented and ubiquitous mediascape. The formal aspects of Soundies may presage the rise of MTV in the 1980s or even the explosion of digital shorts on YouTube in the 2000s, but Soundies' particular shifts in media-scale, evident in their ephemeral circulation and viewing practices, resonate deeply with contemporary discourses on short-form media and small-screen technologies.[3]

Soundies' afterlife migrations and iterations open up issues about the expansive circulation of short-media texts and genres into both new screen spaces and delivery platforms and the prolonged pairing of short-media forms with small, ubiquitous screens. As a pivotal example of short-media and small-screen viewing, Soundies circulation highlights several discursive assumptions about the function and import of short commercial media from both producers and consumers alike. From the Panoram's early experimental phases in the late 1930s, it was designed expressly as a machine for the exhibition of short media. Rather than the company acknowledging the length of a 16mm reel as a constraining factor for the duration of movie-machine entertainment, the SDC positioned the short format as the new, preferred way to consume in the "ever fast and furious" changing American landscape.[4] As Soundies' earliest marketing discourses touted, their films had to be "so good, so rich in fast and concentrated action and meaning" that the "same persons may want to see the very same film fifty or more times!"[5] From an industry standpoint, Soundies' short media potentially were more profitable due to their ability to be repeatedly and ubiquitously consumed. For consumers, they similarly offered flexible commercial entertainment that was both efficient and accessible. Both producers and consumers, then, relied on short-media consumption to be temporally brief in duration and spatially flexible.[6] Soundies' organizing logics of short-media consumption draw upon deep-rooted and long-standing discourses on modernity and efficiency extending from early-twentieth-century production practices through midcentury consumer convenience. These enduring discourses on fast, efficient consumption suggest particular relationships with time and space, where the spaces for media are limitless (aided by mobile technologies and compressed media formats) and the duration of media is rapid and therefore repeatable and multiple.

In our contemporary mediascape, the fragmented and far-reaching dispersion of short media epitomizes and continues to bolster our media consumption. Undergirding these logics of the scale of short media are notions of compression and portability, both of which gesture beyond the formal qualities of short representations to its formatting, technology, and delivery platforms.[7] As Jonathan Sterne states, an emphasis on media formats can provide different "inroads to media history" that reveal "subterranean connections across media."[8] Soundies' short-form circulation highlights transmedia "connections" to short audio formats like popular music recordings, jukeboxes, radio, and digital platforms like iTunes, but Soundies' particular connection to small-screen delivery further throws into relief twenty-first-century discourses continually binding short-form media circulation to screen consumption practices. For instance, a 2013 *New York Times* article entitled "Good Fit for Today's Little Screens: Short Stories" explicitly links short media with small-screen consumption.[9] In the case of digital books, the duration of the moving image is substituted for narrative length. In an excerpt from an interview with novelist Amber Dermont, she states, "The single-serving quality of a short narrative is the perfect art form for the digital age . . . Stories are models of concision, can be read in one sitting, and are infinitely downloadable and easily consumed on screens."[10] Less about its "art form" or its media content, the short story, which boasts a long history in portable print-media newspaper and magazine circulation, is touted for the accessibility of its digital format and platform and the brevity and efficiency in its act of consumption. Although the writer describes the stories as "models of concision," the primary emphasis on user interaction and modes of consumption (downloading) bespeaks the import of the compressed digital formatting more so than of succinct narration. This dynamic of compression/portability is central in organizing discourses on digital-media circulation and delivery formats. However, the repeated inclusion of short-media content into these discussions of format compression and portability exposes an odd though enduring supposition about the function of short media and the attachments between form and format.

The continued pairing of short-form media and the small screen again brings to the fore the logics of media scale—namely, the smaller the media form, the more portable its format and the broader its circulation, an entanglement not necessarily predicated on either technological necessity or aesthetic proclivity. In a direct retort to the author Dermont (quoted above), a *Salon* article entitled "Sorry, the Short Story Boom Is Bogus" argues that such short-form discourses are more of an industry ideal than a consumer-based reality.[11] The author draws attention to this "absurd notion" of conflating levels of media scale: "Because the screens of smartphones are small, people are somehow more inclined to use them to read shorter fiction." In an attempt to dismantle this assumption between form and screen, the article opens up a larger interrogation of digital formatting and argues for the popularity of the portable novel, the nine-hundred-page book that can now be quickly downloaded and carried in your pocket. However unsubstantiated this conflation of short-form media (its duration) with compressed formatting and technological portability (an issue of size and storage space) is becoming in the digital age, the overall persistence of short-media content with small-screen delivery cannot be so easily dismissed by novels on Kindle. Even if the resurgence of the short story is more tempered than e-publishers would like to believe, the profusion of short-media content across digital platforms has indeed shaped how we consume and imagine short media to function and circulate.

Rather than arbitrarily parsing short-form content from their delivery formats and modes of consumption, we need to tend to their intersections and the maintained interconnections of form and format in popular and journalistic discourses on short-media consumption. In the introduction to *Ephemeral Media*, Grainge posits that ephemeral media "implies a relation to screen images as much as . . . any particular form."[12] Soundies' music-screen legacies persist in a variety of contemporary media contexts precisely because of the inextricable connections their form forges with small-screen technologies. The fact that the music video, for instance, was most pronounced as a pop-culture phenomenon in its iteration on 1980s MTV fits well within Soundies' own shifting scale of screen representation and its continuities with the rise of television-screen viewing. However, Soundies' logics of consumption were found less on MTV proper, which was aligned more with cable broadcasting formats, than in ancillary discourses that highlighted the circulation and delivery of music videos as small-screen jukebox technologies.

During this music video boom, several stations sought to capitalize on the popularity of MTV's launch of a twenty-four-hour music-video station in 1981 with their own music video programming, including NBC's *Friday Night Videos* (1983–1992), Superstation WTBS's *Night Tracks* (1983–2002), and HBO's aptly titled *Video Jukebox* (1981–1986). Unlike the other programs that positioned themselves in their opening credits as an extension of the music-recording industry,[13] HBO's iteration of music videos for small-screen delivery used a coin-operated jukebox shaped like a robot. In *Video Jukebox*'s opening segment, the robot feeds a coin into its own mouth as music-video stills flicker on its screen-like body. Rather than early MTV promos that emphasized the musicians appearing in videos, HBO's promo highlights the system of media delivery and further frames small-screen exhibition as economic exchange (fitting for premium cable). The robot-as-video jukebox provides a somewhat futuristic image of short-media delivery while still relying on the very name "jukebox" and its coin operation.[14] This conflating of old jukebox technology with images of a robot-screen brings together images of old and new forms of media distribution within the amalgamated format of the hybrid video jukebox.

The envisioning of television music as a video jukebox endures beyond the age of MTV and the music short's televisual resurgence. Soundies' coin-operated discourses of self-selection continue to inform more ancillary, fragmented, and ubiquitous screen practices and align well with contemporary internet consumption. For instance, several self-proclaimed "video jukebox" channels populate YouTube, which has become a primary site for viewing music videos.[15] YouTube's iteration of the virtual video jukebox similarly points to the enduring association between music shorts and residual playback technologies. However obsolete these technological attachments and associations may be (think the virtual bookshelf for e-books or the remediated Polaroid on Instagram), these representations evoke particular modes of media consumption and suggest continuities across delivery platforms. The persistent logics of music video screen exhibition as jukebox delivery highlights media consumption as user-activated and individualized, which works well within user-generated internet platforms like YouTube. It is especially fitting as many of these "video jukebox" channels on YouTube are both played by individual consumers and programmed and maintained by them as well.

These video jukebox logics have far from disappeared and continue to organize portable and ubiquitous screen platforms. In April 2013, some fifty years after the Scopitone's film jukebox, *Vending Times* announced the launch of a digital, music video jukebox by retailer AMI Entertainment. Couched similarly in the language of revival, the article states, "The music video category, once nearly obsolete, is now making a comeback, thanks to YouTube and other Internet sources."[16] As AMI president and chief executive Mike Maas declares, "The time is right to bring music video to jukeboxes." Providing yet another pairing of short visual media for small-screen circulation, this particular relaunch of the music video jukebox is attributed to small-screen delivery platforms (namely, YouTube and the internet). In fact, rather than framing itself as a video jukebox, the company seeks to redefine their jukebox as such a platform. Resembling a large iPhone, this nouveau digital jukebox is, according to Maas, "more than a jukebox . . . it's a long-term platform that could be augmented with skins and technology." Boasting adaptability and multimedia capabilities, this site-specific, coin-operated "platform" can even be dressed in "nostalgia" jukebox "skins."[17]

The revival of music videos on a digital jukebox speaks partly to a culture of nostalgia but more so to the profusion of delivery platforms that support short-media circulation. The return of the music video as multiplatform, small-screen content provides more than just rumination on its enduring, generic aspects of screen music. Recent collections like *Medium Cool* and *Ephemeral Media* have highlighted that the ongoing and pervasive circulation of short media like music videos through mobile, wireless, and digital platforms into new consumer spaces makes short-form media relevant and in need of critical attention. As both an industrial and cultural practice, the proliferation of short-media ephemera and their circulation on small-screen technologies have supported and sustained a ubiquitous media culture precisely because of its interstitial transmedia positioning. Driven by both the demand for 24/7 content on a host of delivery platforms and screen technologies as well as consumer desire for greater media mobility and adaptability, these betwixt-and-between products of Hollywood, television, and the music industries shape the logics of media by filling in both temporal and spatial gaps in our mediascape. The history of Soundies as short form and screen format informs these understandings of contemporary screen culture and the ubiquitous conditions of media consumption. Couched inadvertently in discourses involving, for instance, furloughed soldiers' leisure time or a factory worker's lunch hour, Soundies screening practices help materialize overlooked but pervasive media networks. Animating areas and possibilities in screen dynamics where the screen is not necessarily a stand-alone phenomenon but is interwoven into the fabric of the everyday, Soundies enacted, while helping to further imagine, this shift in the scale of contemporary media culture.

Acknowledgments

This book would not have been possible without the support of many colleagues, friends, and institutions. First of all, Auburn University's School of Communication and Journalism has provided me with the resources and the time to complete this book. With last-minute help from Jennifer Adams, I was fortunate enough to receive a semester release from Auburn University's College of Liberal Arts. I also was grateful to receive support from the Broncyz fund for additional archival research. My colleagues throughout Auburn University and especially within the Media Studies Program have made Auburn a welcoming place to work. Susan Brinson has provided guidance and friendship; Hollie Lavenstein has kept me motivated with her zeal and constant curiosity; and George Plasketes has shared warm, writerly encouragement often in the form of a song lyric. My graduate research assistants, Kayleigh Murdock and Kesha James, have taken on some tough research tasks with aplomb and enthusiasm, and I am so grateful for their willingness to gather sources and create databases within the confines of their schedules.

I first discovered Soundies as a graduate student doing research at Indiana University's Black Film Center/Archive when I came across a short film of Dorothy Dandridge performing "Cow Cow Boogie." This serendipitous finding evolved into a seminar paper and a conference presentation and eventually guided me to this larger research project. My dissertation advisor, Greg Waller, was instrumental in helping me develop this research, which would never have happened without his urging. I have learned so much about film and media history in working with him, and I can't thank him enough for his time and generosity, our lengthy talks, his careful readings, the delicious food, and his continued advice and mentoring. Additionally, Barb Klinger, Ted Striphas, and Susan Courtney offered thoughtful and useful suggestions during various phases of this project. I have also been lucky to receive advice and support from generous scholars like Haidee Wasson, whose work has inspired much of my interrogation of screens, culture, and scale.

Lisa Banning and Alissa Zarro at Rutgers University Press have made the publishing process run smoothly and transparently. I am grateful for their professionalism and support. Leslie Mitchner's enthusiasm for Soundies helped remind me of why I started researching these films in the first place. I am incredibly grateful for Bethany Luckenbach's thorough and thoughtful editing of the final stages of the manuscript. In terms of research, the Margaret Herrick Library at the Academy of Motion Pictures has one of the few archives of Soundies production materials and photographs and is truly an invaluable resource. As most people have not seen a lot of the Soundies, the production photographs appearing in this book offer a sense of the staging and overall feel of these short films. For me, they are vital to understanding the cultural work that Soundies do. Both Faye Thompson and Kristine Krueger were beyond helpful and conscientious in assisting me with research materials and image acquisitions.

Thanks to all my friends who sat across tables from me in libraries, offices, and coffee shops across Bloomington and Auburn during various phases of this project—especially Jeremiah Donovan, Noelle Griffis, Mack Hagood, Megan MacDonald, James Paasche, Landon Palmer, Justin Rawlins, Zeynep Yasar, and Anna Weinstein. Without these writing dates and lunch breaks, I am pretty sure this project would have been far more daunting and less interesting to pursue. I especially want to thank Seth Friedman and Travis Vogan, who continually share their keen insights, encouragement, and friendship while navigating the various phases of academic life.

I cannot adequately express how fortunate I am to have a family that has shown me unconditional love and support in this and in every endeavor. My mother, Mary Ringenberg, encouraged me to return to school for graduate work and, because she understands me more than I do myself, has helped to give my life direction even when I resisted it. My sister, Ali Crawford, has cheered me on with her constant enthusiasm, spirit, and amazing sense of humor. My dad, Steve Ringenberg, introduced me to a world of music, record collections, and movies and has shaped my outlook and approach to media. My brother, Ben Ringenberg, has always been a source of encouragement, kindness, and connection. Finally, my husband, Bay Kelley, moved to Bloomington with some vague promise of a grad-school finish line that constantly shifted and left us often in limbo. He then willingly embraced the move to Auburn, Alabama. In the interim, he convinced me to get married, have a kid, and set work aside from time to time. Thanks for your patience and willingness to talk about the process while helping me realize that you can get on with an amazing life while pursuing academic research. When I began to research Soundies, I was pregnant. I now have a smart and inspiring eight-year-old daughter who is growing up in an immersive world of small-screen entertainment. May she continue to enjoy it but not take it at face value.

An earlier version of chapter 1 appeared as the article "From Attraction to Distraction: The Panoram Machine and Emerging Modes of Multi-Sited Screen Consumption," in *Continuum* 28, no. 3 (2014): 330–341. An earlier version of chapter 2 appeared as the article "'A Revolution in the Atmosphere': The Dynamics of Site and Screen in 1940s Soundies," in *Cinema Journal* 54, no. 2 (2015): 72–93, and portions of chapter 3 appeared in "Mobilizing the Moving Image," in *Cinema's Military Industrial Complex*, ed. Lee Grieveson and Haidee Wasson (Berkeley: University of California Press, 2018), 44–60. Thanks to Taylor & Francis, University of Texas Press, and University of California Press for the rights to reuse phrases and ideas published in these earlier pieces.

Notes

Introduction

1 "Jimmie's Peep Shows," *Time*, March 4, 1940, 67.
2 Lee Shippey, "Lee Side o' L.A.," *Los Angeles Times*, November 23, 1940, A4.
3 Other mash-up figures can be found in Soundies like *Hula Rumba* (1946), *Cow Cow Boogie* (1942), *He's a Latin from Staten Island* (1941), and *Rigoletto* (1945). Many of these films will be discussed in detail in chapters 2 and 5.
4 See Thomas Schatz, *Boom and Bust: American Cinema in the 1940s* (Berkeley: University of California Press, 1999), 461–462.
5 Film history collections like *Useful Cinema* and *Learning with the Lights Off* centralize educational and institutional film genres and exhibition practices and expand the complex dynamics and scope of moving-image culture in the early to mid-twentieth century. Charles Acland and Haidee Wasson, eds., *Useful Cinema* (Durham: Duke University Press, 2011), and Devin Oregron, Marsha Oregron, and Dan Streible, eds., *Learning with the Lights Off: Educational Film in the United States* (New York: Oxford University Press, 2012).
6 For works that foreground 16mm projectors and their organizing discourse within 1930s and 1940s expansion of cinema culture, see Gregory A. Waller, "Projecting the Promise of 16mm, 1935–45," in *Useful Cinema*, and Haidee Wasson, "The Other Small Screen: Moving Images at New York's World Fair, 1939," *Canadian Journal of Film Studies* 21, no. 1 (Spring 2012): 81–103.
7 Additional details on the formation and the in-flux organization of Soundies and Mills's business structure are available in Scott MacGillivray and Ted Okuda, *The Soundies Book: A Revised and Expanded Guide to the "Music Videos" of the 1940s* (New York: iUniverse, Inc., 2007).
8 Wally Hose, *Soundies* (St. Louis: Wally's Multimedia LLC, 2007), 7.
9 See Hose, 8.
10 See Hose, 10.
11 For a numerical breakdown of Soundies music genres, see Hose, 15.
12 Eric Smoodin, "The History of Film History," in *Looking Past the Screen: Case Studies in American Film History and Method*, ed. Jon Lewis and Eric Smoodin (Durham: Duke University Press, 2007), 17.

13 Both Henri Lefebvre's *Production of Space*, which argues for space as socially situated and always in formation, and Michel de Certeau's essay "Spatial Stories," which conducts spatial analyses as tours through lived practices and embodied experiences, have informed recent scholarship invested in situating media practices within lived spaces and the everyday dynamics of media engagement. Henri Lefebvre, *The Production of Space* (Oxford: Blackwell, 1991), and Michel de Certeau, *The Practice of Everyday Life* (Berkeley: University of California Press, 1984). For an application of Lefebvre's work on space in media studies, see *MediaSpace: Place, Scale and Culture in a Media Age*, ed. Nick Couldry and Anna McCarthy (London: Routledge, 2004).

14 Anna McCarthy, *Ambient Television: Visual Culture and Public Space* (Durham: Duke University Press, 2001), 2.

15 A. O. Scott, "The Screening of America," *New York Times*, November 22, 2008, MM21.

Chapter 1 The Look-Listening Machine

1 Wally Hose, *Soundies* (St. Louis: Wally's Multimedia LLC, 2007), 10. Hose explains that the Panoram and Soundies were considered part of the jukebox industry at the time of the AFM's recording ban instating no performance of recorded music after August 1, 1942, which did not apply to the motion picture industry and armed forces. Hose states, "Although originally reported to be considered motion pictures, Soundies were deemed to be part of the juke box industry in the eyes of the AFM and were thus included in the ban." Had the Panoram still been considered primarily a film technology, it would have been spared the restrictions and the accompanying financial turmoil.

2 Michelle Henning, "New Lamps for Old: Photography, Obsolescence, and Social Change," in *Residual Media*, ed. Charles R. Acland (Minneapolis: University of Minnesota Press, 2007), 49.

3 Lisa Gitelman, *Always Already New: Media, History and the Data of Culture* (Cambridge: MIT Press, 2006), 7.

4 I am borrowing the term "ambient" from Anna McCarthy's *Ambient Television* to define the more quotidian conditions of nontheatrical exhibition practices. Although McCarthy investigates the placement of television in nondomestic (or public) spaces, her study is invaluable for thinking through how spatial dynamics shape our media consumption. See McCarthy, *Ambient Television*.

5 Tom Gunning, "Now You See It, Now You Don't: The Temporality of the Cinema of Attractions," in *Silent Film*, ed. Richard Abel (New Brunswick: Rutgers, 1996), 71–84.

6 Jonathan Sterne, *The Audible Past: Cultural Origins of Sound Reproduction* (Durham: Duke University Press, 2003), 25.

7 *Panoram with Soundies: RCA Recorded and Projected* (Chicago: Mills Novelty Company, 1940).

8 Anna McCarthy, *Ambient Television: Visual Culture and Public Space* (Durham: Duke University Press, 2001), 71. McCarthy discusses how the presence of screens in public places, particularly in retail spaces, contributes to a mechanization of the consumer's experience.

9 *Panoram with Soundies*.

10 Similar discourses of efficiency coupled with leisure appear alongside Soundie promotional ads. For example, a photo of Coke vending machines with the caption "Time-out Period Steps up Production" appears in *Billboard*, January 31, 1942, 95.

11 See "Jimmy's Got It Again," *Look*, November 19, 1940, 12; "Movie Juke Boxes... What about Them?," *Billboard Music Year Book*, 1943, 73; Maynard Reufer, "The Future of Juke Box Pictures," *Billboard Music Year Book*, January 1, 1944, 124; "Soundies for Vets," *Tide*, July 1, 1944, 72; and *Panoram with Soundies*.

12 Soundies Catalog, 1942–1943, 176.

13 *Panoram with Soundies*.

14 Earl J. Morris, "Grand Town: Day and Night," *Pittsburgh Courier*, September 28, 1940, 21.

15 The gender dynamics are indicative of trade accounts of Panoram exhibition, typically catering to audiences of men (particularly GIs) with their emphasis on women as on-screen commodities. A few accounts of the Panoram mention GIs as their target audiences, including "Arcades Find Pan-O-Rams Successful Attraction," *Billboard*, January 1, 1944, 56; Sgt. Milton Lehman, "Home from the Wars to a Friendly Town," *New York Times*, July 8, 1945, 51; and "Movie Machines' Public Service," *Billboard*, June 16, 1945, 65.

16 *Panoram with Soundies*.

17 Acland, "Introduction: Residual Media," in *Residual Media*, ed. Charles R. Acland (Minneapolis: University of Minnesota Press, 2007), xix.

18 Jack Barry, "This New Showmanship," *Billboard*, January 31, 1942, 89.

19 James "Jimmy" Roosevelt, FDR's oldest son, was head of Globe Productions and the initial producer of Soundies films until he was called to duty during World War II. Considering the Roosevelt administration's advocacy of motion pictures during the war era, it is fitting that Jimmy Roosevelt touts the spread of motion pictures and that his production company should become the front-runner in the emerging film-jukebox industry. For more information on the government's support of Hollywood during World War II, see Thomas Doherty, *Projections of War* (New York: Columbia University Press, 1993), and Thomas Schatz, *Boom and Bust: American Cinema in the 1940s* (Berkeley: University of California Press, 1999), especially 262–281.

20 "Organized Exhibitor Action Opens against Roosevelt's 'Nickel Movies,'" *Motion Picture Herald*, March 3, 1940.

21 "Jimmie's Peep Shows," *Time*, March 4, 1940.

22 *Panoram with Soundies*.

23 Barry, "This New Showmanship."

24 For multiple reasons discussed in chapter 4, Soundies develop a small-screen, juke-film aesthetic that is conducive to both the machine's viewing parameters and the style of music being represented on the screen.

25 More of a mode of consumption, "attractions" account for a "configuration of spectatorial involvement" more than short-film forms do (37). See Tom Gunning, "Attractions: How They Came into the World," in *Cinema of Attractions Reloaded*, ed. Wanda Strauven (Amsterdam: Amsterdam University press, 2006), 31–38. See also Tom Gunning, "'Now You See It, Now You Don't': The Temporality of the Cinema of Attractions," in *Silent Film*, ed. Richard Abel (New Brunswick: Rutgers, 1996), 71–84.

26 "James Roosevelt Introduces His New 'Soundies,'" *Los Angeles Times*, September 17, 1940, 15.

27 *Soundies: A Musical History*, directed by Chris Lamson (2007; Los Angeles, CA: Liberation Entertainment, 2007), DVD.

28 Morris, "Grand Town: Day and Night."

29 The following chapter engages with specific spaces where Panorams circulated to better nuance the machine's viewing dynamics.

30 "Sight and Sound Jukeboxes Expected to Appeal Most to Hinterlanders Where Bands in Person Are a Rarity," *Variety*, December 4, 1940, 17.

31 Robert Allen defines "rusticity," rather than the "rural," as the "lived experience of place" and argues for a better situating of cinema history in the material conditions of culture. See Robert C. Allen, "Relocating American Film History: The 'Problem' of the Empirical," *Cultural Studies* 20, no. 1 (January 2006): 65.

32 For critiques of film and media scholarship's privileging of the visual, see Rick Altman, "Evolution of Sound Technology," in *Film Sound: Theory and Practice*, ed. Elisabeth Weis and John Belton (New York: Columbia University Press, 1985), 44–54, and Sterne, *Audible Past*, 15.

33 Maynard Reufer, "The Future of Juke Box Pictures," 124.

34 "Sight and Sound Jukeboxes," 17.

35 "'Juke Box' Soundies Opening New Outlet for Colored Bands," *Pittsburgh Courier*, November 22, 1941, 20.

36 Drinking is often cited as an activity to accompany Panoram viewing. Douglas W. Churchill claims that when you watch a Soundie, you "get Artie Shaw with your beer" in "Hollywood Strikes Back," *New York Times*, September 29, 1940, 121.

37 Amy Herzog, "Illustrating Music: The Impossible Embodiments of the Jukebox Film," in *Medium Cool: Music Videos from Soundies to Cellphones*, ed. Roger Beebe and Jason Middleton (Durham: Duke University Press, 2007), 30–58.

38 "Phonograph, Movie Machine Combination Is Developed," *Billboard*, January 31, 1942, 67.

39 For various historical approaches to film production technologies, see Robert Allen and Douglass Gomery, *Film History: Theory and Practice* (New York: McGraw-Hill, 1985); John Belton, "Technology and Aesthetics of Film Sound," in *Film Sound: Theory and Practice*, ed. Elisabeth Weis and John Belton (New York: Columbia University Press, 1985), 63–72; and David Bordwell, Janet Staiger, and Kristin Thompson, *The Classical Hollywood Cinema: Film Style & Mode of Production to 1960* (New York: Columbia University Press, 1985).

40 In addition to the aforementioned essays by Haidee Wasson like the "Protocols of Portability," in *Film History: An International Journal* 25, no. 1–2 (2013): 236–247, and Greg Waller's "Projecting the Promise," in *Useful Cinema*, see Charles Acland's "Curtains, Carts and the Mobile Screen," in *Screen* 50, no. 1 (Spring 2009): 148–166.

41 Wasson, "Protocols of Portability," 244.

Chapter 2 The Sites of Soundies

1 "Detroit," *Billboard*, February 26, 1944, 92. The Soundie *Move It Over* (1943) stars Betty Bartley and Madeline Lee, who "appear as part of an auto unit touring army camps," according to its *Billboard* review. See "Movie Machine Review," *Billboard*, February 19, 1944, 59.

2 For detailed accounts of the proliferation of small-gauge film technologies in the 1940s, see Haidee Wasson, "Suitcase Cinema," in *Cinema Journal* 51, no. 2 (2012), and Gregory Waller, "Projecting the Promise of 16mm, 1933–45," in *Useful Cinema*,

ed. Charles Acland and Haidee Wasson (Durham: Duke University Press, 2011), 125–148.

3 Haidee Wasson, "The Other Small Screen: Moving Images at New York's World Fair, 1939," *Canadian Journal of Film Studies* 21, no. 1 (2012): 83.

4 Nick Couldry and Anna McCarthy, eds., *MediaSpace: Space, Place and Culture in a Media Age* (London: Routledge, 2004), 2.

5 Henri Lefebvre, *The Production of Space* (Oxford: Blackwell, 1991), 27. For a specific discussion on the import of addressing the materiality of film historical practices, see Robert C. Allen, "Relocating American Film History: The 'Problem' of the Empirical," *Cultural Studies* 20, no. 1 (2006): 48–88.

6 Anna McCarthy, *Ambient Television* (Durham: Duke University Press, 2001), 18, 47.

7 The following chapter more thoroughly examines the Panoram as a wartime technology employed by the U.S. military.

8 Vivian Sobchack, "Lounge Time: Postwar Crisis and the Chronotope of Film Noir," in *Refiguring American Film Genres*, ed. Nick Browne (Berkeley: University of California Press, 1998), 129–169. For a historical case study exploring everyday living conditions and the constraints to personal time and space on the home front, see Perry R. Duis, "No Time for Privacy: World War II and Chicago's Families," in *The War in American Culture: Society and Consciousness during World War II*, ed. Lewis A. Erenberg and Susan E. Hirsch (Chicago: University of Chicago Press, 1996), 17–45.

9 Quoted in *Motion Picture Herald*, January 18, 1941, 106–107.

10 "Exhibitors, Authorities Hit Slot-Machine Films," *Motion Picture Herald*, August 17, 1940, 27. See also Lee Shippey, "Lee Side o' L.A.," *Los Angeles Times*, November 23, 1940, A4.

11 "Movie Juke Boxes . . . What about Them?," *Billboard Music Year Book*, 1943, 73. "Exhibitors Fighting 'Slot-Machine' Movies" also mentions Soundies doing well in "higher class" Minneapolis restaurants in *Motion Picture Herald*, January 25, 1941, 60.

12 "Music as Written," *Billboard*, April 27, 1946, 26, and Leonard Spinrad, "Movie Going Down Guatemala Way," *New York Times*, July 7, 1946, 41.

13 "Sight and Sound Jukeboxes Expected to Appeal Most to Hinterlanders Where Bands in Person Are a Rarity," *Variety*, December 4, 1940, 17.

14 Chapter 4 addresses the reasons for these changes in Soundies' representations, which include the AFM recording ban, shifting popular music styles, and the development of a small-screen aesthetic with more intimate modes of address.

15 Jack Barry, "This New Showmanship," *Billboard*, January 31, 1942, 89.

16 Chapter 6 offers a discussion of Soundies circulation on television in the late 1940s.

17 See "$30,000 Weekly Slot-Movie Gross Troubles New England Exhibitors," *Motion Picture Herald*, May 24, 1941, 15; "Panorams Hit Favor with Armory Employees in Mass," in *Billboard*, November 11, 1944, 72, where armory employees enjoy the "relaxing benefits" of a Soundie with their meal; and "Industry in Pittsburgh Attacks 16mm. Shows," *Motion Picture Herald*, August 10, 1940, 26, which features early accounts of Panoram-style slot-machine movies being shown at the Circus Inn Café in Homewood, Pennsylvania, and at Isalay's Ice Cream and Dairy in South Park, Pennsylvania, with very favorable reception.

18 "Roosevelt Name Draws Publicity; Jukebox Operators Irritated," *Variety*, March 5, 1941, 45.

19 "Movie Juke Boxes . . . What about Them?," *Billboard Music Year Book*, 1943, 73.
20 *Soundies: A Musical History*, directed by Chris Lamson (2007; Los Angeles, CA: Liberation Entertainment, 2007), DVD.
21 Joseph Driscoll, *Pacific Victory, 1945* (Philadelphia: J. B. Lippincott Company, 1945), 107.
22 Driscoll, 108.
23 Driscoll, 108.
24 "Movie Machine Review," *Billboard*, February 19, 1944, 59. The aforementioned Soundie *Move It Over* also appears on this reel.
25 "Movie Machine Review," *Billboard*, July 24, 1943, 66.
26 The song title is derived from "She's a Latin from Manhattan," a song performed by Al Jolsen in *Go into Your Dance* (Archie Mayo, 1935).
27 U.S. historian Lewis Erenberg similarly comingles acts of identity tourism within the emerging social spaces of nightlife hubs in the 1920s. With the popularity of nightclubs and cabarets featuring themed décor and often appropriating exotic, touristic motifs, the very atmosphere encourages identity play and allows for a "new social informality" to emerge. See Lewis A. Erenberg, *Steppin' Out: New York Nightlife and the Transformation of American Culture, 1890–1930* (Westport: Greenwood Press, 1981), xiii.
28 David Stowe, *Swing Changes: Big-Band Jazz in New Deal America* (Cambridge: Harvard University Press, 1994), 73.
29 Adam Knee, "Class Swings: Music, Race and Social Mobility in *Broken Strings*," in *Soundtrack Available*, ed. Pamela Robertson Wojcik and Arthur Knight (Durham: Duke University Press, 2001), 272.
30 Roger Butterfield, "Los Angeles," *Life*, November 22, 1943, 117.
31 "Movie Machine Review," *Billboard*, October 20, 1945, 76.
32 Alongside often demeaning tropes of women and nonwhite Americans found in some of these films, a fair number of Soundies (far proportionate to theatrical films showcasing diverse musicianship) featured African American artists as well as all-women bands like the Sweethearts of Rhythm. Seeing these artists perform on the Panoram could have furthered the democratizing impulse of these films while simultaneously catering to the idealized fantasies of white male viewers. Both Kristin McGee's *Some Liked It Hot: Jazz Women in Film and Television, 1928–1959* (Middletown: Wesleyan University Press, 2009) and Sherrie Tucker's *Swing Shift: "All-Girl" Bands of the 1940s* (Durham: Duke University Press, 2000) provide detailed analyses of gendered jazz representations during the swing era.
33 Wasson, "The Other Small Screen," 87.
34 "Industry Mentions," *Billboard*, October 30, 1943, 71.
35 For a discussion of the war's role in supporting a future-thinking ideology based upon notions of technological and economic progress, see Alan Brinkley, "World War II and American Liberalism," in *The War in American Culture: Society and Consciousness during World War II*, ed. Lewis A. Erenberg and Susan E. Hirsch (Chicago: University of Chicago Press, 1996), 313–330.
36 Sgt. Milton Lehman, "Home from the Wars to a Friendly Town" *New York Times*, July 8, 1945, 51.
37 Lehman, 51.
38 Fictional character Holden Caulfield of *Cather in the Rye* fame experiences a momentary respite at Grand Central in the mid-1940s as he harbors his own

interpretation of the Burns' poem "Comin' Thro' the Rye." Holden also has a similarly ambivalent relationship toward watching movies.

39 McCarthy, *Ambient Television*, 15.

40 "Soundies for War Plants," *Billboard*, February 13, 1943, 61.

41 "Soundies for War Plants," 61.

42 "Soundies for War Plants," 61.

43 "Movie Machine Review," *Billboard*, February 27, 1943, 104.

44 "Movie Machine Review," 104.

45 "Soundies for War Plants," 61. Although this source does not indicate the size of the enlarged screen, another Billboard account of a Soundies public exhibition describes a four-by-five-foot screen being attached to the Panoram for greater viewing capacity. See "Panoram Used in Red Crosses' Drive for Nurses, Aids," *Billboard*, May 15, 1943, 65.

46 Photo caption, *Billboard*, February 14, 1942, 57.

47 "Mills Novelty Penalized for WPB Violation," *Chicago Daily Tribune*, April 14, 1942, 23.

48 "Movie Machines' Public Service," *Billboard*, June 16, 1945, 65.

49 See Brownell, "'It Is Entertainment, and It Will Sell Bonds!': 16mm Film and the World War II War Bond Campaign," *Moving Image* 10, no. 2 (2010): 60–82.

50 See Charles Acland and Haidee Wasson, eds., *Useful Cinema* (Durham: Duke University Press, 2011) for case studies addressing the civic and educational uses of film in the 1930s and 1940s.

51 "Machines for Recruiting," *Billboard*, March 18, 1944, 70.

52 "'We'll Slap the Japs' Rings Out in Chi City Hall," *Billboard*, January 24, 1942, 71.

53 Photo caption, *Billboard*, January 24, 1942, 80.

54 "Movie Machines' Public Service," 65.

55 "Movie Machines' Public Service," 65.

56 "'We'll Slap the Japs,'" 71.

57 "Movie Machines' Public Service," 65.

58 "3 Panorams Draw 600,000 at 20-Day Det. Army Air Show," *Billboard*, July 15, 1944, 69.

59 "Panoram Used in Red Crosses' Drive," 65.

60 "Movie Machine Review," *Billboard*, February 28, 1942, 78, and "Movie Machine Review," *Billboard*, February 3, 1945, 64. An actual account of a Panoram in a military hospital also suggests that hospital-themed Soundies like *Angels of Mercy* may have directly correlated to their exhibition sites. See "Movie Machines' Public Service."

61 "Panoram Used in Red Crosses' Drive," 65.

62 Photo, *Billboard*, May 23, 1942, 73.

63 "Panoram for Defense," *Billboard*, March 14, 1942, 85.

64 Marshall Field's (advertisement), *Chicago Daily Tribune*, October 9, 1942, 2.

65 McCarthy, *Ambient Television*, 63. For further elaboration on early uses of site-specific screens in 1940s department stores, see chapter 2, "Gendered Fantasies of TV Shopping in the Postwar Department Store," which includes analyses of both film and TV in 1940s retail spaces. Also, for more on department stores and spectatorship, see Anne Friedberg's *Window Shopping: Cinema and the Postmodern* (Berkeley: University of California Press, 1993). See *Business Screen* 3, no. 3 (1941): 8 on the potential for coin-operated movies to function as sales devices. For postwar

plans to make Panoram-like machines into sales devices, see Henry Clay Gipson, *Films in Business and Industry* (New York: McGraw-Hill, 1947), 93.

66 "OWI Pics for Soundie Fans," *Billboard*, June 17, 1944, 68.

67 "Soundies Plug Bonds during the 6th War Loan Drive," *Billboard*, December 2, 1944, 97.

68 "OWI Pics," 68.

69 As Katherine Brownell argues, government producers "changed the nature of the films from a source of information to a commercial medium focusing more attention on entertainment." Brownell, "It Is Entertainment," 77.

70 "Movie Machine Review," *Billboard*, March 25, 1944, 93.

71 "Movie Machine Review," *Billboard*, September 30, 1944, 64.

72 "OWI Pics," 68.

73 "Movie Machine Reviews," *Billboard*, December 23, 1944, 67.

74 Arlene Wolf, "Milady Dreams of Post-War 'Utopia,'" *Canton Repository*, January 1, 1944, 10.

75 Christopher Anderson, "Television and Hollywood in the 1940s," in *Boom and Bust: American Cinema in the 1940s*, ed. Thomas Schatz (Berkeley: University of California Press, 1999), 424.

76 Anderson similarly links ancillary film practices with the rise of television in his discussion on how small, independent film studios were among the earliest producers of television programming. See Christopher Anderson, "Television and Hollywood in the 1940s," 422–444.

77 In chapter 6, I discuss how Soundies proved to be highly adaptable to fledging television, particularly with their images scaled for small-screen consumption. See, for example, "'Soundies' Getting Air-Pix Test," *Billboard*, November 11, 1944, 63, and "Old Soundies, Costing 300G, Bring in 700G," *Billboard*, February 3, 1951, 6.

Chapter 3 Mobilizing Space

1 "Movie Machine Review Program 10 68," *Billboard*, May 30, 1942, 92.

2 "Movie Juke Boxes . . . What about Them?," *Billboard Music Year Book*, 1943, 73.

3 "Equipment Field Notes," *Film Daily*, September 10, 1943, 1.

4 Wasson, "Protocols of Portability," *Film History: An International Journal* 25, no. 1–2 (2013): 236–247.

5 The company was initially called Mills-Globe Company after Jimmy Roosevelt's Globe Productions and Fred Mills of the Mills Novelty Company. See Wally Hose, *Soundies* (St. Louis: Wally's Multimedia LLC, 2007), 7. Additional details on the in-flux organization of Soundies and the Mills business structure are available in Scott MacGillivray and Ted Okuda, *The Soundies Book: A Revised and Expanded Guide to the "Music Videos" of the 1940s* (New York: iUniverse, Inc., 2007).

6 "Expect Priority to Build Capt. Jimmy's Jukes," *Chicago Daily Tribune*, August 31, 1941, 1.

7 See Thomas Doherty's *Projections of War* and Kathryn Cramer Brownell's "'It Is Entertainment, and It Will Sell Bonds!': 16mm Film and the World War II War Bond Campaign," *Moving Image* 10, no. 2 (2010): 60–82.

8 Peter Lester, "'Sweet Sixteen' Goes to War: Hollywood, the NAAF and 16mm Film Exhibition in Canada during World War II," *Canadian Journal of Film Studies* 19, no. 1 (Spring 2010): 2–19.

9 Westbrook Pegler, "James Roosevelt as a Partner: Manufacturers of 'One-Arm Bandits' Welcomed Him in Gala Party Brochure," *San Diego Union*, September 19, 1950, 20.

10 As one of the largest bases in the United States, Camp Kilmer contained expansive recreational facilities, including 20 softball diamonds, 30 volleyball courts, and 160 horseshoe courts. The camp also had its own band, orchestra, and football team. "The National Archives at New York City, Camp Kilmer," U.S. National Archives and Records Administration, http://www.archives.gov/nyc/exhibit/camp-kilmer (March 6, 2015)

11 Mary Jane Medlin, "A Community Project in Service Men's Recreation," *Journal of Health and Physical Education* 14 (1943): 364, 402.

12 Medlin, 364.

13 Photo, *Billboard*, June 6, 1942, 66.

14 In *Soundies: A Musical History*, a similar account of Soundie viewing describes people watching with their noses up to the screen. Hugh Hefner also tells of watching Soundies at PXs. See *Soundies: A Musical History*, directed by Chris Lamson (2007; Los Angeles, CA: Liberation Entertainment, 2007), DVD.

15 "Movie Machine Reviews," *Billboard*, June 6, 1942, 67.

16 In using the term "ambient," I again am evoking Anna McCarthy's *Ambient Television*, in which she provides a conceptual framework for, and historical overview of, the ways in which nondomestic television screens were integrated into various public spaces in the United States. See Anna McCarthy, *Ambient Television* (Durham: Duke University Press, 2001).

17 Lloyd Norman, "Penny-in-Slot Devices Now Pay Death-To Axis," *Chicago Daily Tribune*, August 9, 1942, A10.

18 Raymond Williams, *Television: Technology and Cultural Form* (London: Routledge, 1974), 140.

19 Col. Emmanuel Cohen, "Film Is a Weapon," *Business Screen: Army Pictorial Issue*, no. 1 (1946): 43, 72, and 74, and *Business Screen*, no. 5 (1945): 72.

20 Cohen, 43.

21 *Business Screen: Army Pictorial Issue*, no. 1 (1946): 59.

22 Cohen, "Film Is a Weapon," 43.

23 Mills Novelty Company (advertisement), *Business Screen* 5, no. 1 (1943): 31.

24 Mills Novelty Company (advertisement), 31.

25 Roger W. Babson, "Preparing for Jobs," *Washington Post*, April 2, 1945, 12.

26 "Dayroom Information Centers Feature Shaw Field Program," *Digest*, May 1944, 4–5.

27 "Dayroom Information Centers," 5.

28 Lt. Claude A. Eggertsen, "Education Home from the Wars," *Educational Administration & Supervision* 31 (1945): 483–494.

29 Eggertsen, 492.

30 For further analysis of the role of film in educational settings, see Devin Orgeron, Marsha Orgeron, and Dan Streible, eds., *Learning with the Lights Off: Educational Film in the United States* (New York: Oxford University Press, 2012), an anthology offering historic case studies on educational film usage and disrupting oversimplified understandings of the nontheatrical film by complicating notions of film in educational settings being used solely for didactic functions.

31 Eggertsen, "Education Home from the Wars," 492.

32 General Electric (advertisement), *Business Screen* 7, no. 6 (1945): 10. This ad for a GE projector contains a photo of GIs gathered for a screening in an outdoor amphitheater.
33 Cohen, "Film Is a Weapon," 43.
34 For more on efficient learning in postwar instructional film discourse, see Charles Acland, "Curtains, Carts and the Mobile Screen," *Screen* 50, no. 1 (2009): 148–166.
35 "Films as Medicine," *Business Screen: Army Pictorial Issue*, no. 1 (1946): 46.
36 "Films as Medicine," 46.
37 "Films as Medicine," 46.
38 "Films as Medicine," 46.
39 "Films as Medicine," 46.
40 "Soundies Fetes Wounded Vets," *Billboard*, May 13, 1944, 76.
41 "Soundies Fetes Wounded Vets," 76.
42 "Movie Machines' Public Service."
43 "Movie Machines' Public Service."
44 "Movie Machines' Public Service."
45 "Films as Medicine," 46.
46 For an analysis of our contemporary fascination with the notions of "portability" and "screen mobility" within 1940s instructional film materials, see Charles Acland, "Curtains, Carts and the Mobile Screen."
47 "Movie Machines' Public Service."
48 "Soundies Fetes Wounded Vets," 76.
49 "Movie Machines' Public Service," *Billboard*, June 16, 1945, 65.
50 For an exceptionally detailed history of the United States' socioeconomic transition from World War II to postwar prosperity, see Lizabeth Cohen's *A Consumer's Republic* (New York: Vintage Books, 2003). For Cohen's discussion on GI incentives and favoritism, see especially chapter 3, "Reconversion," 112–165.
51 "Vet's Plan, Better Pix, Service School and Venue from Ads Spotlight Soundies Post-War Plans" *Billboard*, April 22, 1944, 64. See also "Soundies for Vets," *Tide*, July 1, 1944, 72–73.
52 "Vet's Plan."
53 "Vet's Plan."
54 "Sono-vision" (advertisement), *Business Screen* 6, no. 5 (1945): 87.
55 "Sono-vision" (advertisement), 87.
56 "Sono-vision" (advertisement), 87.
57 "Sono-vision" (advertisement), *Business Screen* 7, no. 2 (1946): 7.
58 "Sono-vision" (advertisement), 7.
59 Henry Clay Gipson, *Films in Business and Industry* (New York: McGraw-Hill, 1947), 93.
60 For further cultural analysis of the war's role in supporting a future-thinking ideology based upon notions of technological progress, see Alan Brinkley, "World War II and American Liberalism," in *The War in American Culture: Society and Consciousness during World War II*, ed. Lewis A. Erenberg and Susan E. Hirsch (Chicago: University of Chicago Press, 1996), 313–330.

Chapter 4 Up Close and Personal

1 Tim Anderson examines in detail this shift from a performance- to recording-based music economy in postwar America. See Tim Anderson, *Making Easy Listening:*

Material Culture and Postwar American Recording (Minneapolis: University of Minnesota Press, 2006). Additionally, historian Adam Green explores this transition in the music industry in the 1930s and 1940s in relation to the emergence of black recording artists and deejays. See Adam Green, *Selling the Race: Culture, Community, and Black Chicago, 1940–1955* (Chicago: University of Chicago Press, 2009). For a comprehensive overview of the U.S. music industry, see Russell Sanjek, *Pennies from Heaven: The American Popular Music Business in the Twentieth Century* (New York: De Capo Press, 1996).

2 "Petrillo Lifts Ban on Hiring of Union Men by Soundies," *Billboard*, November 6, 1943, 62. Although the AFM lifts the ban on Soundies and several smaller record labels by November 1943, Victor and Columbia, the two major recording labels, held out until November 1944.

3 See Green, *Selling the Race*, especially 56–57. For an industry history of the expansion of popular music genres, see Russell Sanjek, *Pennies from Heaven*.

4 Philip K. Scheuer, "Town Called Hollywood," *Los Angeles Times*, November 29, 1942, C3.

5 Scheuer, C3.

6 See Katherine Spring, *Saying It with Songs: Popular Music and the Coming of Sound to Hollywood Cinema* (New York: Oxford University Press, 2013), and Rob King, *Hokum!: The Early Sound Slapstick Short and Depression-Era Mass Culture* (Berkeley: University of California Press, 2017).

7 Charles Wolfe further examines the relationship between popular music in Vitaphone Shorts and its integration in feature films during this era. Charles Wolfe, "Vitaphone Shorts and *The Jazz Singer*," *Wide Angle* 12, no. 3 (July 1990): 58–78.

8 "Music: Soundies," *Time*, September 16, 1940.

9 "'No Competition,' 16mm Men Say," *Motion Picture Herald*, June 7, 1941, 24.

10 "Roosevelt-Mills' Juke-Box Pix to Entail Cost of $1,000,000 a Yr.," *Variety*, March 13, 1940, 4.

11 "Jimmy's Got It Again," *Look*, November 19, 1940, 14.

12 "Mills Novelty and Jas. Roosevelt's Classy N.Y. Preem for 'Soundies,'" *Variety*, October 23, 1940, 18. See also "'Juke-boxes' Jammed in Bottleneck of Insufficient Product Backlog," *Motion Picture Herald*, March 22, 1941, 48.

13 "Music: Soundies."

14 "Roosevelt-Mills' Juke-Box Pix," 4.

15 "'Jimmy' Not A-drift," *Motion Picture Herald*, November 23, 1940, 9.

16 "Roosevelt Name Draws Publicity; Jukebox Operators Irritated," *Variety*, March 5, 1941, 45.

17 Jack Barry, "This New Showmanship," *Billboard*, January 31, 1942, 89.

18 For more on the dynamics of television sound, see Michel Chion, *Audio-Vision: Sound on Screen* (New York: Columbia University Press, 1994). Lynn Spigel also explores the dynamics of sound and image on early television in *TV by Design: Modern Art and the Rise of Network Television* (Chicago: University of Chicago Press, 2008).

19 *Frim Fram Sauce* (1945), a King Cole Trio Soundie, uses this same gag of live performer interacting with his mediated self on the Panoram screen, drawing attention to the Panoram's nontheatrical spaces of exhibition and perhaps similarly commenting upon the perceived threat of performers having to compete with the prevalence of recorded music.

20 Anderson, *Making Easy Listening*, 7.

21 "Both Sides Are Cautious," *Billboard*, July 25, 1942, 6, 9.
22 "Movie Juke Boxes . . . What about Them?," *Billboard Music Year Book*, 1943, 73.
23 "Soundies Company Now Going into Production," *Billboard*, March 6, 1943, 71.
24 Black representations and increased circulation of African American music in Soundies is discussed in detail in chapter 5. Adam Green's history of black music in Chicago provides a nuanced intervention to the accounts of music industry turmoil and argues that these conditions helped popularize more forms of black music during the time. See Green, *Selling the Race*.
25 Not immune to black entertainment stereotypes, even within an all-black context, *Caravan* shows a man eating watermelon and other demeaning archetypes for comedic appeal.
26 "Move Machine Review," *Billboard*, October 17, 1942, 68.
27 According to historian Peter Townsend, using vocal talent to emulate instrumentation was one among many tactics used by record companies during the ban. See Peter Townsend, *Pearl Harbor Jazz: Change in Popular Music in the Early 1940s* (Jackson: University Press of Mississippi, 2007), 175.
28 Another comedic Soundie, Spike Jones and his City Slickers' *Clink! Clink! Another Drink!* (1942), further plays upon the joke of using trick vocalists by having a woman lip sync to the sounds of a horn among several misplaced sonic cues throughout the film (which also features a sing-along to a Panoram).
29 "Move Machine Review," 68.
30 "G.I.'s Select Their Favorite Records; Still Kids at Heart," *Billboard*, September 23, 1944, 72.
31 Townsend, *Pearl Harbor Jazz*. Townsend counters the tendency in recent jazz histories to overlook the presence of the vocalist in big-band jazz recordings and overemphasize the effects of the recording ban. Although his assertions run counter to my contentions that the ban had a tremendous impact on the kinds of Soundies that could be filmed, I also recognize certain historical continuums with the role of vocalists in recorded popular music. See pages 178 and 179.
32 "Jukes Helped Disk Firms Recover from Sales Slump," *Billboard*, November 6, 1943, 63.
33 Anderson, *Making Easy Listening*, xx.
34 Wally Hose, *Soundies* (St. Louis: Wally's Multimedia LLC, 2007), 15.
35 Townsend, *Pearl Harbor Jazz*, 180.
36 Sanjek, *Pennies from Heaven*, 305.
37 Chris Rasmussen, "'People's Orchestra': Jukeboxes as the Measure of Popular Musical Taste in the 1930s and 1940s," in *Sound in the Age of Mechanical Reproduction*, ed. David Suisman and Susan Strasser (Philadelphia: University of Pennsylvania Press, 2010), 185.
38 "Jukes Helped Disk Firms Recover," 63. See also "G.I.'s Select Their Favorite Records," 20 and 72.
39 Rasmussen, "'People's Orchestra,'" 192.
40 "Movie Machine Reviews," *Billboard*, December 11, 1943, 67.
41 Paddy Scannell, *Radio, Television and Modern Life* (Cambridge: Blackwell, 1996), 68.
42 Scannell, 69.
43 Scannell, 64. In his analysis of the 1940s British vocalist Vera Lynn, Scannell similarly compares the intimacy-evoking tendencies of the screen's close-up with the sincere-styled vocalist.

44 Michael Ritchie discusses how early television also was stymied by an AFM ban headed by James Petrillo from 1945 to 1948. Using similar strategies and resources to counter the ban, early television producers had to rely on amateur talent and variety programming. See Michael Ritchie, "The Day the Music Died," *Please Stand By: A Prehistory of Television* (Woodstock: Overlook Press, 1994), 185–189.

45 Music historian Elijah Wald also cites new amplification systems that allowed for more intimate tones to be heard, thereby adding to the King Cole Trio's aesthetic of engagement. See Elijah Wald's *How the Beatles Destroyed Rock 'n' Roll: An Alternative History of American Popular Music* (Oxford: Oxford University Press, 2009), 148–149.

46 Rasmussen, "'People's Orchestra,'" 195.

47 "Panorams Hit Favor with Armory Employees in Mass," *Billboard*, November 11, 1944, 72.

48 "Soundies for Vets," *Tide*, July 1, 1944, 51. See also "Syndicated Film Video Segs Eyed by ET Orgs as Future Market," *Billboard*, June 22, 1946, 19.

49 "'Soundies' Getting Air-Pix Test," *Billboard*, November 11, 1944, 12, 63.

50 "'Soundies' Getting Air-Pix Test," 63.

51 "Old Soundies, Costing 300G, Bring in 700G," *Billboard*, February 3, 1951, 6.

52 "Filmmusic Shorts for TV in Golden Sweep, 30G to 100G," *Billboard*, July 15, 1950, 7. See also "AFM to Collect on Oldies in Fresh 'Official' Pact," *Billboard*, November 11, 1950, 12.

53 Chapter 6 further examines the remediation of Soundies on television in the 1950s.

54 *Panoram with Soundies: RCA Recorded and Projected* (Chicago: Mills Novelty Company, 1940).

55 *Panoram with Soundies*.

56 "Mills Novelty,'" 18.

57 "Further Analysis Cues Jukebox Take Nearer $150,000,000 a Year," *Variety*, August 21, 1940, 49, 60.

58 Rick Altman, "Cinema and Popular Song: The Lost Tradition," in *Soundtrack Available*, ed. Pamela Robertson Wojcik and Arthur Knight (Durham: Duke University Press, 2001), 25.

59 "Mills Novelty,'" 18.

60 "Yermi Stern's Juke-box Shorts Points Up New Gadgets Sundry Deficiencies," *Variety*, August 7, 1940, 16.

61 "Further Analysis Cues Jukebox Take Nearer $150,000,000 a Year," *Variety*, August 21, 1940 49, 60.

62 Maynard Reufer, "The Future of Juke Box Pictures," *Billboard Music Year Book*, January 1, 1944, 124.

63 "Soundies for Vets," 51.

64 "Soundies Subjects May Be Selected," *Billboard*, August 22, 1942, 65.

65 "Jerkbox?," *Variety*, March 22, 1944, 38.

66 For early accounts on domestic media engagement and discourses of control, see William Boddy, "Wireless Nation: Defining Radio as a Domestic Technology," *New Media and Popular Imagination: Launching Radio, Television, and Digital Media in the United States* (Oxford: Oxford University Press, 2004), 16–43.

Chapter 5 "A Swing Half Breed"

1 Wally Hose, *Soundies* (St. Louis: Wally's Multimedia LLC, 2007), 5.

2 See, for example, Thomas Cripps, *Slow Fade to Black: The Negro in American Film, 1900–1942* (New York: Oxford University Press, 1993), and Scott Yanow, *Jazz on Film* (San Francisco: Backbeat Books, 2004).

3 "Shine" was also featured the following year in the black-cast musical *Cabin in the Sky* (1943), where it is performed by John "Bubbles" Sublett. Arthur Knight suggests that this filmed performance of the song evokes the African American trickster figure, Shine, rather than Armstrong's "more 'innocent' clowning." See Arthur Knight, *Disintegrating the Musical: Black Performance and American Musical Film* (Durham: Duke University Press, 2002), 154.

4 Amy Herzog, "Illustrating Music: The Impossible Embodiments of the Jukebox Film," in *Medium Cool: Music Videos from Soundies to Cellphones*, ed. Roger Beebe and Jason Middleton (Durham: Duke University Press, 2007), 30–58.

5 Gleason offers a useful, in-depth analysis of the ambiguous and contradictory American rhetoric of the era. See Philip Gleason, "Americans All: World War II and the Shaping of American Identity," *Review of Politics* 43 (October 1981): 498–518. See also Gary Gerstle, *American Crucible: Race and Nation in the 20th Century* (Princeton: Princeton University Press, 2002), and *The War in American Culture: Society and Consciousness during World War II*, ed. Lewis A. Erenberg and Susan E. Hirsch (Chicago: University of Chicago Press, 1996).

6 "Move Machine Reviews," *Billboard*, February 9, 1946, 91.

7 Gleason, "Americans All," 502–503.

8 For a more detailed exploration of Latin American representations during the Good Neighbor Policy, see Ana Lopez, "Are All Latins from Manhattan?: Hollywood, Ethnography and Cultural Colonialism," in *Unspeakable Images: Ethnicity and the American Cinema*, ed. Lester D. Friedman (Urbana: University of Illinois Press, 1991). For an in-depth analysis of miscegenation tensions enacted through GI fantasies in South Sea's films, see Susan Courtney's *Hollywood Fantasies of Miscegenation: Spectacular Narratives of Gender and Race, 1903–1967* (Princeton: Princeton University Press, 2005), especially chapter 3.

9 There are a few exceptions to the dominant representations of white-passing, as evidenced by the Dorothy Dandridge Soundies (discussed later on), as well as the Delta Rhythm Boys' *Snoqualomie Jo Jo* (1945). In this Soundie, an African American male poses as an American Indian chief draped in two American flags. See Scott MacGillivray and Ted Okuda, *The Soundies Book: A Revised and Expanded Guide to the "Music Videos" of the 1940s* (New York: iUniverse, Inc., 2007), 67.

10 Ana Lopez interrogates the mainstreaming of Latin representation in the United States, specifically claiming that Hollywood positions itself as an ethnographer in its management of representations of Latin America during this era. See Lopez, "Are All Latins from Manhattan?"

11 This song title borrows from the song "She's a Latin from Manhattan," featured in *Go into Your Dance* (1935), a film starring Al Jolson, wherein he sings a song about a chorus girl who poses as a Latin dancer. In a nightclub routine, Dot Wayne (Ruby Keeler) is introduced as Senorita Delores, only to be jokingly exposed by Jolson's song: "She's a Latin from Manhattan, but not Havana. Though she does the Rumba for us, and she calls herself Dolores, she was in a Broadway chorus known as Susie Donahue."

12 An anecdotal account by jazz historian Dan Morgenstern indicates that Panorams may have been on the Staten Island Ferry, lending further import to the chosen locale for this Soundie. See *Soundies: A Musical History*, directed by Chris Lamson (2007; Los Angeles, CA: Liberation Entertainment, 2007), DVD.

13 For an in-depth analysis of the negotiated masculinity of the "Latin Lover," see Miriam Hansen's study of Rudolph Valentino in *Babel and Babylon: Spectatorship in American Silent Film* (Cambridge: Harvard University Press, 1991), especially chapter 11, "Male Star, Female Fans." Utilizing star and reception discourses, Hansen explains how Valentino's image of ethnic other was tempered by claims of European descent and how his masculinity was feminized in various ways through an emphasis on his beauty, which in turn helped displace miscegenation anxieties.

14 MacGillivray and Okuda, *The Soundies Book*, 224–225.

15 Michael Paul Rogin, *Blackface, White Noise: Jewish Immigrants in the Hollywood Melting Pot* (Berkeley: University of California Press, 1996), 183.

16 Not to force a direct lineage between nineteenth-century minstrelsy practices and Soundie representations, but it should be noted that, in addition to their thematizing and circulating racial and ethnic differences through popular cultural forms, blackface minstrelsy and Soundies' programming formats and exhibition contexts contain some synchronicities. As Eric Lott explains, the minstrel show drew upon "folklore, dance, jokes, songs . . . racial and gender cross-dressing or impersonation," similar to Soundies' variety formatting. Also, both Soundies and minstrel shows circulated in a variety of public spaces for diverse (and sometimes racially integrated) audiences. See Eric Lott, *Love & Theft: Blackface Minstrelsy and the American Working Class* (New York: Oxford University press, 1993), 9.

17 Of the 1,850 Soundies, 29 are Irish, 106 are Latin, 40 are Hawaiian, and another 40 are given "foreign" classification. Coupled with the 287 black-cast Soundies, 30 percent of all Soundies feature themes of cultural "difference." For a complete breakdown of Soundies by category, see Wally Hose, *Soundies*, 15.

18 Gleason, "Americans All," 498.

19 Knight, *Disintegrating*, 147.

20 Knight, 147.

21 David Stowe, *Swing Changes: Big-Band Jazz in New Deal America* (Cambridge: Harvard University Press, 1994), 73, 156.

22 This is not to say that issues of African American integration were completely unaddressed in U.S. politics but that Hollywood, with the support of the Roosevelt administration, became recognized as an important site for considering racial identity politics. For instance, the 1942 NAACP convention in L.A. addressed putting more pressure on Hollywood for better African American representation, and, with the support of the OWI, films like *The Negro Soldier* overtly adopted an integrationist agenda. For further analysis of the relationship between Hollywood and the U.S. government during World War II, see Thomas Doherty's *Projections of War* (New York: Columbia University Press, 1993).

23 Adam Knee, "Class Swings: Music, Race and Social Mobility in *Broken Strings*," in *Soundtrack Available*, ed. Pamela Robertson Wojcik and Arthur Knight (Durham: Duke University Press, 2001), 272.

24 Favorable black press coverage frames Gene Krupa as a progressive and unapologetic integrationist. See "Gene Krupa Forgets South, Features Roy," *Chicago Defender*, March 7, 1942, 20.

25 Stowe, *Swing Changes*, 127–128. According to Stowe, Roy Eldridge was cut from *Ball of Fire*, a film featuring Gene Krupa's band.

26 In his analysis of the avant-garde jazz film *Jammin' the Blues* (1944), Arthur Knight argues that the role of dancers in filmed jazz performance visually detracts from the artistry (and therefore the authenticity) of black musicianship and the quality of the film in general. Although it is important to note the ways dance and other modes of performance are aligned with and help configure the visual representations of black musicality, I am not sure that dance unequivocally detracts from or degrades the quality of the film. See Knight, *Disintegrating*, 225.

27 Knight, 148.

28 Knight, 158.

29 Donald Bogle, *Toms, Coons, Mulattoes, Mammies, and Bucks: An Interpretive History of Blacks in American Films* (New York: Continuum, 2002), 18.

30 Bogle, *Toms, Coons, Mulattoes, Mammies, and Bucks*, 118.

31 See Cripps, *Slow Fade to Black*, 229.

32 Knight, *Disintegrating*, 248.

33 For a more in-depth star study involving racial dynamics and crossover appeal, see Richard Dyer's *Heavenly Bodies: Film Stars and Society* (London: Routledge, 2004), particularly his study of Paul Robeson's constructions of black masculinity.

34 "Movie Machine Review," *Billboard*, November 14, 1942, 67.

35 See Donald Bogle, *Dorothy Dandridge: A Biography* (New York: Amistad Press, 1997), and Charlene Regester, *African American Actresses: The Struggle for Visibility, 1900–1960* (Bloomington: Indiana University Press, 2010). Specifically, Regester discusses the melding of Dandridge's screen persona with her personal life, both of which ended untimely and tragically.

36 See Bogle, *Toms, Coons, Mulattoes, Mammies, and Bucks.*

37 "New Stars Being 'Born' as Soundies Make Shorts in Harlem," *New York Amsterdam News*, August 28, 1943, 16.

38 "Pretty Girls Due for Soundie Feature Films," *New York Amsterdam News*, May 22, 1943, 15.

39 *Soundies: A Musical History*.

40 Such discourses on economic opportunism similarly pervade early black press coverage of the Soundies industry. Black film actor Clarence Muse stated, "Colored talent will have a great opportunity in this new field, because some of our best records in the past have been creations by Negro artists." Clarence Muse, "What's Going On in Hollywood," *Chicago Defender*, September 28, 1940, 20. Other reports indicate both the potential profitability and crossover appeal of black music in Soundies: "To be very popular among Negroes the 'Soundies' will have to make a direct appeal by presenting colored personalities . . . Count Basie, Fats Waller, Jimmy Lunceford, right here in Hollywood, have had ofay jitterbugs eating out of their hands." Earl J. Morris, "Grand Town: Day and Night," *Pittsburgh Courier*, September 28, 1940, 21.

41 Robin D. G. Kelley, "The Riddle of the Zoot: Malcolm Little and Black Cultural Politics during World War II," *American Studies: An Anthology*, ed. Janice Radway, et al. (Chichester: Wiley-Blackwell, 2009), 284. Kelley points to the juxtaposition between "wartime rhetoric of equal opportunity and the apparent availability of well-paying jobs for whites with the reality of racist discrimination in the labor market" during the 1940s.

42 Kelley, "The Riddle of the Zoot," 282. Kelley's analysis of the early life of Malcolm X fully explores the cultural significance of the zoot suit during the early 1940s as both in opposition to mainstream white America and the black bourgeoisie.

43 A few accounts suggest Soundies' import to African American communities in circulating representations of prominent African American artists in public spaces. According to cultural historian Delilah Jackson, Soundies were very popular in Harlem, and lines would often form out in the street to watch a Soundie. See *Soundies: A Musical History*. A *Billboard* account of a movie machine exhibition in Norfolk, Virginia, similarly shows that Soundies featuring big-name black artists like Duke Ellington and Cab Calloway proved a tremendous draw to African American audiences: "Crowds almost jammed traffic on the streets trying to get in to patronize the machines." See "Play Goes upward on Movie Machines," *Billboard*, September 19, 1942, 62.

44 Krin Gabbard, *Jammin' at the Margins* (Chicago: University of Chicago Press, 1996), 264. Gabbard claims that Carmichael's relationship with African Americans was more complex than mere minstrelsy. Having performed with a black band on a "race" record in 1929, he held strong relationships with black musicians. Gabbard further argues that Carmichael's association with African American musicians held an influence on his screen persona.

45 In addition to Carmichael's raced performance, *Hong Kong Blues* also features a miniaturized Asian woman dancing on his piano, evoking a confluence of cultural traditions and unsettling—but certainly not atypical—gendered representations.

46 Gabbard, *Jammin' at the Margins*, 240.

47 Gabbard, 264.

48 Susan Gubar, *Racechanges: White Skin, Black Face in American Culture* (New York: Oxford University Press, 1997).

49 Gubar, 10.

50 Gubar, 11.

51 In an analysis of *Paper Doll*, Amy Herzog further adds that this representation of Dandridge is "excessive" and "disquieting" since her spastic dance movements have no correlation to the sounds of the song, thereby offering another instance where Dandridge's representations are unsettled and never fully contained by the logics of the film. See Amy Herzog, "Discordant Visions: The Peculiar Musical Images of the Soundies Jukebox Film," *American Music* 22, no. 1 (Spring 2004): 27–39.

52 MacGillivray and Okuda, *The Soundies Book*, 61.

53 Such self-conscious appropriations of African imagery and jungle themes were popular among black big-band / jazz composers of this era—namely, Duke Ellington. See *Soundies: A Musical History*.

54 According to Hose's *Soundies*, 76 percent (or three-quarters) of all Soundies are western themed.

55 See Richard Slotkin's *Gunfighter Nation: The Myth of the American Frontier* (Norman: University of Oklahoma Press, 1992). Slotkin explains that the cowboy-hero in the popular American mythos serves as a "model" par excellence for "regenerating the lost manliness and vigor" of middle-class white males (37).

56 Stuart Hall, "What Is This 'Black' in Black Popular Culture?," in *Representing Blackness: Issues in Film and Video*, ed. Valerie Smith (London: Anthlone Press, 1997), 129.

57 Homi Bhabha, *The Location of Culture* (London: Routledge, 1994), 7. Bhabha's widely utilized concept of cultural hybridity is often deployed in more specific

articulations of postcolonial discursive formations and issues of translation. Although his concept has come under much debate and scrutiny, I find it to be a useful way to orient the radical potential of in-between identity constructions. Similarly, from an anthropological perspective, Victor Turner asserts the import of the liminal in studying cultural ritual. See, for example, Victor Turner's "Liminality and Communitas," in *The Ritual Process: Structure and Anti-Structure* (New Brunswick: Aldine Transaction Press, 2008).

58 Bogle, *Dorothy Dandridge*, 93.

59 Robyn Weigman, "Black Bodies/American Commodities: Gender, Race and the Bourgeois Ideal in Contemporary Film," in *Unspeakable Images: Ethnicity and the American Cinema*, ed. Lester D. Friedman (Urbana: University of Illinois Press, 1991), 311.

60 For more on the construction and management of utopian impulses in musical films, see Richard Dyer's "Entertainment and Utopia," in *Only Entertainment*, 2nd ed. (London: Routledge, 2002), 19–35.

61 "Movie Machine Review," *Billboard*, November 14, 1942, 67.

62 Lott, *Love & Theft*, 18.

63 Lott, 6.

64 Similar to *Rigoletto*, *Broken Strings* (1940), a race film starring Clarence Muse, plays upon the tensions between classical and swing music through a generational conflict and, according to Adam Knee, operates as a black allegorical response to *The Jazz Singer*. See Knee, "Class Swings," 269–294.

65 *Billboard*'s reviews of Day, Dawn and Dusk's vaudeville routines mention their appeal to mass audiences and how their songs "indicate that the three boys have been signing in the music halls overseas rather than the Harlem hotteries." See "Night Club Reviews," *Billboard*, May 30, 1942, 13, and September 21, 1946, 36.

66 See Knight, *Disintegrating*, 6. Knight claims that in musical films, the task is to restore sight to sound, rather than the predominant logics of synchronized-sound film that seeks to match sound to image.

67 Alice Maurice, *Cinema and Its Shadow: Race and Technology in Early Cinema* (Minneapolis: University of Minnesota Press, 2013), 3.

Chapter 6 Postwar Screens

1 "Cine Juke Box: Just a Novelty?," *Billboard*, July 10, 1965, 45–46.

2 Gary Cross, *An All Consuming Century: Why Commercialism Won in Modern America* (New York: Columbia University Press, 2000), 100.

3 Lizabeth Cohen, *A Consumers' Republic: The Politics of Mass Consumption in Postwar America* (New York: Vintage Books, 2003), 319.

4 Cohen, 309.

5 In orienting this study of Soundies around the "residual," I am borrowing from Raymond Williams's description of cultural formations in *Marxism and Literature*, which addresses the interplay of the dominant, emerging, and residual cultural forms and practices in the always uneven processes of historical change. See Raymond Williams, *Marxism and Literature* (New York: Oxford University Press, 1977). For a more specific positioning of the residual elements in media culture, see Charles R. Acland, "Introduction: Residual Media," in *Residual Media*, ed. Charles R. Acland (Minneapolis: University of Minnesota Press, 2007).

6 "Soundies for Vets," *Tide*, July 1, 1944, 72–73.

7 Scott MacGillivray and Ted Okuda, *The Soundies Book: A Revised and Expanded Guide to the "Music Videos" of the 1940s* (New York: iUniverse, Inc., 2007), 397.
8 "Television? Who Knows What It Will Do to Film Theaters?," *Cleveland Plain Dealer*, February 15, 1948, 15B.
9 "Movies in Taverns Barred in Michigan," *Billboard*, June 19, 1948, 27.
10 "Inroad on Video Market Is Foreseen in Soundies," *Broadcasting*, November 1, 1940, 79.
11 MacGillivray and Okuda, *The Soundies Book*, 403, 405.
12 Scott MacGillivray, *Castle Films: A Hobbyist Guide* (Lincoln: iUniverse, Inc., 2004), xvii.
13 MacGillivray, 140.
14 MacGillivray and Okuda, *The Soundies Book*, 401.
15 "Cash for Your 16mm Sound Films" (advertisement), *Billboard*, August 21, 1948, 48.
16 Advertisement, *Oregonian*, August 23, 1948, 5.
17 Richard A. Peterson, "Why 1955? Explaining the Advent of Rock Music," *Popular Music* 9, no. 1 (January 1990): 113. http://www.jstor.org/stable/852886.
18 "'Instant Soundies' Panned by Jerry," *Rockford Register-Republic*, July 5, 1960, 10B.
19 "'Soundies' Getting Air-Pix Test," *Billboard*, November 11, 1944, 63.
20 Christopher Anderson, "Television and Hollywood in the 1940s," in *Boom and Bust: American Cinema in the 1940s*, ed. Thomas Schatz (Berkeley: University of California Press, 1999), 422–444.
21 Michel Chion, *Audio-Vision: Sound on Screen* (New York: Columbia University Press, 1990), 157.
22 "Coast Philco Distib Set HugeTeleHyp," *Billboard*, September 6, 1947, 13.
23 "'Requestfully Yours' Televised by WATV," *Billboard*, February 5, 1949, 41.
24 "Brenner a Disc Jockey on TV with Soundie Films Instead of Wax," *Variety*, February 2, 1949, 37.
25 "TV: The New Home for Disc Jockeys," *Billboard*, October 7, 1950, 70–71.
26 "Picture Jockeys," *News Week*, July 17, 1950, 48.
27 "Al Jarvis," *Billboard*, September 13, 1947, 15.
28 "On the Square," *Times-Picayune*, April 12, 1950, 23.
29 "Old Soundies, Costing 300G, Bring in 700G," *Billboard*, February 3, 1951, 6. See also "AFM to Collect on Oldies in Fresh 'Official' Pact," *Billboard*, November, 11, 1950, 12.
30 "Filmmusic Shorts for TV in Golden Sweep, 30G to 100G," *Billboard*, July 15, 1950, 7.
31 "TV: The New Home," 70–71.
32 See "Television: The Vault of Hollywood" for television's remediation of Hollywood film in the 1950s in Michele Hilmes, *Hollywood and Broadcasting: From Radio to Cable* (Urbana: University of Illinois Press, 1990).
33 "CBS-TV to Lead Daytime Race; Dumont on Heels," *Billboard*, August 12, 1950, 4.
34 "TV: The New Home," *Billboard*, 70.
35 MacGillivray and Okuda, *The Soundies Book*, 397–399.
36 For example, see "Greg Norman Takes Video Plunge . . . ," *Billboard*, May 19, 1951, 11, and "Don Lee's KHJ-TV Gets 800 Snader Telescripts," *Billboard*, February 9, 1952, 12.
37 One of the major formal influences on 1950s television variety shows is vaudeville. For a residual history of the vaudeville form and its remediation on television, see JoAnne Stober's "Vaudeville: The Incarnation, Transformation, and Resilience of an Entertainment Form," in *Residual Media*.

38 Murray Forman offers an excellent analysis of early television music and explores both the aesthetic shifts and the industrial convergences between popular music, film, radio, and television during this era. Murray Forman, *One Night on TV Is Worth Weeks at the Paramount: Popular Music on Early Television* (Durham: Duke University Press, 2012).

39 "On the Square."

40 For accounts of combination devices added to Panorams and jukeboxes, see "Phonograph, Movie Machine Combination Is Developed," *Billboard*, January 31, 1942, 67, and "Combo Disk-Film Juke Box May Develop Pix Shorts Field for Orks and Singers," *Billboard*, June 15, 1946, 36. For accounts of big-screen attachments to Panorams, see "Night Club Movie Mch. Points Way to Entirely New Location," *Billboard*, August 11, 1945, 65; "Panoram Used in Red Crosses' Drive for Nurses, Aids," *Billboard*, May 15, 1943, 65; and "Soundies for War Plants," *Billboard*, February 13, 1943, 61.

41 "Movie Machine Aids Photog in Snapping Youngsters' Poses," *Billboard*, April 27, 1946, 152.

42 "Speaking of Pictures . . . Susan's Studios Mass-Produce Kid Pictures," *Life*, February 26, 1945, 14.

43 Photo caption, *Billboard*, May 11, 1946, 128.

44 "Movie Machine Aids Photog."

45 For additional accounts of postwar plans for Soundies in sales, see "Vet's Plan, Better Pix, Service School and Venue from Ads Spotlight Soundies Post-War Plans," *Billboard*, April 22, 1944, 64, and "NAVED Meet Set for Chi August 6–7," *Billboard*, June 8, 1946, 114.

46 "Amusement Games Firms Tell Plan for Showing," *Billboard,* January 25, 1947, 87, and "Want Panorams" (classified ad), *Billboard*, December 18, 1948, 110.

47 "Edison Old Bronx Studio Grinding Out 8 Films a Day," *Seattle Sunday Times*, April 23, 1944, 2.

48 "Anniversary of 'Talkies' Recalls Coin Devices' Role in Film Industry's Growth," *Billboard*, May 25, 1946, 126.

49 Westbrook Pegler, "James Roosevelt as a Partner: Manufacturers of 'One-Arm Bandits' Welcomed Him in Gala Party Brochure," *San Diego Union*, September 19, 1950, 20.

50 "Amusement Games Firms."

51 "Want Panorams" (classified ad), *Billboard.*

52 Amy Herzog, "Fetish Machines: Peep-Shows, Co-Optation, and Technological Adaptation," in *Adaptation Theories*, ed. Jillian Saint Jacques (Maastricht: Jan van Eyck Academie, 2011), 71. In mapping the adaptation of the Panoram into a peep-show device in the 1960s, Amy Herzog calls into question theories of adaptation based on the "evolution of media technology" and its successes. Similar to the issues posed in the essay collection *Residual Media*, Herzog seeks models for narrativizing "outmoded, discarded" technologies like the Panoram and its subsequent modifications.

53 Herzog's comparison between the adaptation of an exhibition format and biological mutation is useful in conceptualizing the value of the Panoram as derelict technology, but I find it a limiting comparison when placed within a broader consideration of movie-machine technologies and their enduring continuities beyond just peep shows. Rather than countering narratives of evolutions with devolution and thereby maintaining a strict binary within the technological narrative, the

Panoram's discourses evidence the more uneven and fragmentary dialectics of technological change. See Herzog's "Fetish Machines."

54 Westbrook Pegler, "Jimmy Roosevelt and the Peepshows," *Augusta Chronicle*, October 17, 1950, 4.

55 "4 Cabarets Ordered Closed for Safety," *Seattle Times*, May 10, 1960, 2. For another mention of Panoram machines as peep devices in the 1960s, see *Billboard* classifieds, May 9, 1964, 46.

56 "Arcade Ops" (advertisement), *Billboard*, December 22, 1956, 63. See also "Council Puts Limits on Peep Shows," *Seattle Daily Times*, January 18, 1966, 13, "Auto Dealers Complain of City 'Harassment,'" *Seattle Daily Times*, May 1, 1974, 18, and "Legal Notices" (advertisement), *Seattle Daily Times*, December 14, 1975, E28.

57 See Amy Herzog, "In the Flesh: Space and Embodiment in the Pornographic Peep Show Arcade," in *Velvet Light Trap* 62, no. 1 (2008): 29–43.

58 "'French Scop-i-tone' Is a La 'Soundies,'" *Variety*, September 27, 1961, 21.

59 "Video; The Industry Is Taking a Second Look," *Billboard*, May 28, 1966, 55. For another comparison of the Scopitone to the Panoram, see "Cine Juke Box," 45.

60 "Cine Juke Box," 66.

61 For the sake of clarity, I am using the Scopitone as the generic label for the 1960s movie machine. For an overview of the competing brands, see *Billboard*, May 28, 1966, 55–65, which features multiple articles and ads on this movie-machine revival.

62 Susan Sontag, "Notes on Camp," in *Against Interpretation* (New York: Picador, 2001), 278.

63 "Another Film Co. in Coin Op Picture," *Billboard*, January 29, 1966, 68.

64 Michael Fessier Jr., "Tollvision: Jukebox Films Given LA Demo; Bank of 36 3-Min. Color Pix," *Variety*, Aug 12, 1964, 26.

65 For a detailed description of these emerging advertising trends on 1960s television, see Lawrence Samuels, *Brought to You By: Postwar Television Advertising and the American Dream* (Austin: University of Texas Press, 2001). See especially chapter 5, "Think Young, 1961–1962," and chapter 6, "The Psychic Air We Breathe, 1963–1964."

66 Samuels, *Brought to You By*, 154.

67 "Pictures: Two-Bits Services Girl-Watching Stags," *Variety*.

68 "Color-Sonics" (advertisement), *Billboard*, May 28, 1966, 67.

69 "Rosen to Distribute Cinejukebox World-Wide," *Billboard*, May 28, 1966, 66.

70 "Kaiser Chain Yens 'Visual Disks' for TV Jockeys (V-J)," *Variety*, August 18, 1965, 62.

71 "New Potential for Film Machine?," *Billboard*, 72.

72 "Color-Sonics" (advertisement), 67.

73 "Color-Sonics" (advertisement), 67.

74 "New Potential for Film Machine?"

75 "New Potential for Film Machine?"

76 "Scopitone Turns to the Coin Industry," *Billboard*, May 28, 1966, 65.

77 "Video; The Industry Is Taking a Second Look."

78 Photo, *Billboard*, February 5, 1966, 55.

79 "Hooray for the Yé-Yé Girls," *Life*, May 29, 1964, 39.

80 "Movie Keyed to Record" (photo), *Rocky Mountain News*, February 19, 1965, 96.

81 According to the "Rise and Fall of Scopitone Jukebox," U.S. audiences lost interest in Scopitones partly because of changing music aesthetics from pop to psychedelic in 1966, as well as associations with the Mafia and several technical

problems (like playing wrong selections). See Jennifer Sharpe, "Rise and Fall of Scopitone Jukebox," *NPR*, August 6, 2009.

82 "New Potential for Film Machine?"

83 "Pictures: Two-Bits," 13.

84 Fessier Jr., "Tollvision," 26.

85 Fessier Jr., 26.

86 Fessier Jr., 26.

87 "New Potential for Film Machine?," 72.

88 "Scopitone's Carousel of Stars!" (advertisement), *Billboard*, May 28, 1966, 65.

89 The mechanism of the carousel had been popularized by Kodak in the late 1950s with its slide projector. The adaption of the Kodak "carousel" to film further reorients the Scopitone's new mode of film distribution to small, discreet, easily interchangeable media.

90 "Color-Sonics" (advertisement), 67.

91 "Color-Sonics" (advertisement), 67.

92 For more detail on the record single and its contemporary extensions of privatized media consumption in digital media files, see Eric Harvey, "The Social History of the MP3," www.pitchfork.com, http://pitchfork.com/features/articles/7689-the-social-history-of-the-mp3.

93 "Video; The Industry is Taking a Second Look."

94 "Pictures: Cassette Machines Tested for Trailers," *Variety*, September 1, 1971, 20. Such transitional technologies include this account of a film machine that contains "24 regular 8mm sound film cassettes" that will be placed in theaters, hotels, and airports "to advertise pictures." Although Kodak's Super 8 cartridges hit the market in 1965, Scopitone's use of the cartridge as a playback technology suggests it was an early forerunner in using cartridge systems beyond film production.

Conclusion

1 Thomas Schatz, *Boom and Bust: American Cinema in the 1940s* (Berkeley: University of California Press, 1999).

2 Nick Couldry and Anna McCarthy, "Introduction," in *MediaSpace: Place, Scale and Culture in a Media Age*, ed. Nick Couldry and Anna McCarthy (London: Routledge, 2004), 7. Haidee Wasson similarly utilizes the "trope of scale" to extend understandings of cinema to its material articulations and technologically specific components, such as considerations of the size of the moving-image screen. See Haidee Wasson, "The Other Small Screen: Moving Images at New York's World Fair, 1939," *Canadian Journal of Film Studies* 21, no. 1 (Spring 2012): 81.

3 As Paul Grainge notes in his introduction to *Ephemeral Media: Transitory Screen Culture from Television to YouTube*, analyses of the circulation of short-media texts, or "media at the edges," expose the logics of more dominant media industries in providing intersecting and often indexical media practices. See Paul Grainge, "Introduction," in *Ephemeral Media: Transitory Screen Culture from Television to YouTube*, ed. Paul Grainge (Houndsmill: Palgrave Macmillan, 2011), 9.

4 *Panoram with Soundies: RCA Recorded and Projected* (Chicago: Mills Novelty Company, 1940).

5 *Panoram with Soundies.*

6 Grainge similarly argues that ephemeral media highlight particular relations to both the "regimes of time (duration, shortness, speed)" and the "regimes of transmission (circulation, storage, value)." See Grainge, "Introduction," 9.
7 Jonathan Sterne's *MP3: History of a Format* (Durham: Duke University Press, 2012) explicitly engages with the technical dimensions of MP3 compression to reorient his media history of sound recording around formatting.
8 Sterne, 17.
9 Leslie Kaufman, "Good Fit for Today's Little Screens: Short Stories," *New York Times*, February 15, 2013, accessed February 16, 2013, http://www.nytimes.com/2013/02/16/books/a-good-fit-for-small-screens-short-stories-are-selling.html?emc=eta1.
10 Kaufman.
11 Laura Miller, "Sorry, the Short Story Boom Is Bogus," *Salon*, February 20, 1013, accessed on March 20, 2013, http://www.salon.com/2013/02/21/sorry_the_short_story_boom_is_bogus/.
12 Grainge, "Introduction," 12.
13 For example, the opening titles to TBS's *Night Tracks* from the early 1980s shows a record spinning, and NBC's *Friday Night Videos* opening graphics show a needle on a record.
14 In another *Video Jukebox* promo from 1982, the viewer travels with a coin along its chute into a more traditional music jukebox. Once inside the machine, music instruments are played by robot arms à la Herbie Hancock's *Rockit*.
15 See, for example, user-generated channels like "YouTube Video Jukebox," accessed on April 11, 2013, http://www.youtube.com/playlist?list=PL53A7FBA939D7FED8. Another contemporary example of small-screen jukeboxes includes a "TV Jukebox" column in *Entertainment Weekly*, which features musical moments in popular TV shows from that week. For example, see Lanford Beard, "TV Jukebox: 'Suits,' 'Catfish,' 'Monday Mornings,' and More Music-on-TV Moments," *Entertainment Weekly*, February 20, 2013, accessed on April 15, 2013, http://music-mix.ew.com/2013/02/23/tv-jukebox-feb-23-2013/.
16 Nick Montano, "AMI Entertainment Plans Music Video Service for NGX Jukeboxes; Target Launch Is Q4 2013," *Vending Times* 53, no. 4 (April 2013), accessed on April 10, 2013, http://www.vendingtimes.com/ME2/dirmod.asp?sid=650DC4553F514A848B520ED329F08BA3&nm=Music+%26+Games+Features&type=Publishing&mod=Publications%3A%3AArticle&mid=8F3A7027421841978F18BE895F87F791&tier=4&id=F4405EC1323A4D7C8EFEC295127E856C.
17 Hank Schlesinger, "NGX Introduces Inside and Out Modularity to Rowe Jukeboxes," *Vending Times* 51, no. 4 (April 2011), accessed on April 10, 2013, http://www.vendingtimes.com/me2/dirmod.asp?sid=EB79A487112B48A296B38C81345C8C7F&nm=Vending+Features&type=Publishing&mod=Publications%3A%3AArticle&mid=8F3A7027421841978F18BE895F87F791&tier=4&id=E759FF8FB5D0474DADEC4B0ACF341B11.

Bibliography

Acland, Charles R. "Curtains, Carts and the Mobile Screen." *Screen* 50, no. 1 (Spring 2009): 148–166.

———. Introduction to *Residual Media*, edited by Charles R. Acland. Minneapolis: University of Minnesota Press, 2007.

———, ed. *Residual Media*. Minneapolis: University of Minnesota Press, 2007.

Acland, Charles R., and Haidee Wasson, eds. *Useful Cinema*. Durham: Duke University Press, 2011.

Allen, Robert C. "Relocating American Film History: The 'Problem' of the Empirical." *Cultural Studies* 20, no. 1 (January 2006): 48–88.

Allen, Robert C., and Douglass Gomery. *Film History: Theory and Practice*. New York: McGraw-Hill, 1985.

Altman, Rick. "Cinema and Popular Song: The Lost Tradition." In *Soundtrack Available: Essays on Film and Popular Music*, edited by Pamela Robertson Wojcik and Arthur Knight, 19–30. Durham: Duke University Press, 2001.

———. "Evolution of Sound Technology." In *Film Sound: Theory and Practice*, edited by Elisabeth Weis and John Belton, 44–54. New York: Columbia University Press, 1985.

Anderson, Christopher. "Television and Hollywood in the 1940s." In *Boom and Bust: American Cinema in the 1940s*, edited by Thomas Schatz, 422–444. Berkeley: University of California Press, 1999.

Anderson, Tim J. *Making Easy Listening: Material Culture and Postwar American Recording*. Minneapolis: University of Minnesota Press, 2006.

Babson, Roger W. "Preparing for Jobs." *Washington Post*, April 2, 1945, 12.

Barry, Jack. "This New Showmanship." *Billboard*, January 31, 1942, 89.

Beard, Lanford. "TV Jukebox: 'Suits,' 'Catfish,' 'Monday Mornings,' and More Music-on-TV Moments." *Entertainment Weekly*, February 23, 2013, accessed April 15, 2013. http://ew.com/article/2013/02/23/tv-jukebox-feb-23-2013/.

Belton, John. "Technology and Aesthetics of Film Sound." In *Film Sound: Theory and Practice*, edited by Elisabeth Weis and John Belton, 63–72. New York: Columbia University Press, 1985.

Bhabha, Homi. *The Location of Culture*. London: Routledge, 1994.

Billboard. "AFM to Collect on Oldies in Fresh 'Official' Pact." November 11, 1950, 12.

———. "Al Jarvis." September 13, 1947, 15.
———. "Amusement Games Firms Tell Plan for Showing." January 25, 1947, 87.
———. "Anniversary of 'Talkies' Recalls Coin Devices' Role in Film Industry's Growth." May 25, 1946, 126.
———. "Another Film Co. in Coin Op Picture." January 29, 1966, 68.
———. "Arcade Ops" (advertisement). December 22, 1956, 63.
———. "Arcades Find Pan-O-Rams Successful Attraction." January 1, 1944, 56.
———. "Both Sides Are Cautious." July 25, 1942, 6, 9.
———. "Cash for Your 16mm Sound Films" (advertisement). August 21, 1948, 48.
———. "CBS-TV to Lead Daytime Race; Dumont on Heels." August 12, 1950, 4.
———. "Cine Juke Box: Just a Novelty?" July 10, 1965, 45–46.
———. Classifieds. May 9, 1964, 46.
———. "Coast Philco Distrib Sets HugeTeleHyp." September 6, 1947, 13.
———. "Color-Sonics" (advertisement). May 28, 1966, 67.
———. "Combo Disk-Film Juke Box May Develop Pix Shorts Field for Orks and Singers." June 15, 1946, 36.
———. "Detroit." February 26, 1944, 92.
———. "Don Lee's KHJ-TV Gets 800 Snader Telescripts." February 9, 1952, 12.
———. "Filmmusic Shorts for TV in Golden Sweep, 30G to 100G." July 15, 1950, 7.
———. "G.I.'s Select Their Favorite Records; Still Kids at Heart." September 23, 1944, 20, 72.
———. "Greg Norman Takes Video Plunge . . ." May 19, 1951, 11.
———. "Industry Mentions." October 30, 1943, 71.
———. "Jukes Helped Disk Firms Recover from Sales Slump." November 6, 1943, 63.
———. "Machines for Recruiting." March 18, 1944, 70.
———. "Movie Machine Aids Photog in Snapping Youngsters' Poses." April 27, 1946, 152.
———. "Movie Machine Review." February 28, 1942, 78.
———. "Movie Machine Review." June 6, 1942, 67.
———. "Movie Machine Review." October 17, 1942, 68.
———. "Movie Machine Review." November 14, 1942, 67.
———. "Movie Machine Review." February 27, 1943, 104.
———. "Movie Machine Review." July 24, 1943, 66.
———. "Movie Machine Review." December 11, 1943, 67.
———. "Movie Machine Review." February 19, 1944, 59.
———. "Movie Machine Review." March 25, 1944, 93.
———. "Movie Machine Review." September 30, 1944, 64.
———. "Movie Machine Review." December 23, 1944, 67.
———. "Movie Machine Review." February 3, 1945, 64.
———. "Movie Machine Review." October 20, 1945, 76.
———. "Movie Machine Review." February 9, 1946, 91.
———. "Movie Machine Reviews: Program 1068." May 30, 1942, 92.
———. "Movie Machines' Public Service." June 16, 1945, 65.
———. "Movies in Taverns Barred in Michigan." June 19, 1948, 27.
———. "Music—as Written." April 27, 1946, 26.
———. "NAVED Meet Set for Chi August 6–7." June 8, 1946, 114.
———. "New Potential for Film Machine?" November 11, 1967, 72.
———. "Night Club Movie Mch. Points Way to Entirely New Location." August 11, 1945, 65.
———. "Night Club Reviews." May 30, 1942, 13.
———. "Night Club Reviews." September 21, 1946, 36.
———. "Old Soundies, Costing 300G, Bring in 700G." February 3, 1951, 6.

———. "OWI Pics for Soundie Fans." June 17, 1944, 68.
———. "Panoram for Defense." March 14, 1942, 85.
———. "Panorams Hit Favor with Armory Employees in Mass." November 11, 1944, 72.
———. "Panoram Used in Red Crosses' Drive for Nurses, Aids." May 15, 1943, 65.
———. "Petrillo Lifts Ban on Hiring of Union Men by Soundies." November 6, 1943, 62.
———. "Phonograph, Movie Machine Combination Is Developed." January 31, 1942, 67.
———. Photograph caption. January 24, 1942, 80.
———. Photograph caption. February 14, 1942, 57.
———. Photograph. May 23, 1942, 73.
———. Photograph. June 6, 1942, 66.
———. Photograph. February 5, 1966, 55.
———. Photograph caption. May 11, 1946, 128.
———. "Play Goes upward on Movie Machines." September 19, 1942, 62.
———. "'Requestfully Yours' Televised by WATV." February 5, 1949, 41.
———. "Rosen to Distribute Cinejukebox World-Wide." May 28, 1966, 66.
———. "Scopitone's Carousel of Stars!" (advertisement). May 28, 1966, 65.
———. "Scopitone Turns to the Coin Industry." May 28, 1966, 65.
———. "Soundies Company Now Going into Production." March 6, 1943, 71.
———. "Soundies Fetes Wounded Vets." May 13, 1944, 76.
———. "Soundies for War Plants." February 13, 1943, 61.
———. "'Soundies' Getting Air-Pix Test." November 11, 1944, 12, 63.
———. "Soundies Plug Bonds during the 6th War Loan Drive." December 2, 1944, 97.
———. "Soundies Subjects May Be Selected." August 22, 1942, 65.
———. "Syndicated Film Video Segs Eyed by ET Orgs as Future Market." June 22, 1946, 19.
———. "3 Panorams Draw 600,000 at 20-Day Det. Army Air Show." July 15, 1944, 69.
———. "Time-Out Period Steps Up Production." January 31, 1942, 95.
———. "TV: The New Home for Disc Jockeys." October 7, 1950, 70–71.
———. "Vet's Plan, Better Pix, Service School and Venue from Ads Spotlight Soundies Post-War Plans." April 22, 1944, 64.
———. "Video: The Industry is Taking a Second Look." May 28, 1966, 55.
———. "Want Panorams" (classified advertisement). December 18, 1948, 110.
———. "'We'll Slap the Japs' Rings Out in Chi City Hall." January 24, 1942, 71.
Billboard Music Year Book. "Movie Juke Boxes . . . What about Them?" 1943, 73.
Boddy, William. *New Media and Popular Imagination: Launching Radio, Television, and Digital Media in the United States*. Oxford: Oxford University Press, 2004.
Bogle, Donald. *Dorothy Dandridge: A Biography*. New York: Amistad Press, 1997.
———. *Toms, Coons, Mulattoes, Mammies, and Bucks: An Interpretive History of Blacks in American Films*. New York: Continuum, 2002.
Bordwell, David, Janet Staiger, and Kristin Thompson. *The Classical Hollywood Cinema: Film Style and Mode of Production to 1960*. New York: Columbia University Press, 1985.
Brinkley, Alan. "World War II and American Liberalism." In *The War in American Culture: Society and Consciousness During World War II*, edited by Lewis A. Erenberg and Susan E. Hirsch, 313–330. Chicago: University of Chicago Press, 1996.
Broadcasting. "Inroad on Video Market Is Foreseen in Soundies." November 1, 1940, 79.
Brownell, Kathryn Cramer. "'It Is Entertainment, and It Will Sell Bonds!': 16mm Film and the World War II War Bond Campaign." *Moving Image* 10, no. 2 (2010): 60–82.
Business Screen: Army Pictorial Issue, no. 1 (1946): 59.
Business Screen, no. 5 (1945): 72.
Butterfield, Roger. "Los Angeles." *Life*, November 22, 1943, 117.

Certeau, Michel de. *The Practice of Everyday Life*. Berkeley: University of California Press, 1984.
Chicago Daily Tribune. "Expect Priority to Build Capt. Jimmy's Jukes." August 31, 1941, 1.
———. Marshall Field's (advertisement). October 9, 1942, 2.
———. "Mills Novelty Penalized for WPB Violation." April 14, 1942, 23.
Chicago Defender. "Gene Krupa Forgets South, Features Roy." March 7, 1942, 20.
Chion, Michel. *Audio-Vision: Sound on Screen*. New York: Columbia University Press, 1990.
Chris Lamson, dir. *Soundies: A Musical History*. 2007; Los Angeles, CA: Liberation Entertainment, 2007. DVD.
Churchill, Douglas W. "Hollywood Strikes Back." *New York Times*, September 29, 1940, 121.
Cleveland Plain Dealer. "Television? Who Knows What It Will Do to Film Theaters?" February 15, 1948, 15B.
Cohen, Col. Emmanuel. "Film Is a Weapon." *Business Screen: Army Pictorial Issue*, no. 1 (1946): 43, 72, 74.
Cohen, Lizabeth. *A Consumers' Republic: The Politics of Mass Consumption in Postwar America*. New York: Vintage Books, 2003.
"Coin Machine Movies." *Business Screen* 3, no. 3 (1941): 8.
Couldry, Nick, and Anna McCarthy, eds. *MediaSpace: Place, Scale and Culture in a Media Age*. London: Routledge, 2004.
Couldry, Nick, and Anna McCarthy. "Introduction; Orientations: Mapping MediaSpace." In *MediaSpace: Place, Scale and Culture in a Media Age*, edited by Nick Couldry and Anna McCarthy, 1–18. London: Routledge, 2004.
Courtney, Susan. *Hollywood Fantasies of Miscegenation: Spectacular Narratives of Gender and Race, 1903–1967*. Princeton: Princeton University Press, 2005.
Cripps, Thomas. *Slow Fade to Black: The Negro in American Film, 1900–1942*. New York: Oxford University Press, 1977.
Cross, Gary. *An All-Consuming Century: Why Commercialism Won in Modern America*. New York: Columbia University Press, 2000.
Digest. "Dayroom Information Centers Feature Shaw Field Program." May 1944, 4–5.
Doherty, Thomas. *Projections of War*. New York: Columbia University Press, 1993.
Driscoll, Joseph. *Pacific Victory, 1945*. Philadelphia: J. B. Lippincott Company, 1945.
Duis, Perry R. "No Time for Privacy: World War II and Chicago's Families." In *The War in American Culture: Society and Consciousness during World War II*, edited by Lewis A. Erenberg and Susan E. Hirsch, 17–45. Chicago: University of Chicago Press, 1996.
Dyer, Richard. *Heavenly Bodies: Film Stars and Society*. London: Routledge, 2004.
———. *Only Entertainment*. 2nd ed. London: Routledge, 2002.
Eggertsen, Lt. Claude A. "Education Home from the Wars." *Educational Administration and Supervision* 31 (1945): 483–494.
Erenberg, Lewis A. *Steppin' Out: New York Nightlife and the Transformation of American Culture, 1890–1930*. Westport: Greenwood Press, 1981.
Erenberg, Lewis A., and Susan E. Hirsch, eds. *The War in American Culture: Society and Consciousness during World War II*. Chicago: University of Chicago Press, 1996.
Fessier, Michael, Jr. "Tollvision: Jukebox Films Given LA Demo; Bank of 36 3-Min. Color Pix." *Variety*, August 12, 1964, 26.
Film Daily. "Equipment Field Notes." September 10, 1943, 1.
"Films as Medicine." *Business Screen: Army Pictorial Issue*, no. 1 (1946): 46.
Forman, Murray. *One Night on TV Is Worth Weeks at the Paramount: Popular Music on Early Television*. Durham: Duke University Press, 2012.
Friedberg, Anne. *Window Shopping: Cinema and the Postmodern*. Berkeley: University of California Press, 1993.

Gabbard, Krin. *Jammin' at the Margins*. Chicago: University of Chicago Press, 1996.

General Electric (advertisement). *Business Screen* 7, no. 6 (1945): 10.

Gerstle, Gary. *American Crucible: Race and Nation in the 20th Century*. Princeton: Princeton University Press, 2002.

Gipson, Henry Clay. *Films in Business and Industry*. New York: McGraw-Hill, 1947.

Gitelman, Lisa. *Always Already New: Media, History and the Data of Culture*. Cambridge: MIT Press, 2006.

Gleason, Philip. "Americans All: World War II and the Shaping of American Identity." *Review of Politics* 43 (October 1981): 498–518.

Grainge, Paul. Introduction to *Ephemeral Media: Transitory Screen Culture from Television to YouTube*, edited by Paul Grainge, 1–17. Houndsmill: Palgrave Macmillan, 2011.

Green, Adam. *Selling the Race: Culture, Community, and Black Chicago, 1940–1955*. Chicago: University of Chicago Press, 2009.

Gubar, Susan. *Racechanges: White Skin, Black Face in American Culture*. New York: Oxford University Press, 1997.

Gunning, Tom. "Attractions: How They Came into the World." In *Cinema of Attractions Reloaded*, edited by Wanda Strauven, 31–38. Amsterdam: Amsterdam University Press, 2006.

———. "'Now You See It, Now You Don't': The Temporality of the Cinema of Attractions." In *Silent Film*, edited by Richard Abel, 71–84. New Brunswick: Rutgers University Press, 1996.

Hall, Stuart. "What Is This 'Black' in Black Popular Culture?" In *Representing Blackness: Issues in Film and Video*, edited by Valerie Smith, 123–134. London: Anthlone Press, 1997.

Hansen, Miriam. *Babel and Babylon: Spectatorship in American Silent Film*. Cambridge: Harvard University Press, 1991.

Harvey, Eric. "The Social History of the MP3." *Pitchfork*, August 24, 2009, accessed October 3, 2011. http://pitchfork.com/features/articles/7689-the-social-history-of-the-mp3.

HBO. "HBO's Video Jukebox Opener." YouTube video, 0:31. July 2, 2009. Accessed April 11, 2013. https://youtu.be/JB01X5hwpJ8.

Henning, Michelle. "New Lamps for Old: Photography, Obsolescence, and Social Change." In *Residual Media*, edited by Charles R. Acland and Haidee Wasson, 48–65. Minneapolis: University of Minnesota Press, 2007.

Herzog, Amy. "Discordant Visions: The Peculiar Musical Images of the Soundies Jukebox Film." *American Music* 22, no. 1 (Spring 2004): 27–39.

———. "Fetish Machines: Peep-Shows, Co-Optation, and Technological Adaptation." In *Adaptation Theories*, edited by Jillian Saint Jacques, 45–86. Maastricht: Jan van Eyck Academie, 2011.

———. "Illustrating Music: The Impossible Embodiments of the Jukebox Film." In *Medium Cool: Music Videos from Soundies to Cellphones*, edited by Beebe and Middleton, 30–58. Durham: Duke University Press, 2007.

———. "In the Flesh: Space and Embodiment in the Pornographic Peep Show Arcade." *Velvet Light Trap* 62, no. 1 (2008): 29–43.

Hilmes, Michele. *Hollywood and Broadcasting: From Radio to Cable*. Urbana: University of Illinois Press, 1990.

Hose, Wally. *Soundies*. St. Louis: Wally's Multimedia LLC, 2007.

Kaufman, Leslie. "Good Fit for Today's Little Screens: Short Stories." *New York Times*, February 15, 2013, A1.

Kelley, Robin D. G. "The Riddle of the Zoot: Malcolm Little and Black Cultural Politics during World War II." In *American Studies: An Anthology*, edited by Janice Radway,

Kevin K. Gaines, Barry Shank, and Penny von Eschen, 280–289. Chichester: Wiley-Blackwell, 2009.

King, Rob. *Hokum!: The Early Sound Slapstick Short and Depression-Era Mass Culture*. Berkeley: University of California Press, 2017.

Knee, Adam. "Class Swings: Music, Race and Social Mobility in *Broken Strings*." In *Soundtrack Available: Essays on Film and Popular Music*, edited by Pamela Robertson Wojcik and Arthur Knight, 269–294. Durham: Duke University Press, 2001.

Knight, Arthur. *Disintegrating the Musical: Black Performance and American Musical Film*. Durham: Duke University Press, 2002.

Lefebvre, Henri. *The Production of Space*. Oxford: Blackwell, 1991.

Lehman, Sgt. Milton. "Home from the Wars to a Friendly Town." *New York Times*, July 8, 1945, 51.

Lester, Peter. "'Sweet Sixteen' Goes to War: Hollywood, the NAAF, and 16mm Film Exhibition in Canada during World War II." *Canadian Journal of Film Studies* 19, no. 1 (Spring 2010): 2–19.

Life. "Hooray for the Yé-Yé Girls." May 29, 1964, 39.

———. "Speaking of Pictures . . . Susan's Studios Mass-Produce Kid Pictures." February 26, 1945, 14.

LisiBee [username]. "YouTube Video Jukebox." YouTube playlist. Last updated on November 18, 2011, accessed April 11, 2013. https://www.youtube.com/playlist?list=PL53A7FBA939D7FED8.

Look. "Jimmy's Got It Again." November 19, 1940, 12–14.

Lopez, Ana. "Are All Latins from Manhattan?: Hollywood, Ethnography, and Cultural Colonialism." In *Unspeakable Images: Ethnicity and the American Cinema*, edited by Lester D. Friedman, 404–424. Urbana: University of Illinois Press, 1991.

Los Angeles Times. "James Roosevelt Introduces His New 'Soundies,'" September 17, 1940, 15.

Lott, Eric. *Love & Theft: Blackface Minstrelsy and the American Working Class*. New York: Oxford University Press, 1993.

MacGillivray, Scott. *Castle Films: A Hobbyist Guide*. Lincoln: iUniverse, Inc., 2004.

MacGillivray, Scott, and Ted Okuda. *The Soundies Book: A Revised and Expanded Guide to the "Music Videos" of the 1940s*. New York: iUniverse, Inc., 2007.

Maurice, Alice. *Cinema and Its Shadow: Race and Technology in Early Cinema*. Minneapolis: University of Minnesota Press, 2013.

McCarthy, Anna. *Ambient Television: Visual Culture and Public Space*. Durham: Duke University Press, 2001.

McGee, Kristin. *Some Liked It Hot: Jazz Women in Film and Television, 1928–1959*. Middletown: Wesleyan University Press, 2009.

Medlin, Mary Jane. "A Community Project in Service Men's Recreation." *Journal of Health and Physical Education* 14 (1943): 362–402.

Miller, Laura. "Sorry, the Short Story Boom Is Bogus." *Salon*, February 20, 2013, accessed March 20, 2013. http://www.salon.com/2013/02/21/sorry_the_short_story_boom_is_bogus/.

Mills Novelty Company (advertisement). *Business Screen* 5, no. 1 (1943): 31.

Montano, Nick. "AMI Entertainment Plans Music Video Service for NGX Jukeboxes; Target Launch Is Q4 2013." *Vending Times* 53, no. 4 (April 2013), accessed April 10, 2013. http://www.vendingtimes.com/ME2/dirmod.asp?nm=Vending+Features&type=Publishing&mod=Publications%3A%3AArticle&tier=4&id=F4405EC1323A4D7C8EFEC295127E856C.

Morris, Earl J. "Grand Town: Day and Night." *Pittsburgh Courier*, September 28, 1940, 21.

Motion Picture Herald. "Exhibitors, Authorities Hit Slot-Machine Films." August 17, 1940, 27.

———. "Exhibitors Fighting 'Slot-Machine' Movies." January 25, 1941, 60.

———. "Industry in Pittsburgh Attacks 16mm. Shows." August 10, 1940, 26.

———. January 18, 1941, 106–107.

———. "'Jimmy' Not A-drift." November 23, 1940, 9.

———. "'Juke-boxes' Jammed in Bottleneck of Insufficient Product Backlog." March 22, 1941, 48.

———. "'No Competition,' 16mm Men Say." June 7, 1941, 24.

———. "Organized Exhibitor Action Opens Against Roosevelt's 'Nickel Movies.'" March 3, 1940.

———. "$30,000 Weekly Slot-Movie Gross Troubles New England Exhibitors." May 24, 1941, 15.

Muse, Clarence. "What's Going On in Hollywood." *Chicago Defender*, September 28, 1940, 20.

"The National Archives at New York City: Camp Kilmer" (website). U.S. National Archives and Records Administration. Accessed March 6, 2015. http://www.archives.gov/nyc/exhibit/camp-kilmer.

News Week. "Picture Jockeys." July 17, 1950, 48.

New York Amsterdam News. "New Stars Being 'Born' as Soundies Make Shorts in Harlem." August 28, 1943, 16.

———. "Pretty Girls Due for Soundie Feature Films." May 22, 1943, 15.

Norman, Lloyd. "Penny-in-Slot Devices Now Pay Death-To Axis." *Chicago Daily Tribune*, August 9, 1942, A10.

Oregonian. Advertisement. August 23, 1948, 5.

Orgeron, Devin, Marsha Orgeron, and Dan Streible, eds. *Learning with the Lights Off: Educational Film in the United States*. New York: Oxford University Press, 2012.

Panoram with Soundies: RCA Recorded and Projected. Chicago: Mills Novelty Company, 1940.

Pegler, Westbrook. "James Roosevelt as a Partner: Manufacturers of 'One-Arm Bandits' Welcomed Him in Gala Party Brochure." *San Diego Union*, September 19, 1950, 20.

———. "Jimmy Roosevelt and the Peepshows." *Augusta Chronicle*, October 17, 1950, 4.

Peterson, Richard A. "Why 1955? Explaining the Advent of Rock Music." *Popular Music* 9, no. 1 (January 1990): 97–116.

Pittsburgh Courier. "'Juke Box' Soundies Opening New Outlet for Colored Bands." November 22, 1941, 20.

Rasmussen, Chris. "'The People's Orchestra': Jukeboxes as the Measure of Popular Musical Taste in the 1930s and 1940s." In *Sound in the Age of Mechanical Reproduction*, edited by David Suisman and Susan Strasser, 181–198. Philadelphia: University of Pennsylvania Press, 2010.

Regester, Charlene. *African American Actresses: The Struggle for Visibility, 1900–1960*. Bloomington: Indiana University Press, 2010.

Reufer, Maynard. "The Future of Juke Box Pictures." *Billboard Music Year Book*, January 1, 1944, 124.

Ritchie, Michael. *Please Stand By: A Prehistory of Television*. Woodstock: The Overlook Press, 1994.

Rockford Register-Republic. "'Instant Soundies' Panned by Jerry." July 5, 1960, 10B.

Rocky Mountain News. "Movie Keyed to Record" (photograph). February 19, 1965, 96.

Rogin, Michael Paul. *Blackface, White Noise: Jewish Immigrants in the Hollywood Melting Pot*. Berkeley: University of California Press, 1996.

Samuels, Lawrence. *Brought to You By: Postwar Television Advertising and the American Dream*. Austin: University of Texas Press, 2001.

Sanjek, Russell. *Pennies from Heaven: The American Popular Music Business in the Twentieth Century*. New York: De Capo Press, 1996.

Scannell, Paddy. *Radio, Television and Modern Life*. Cambridge: Blackwell, 1996.

Schatz, Thomas. *Boom and Bust: American Cinema in the 1940s*. Berkeley: University of California Press, 1999.

Scheuer, Philip K. "Town Called Hollywood." *Los Angeles Times*, November 29, 1942, C3.

Schlesinger, Hank. "NGX Introduces Inside and Out Modularity to Rowe Jukeboxes." *Vending Times* 51, no. 4 (April 2011), accessed April 10, 2013. http://www.vendingtimes.com/me2/dirmod.asp?sid=EB79A487112B48A296B38C81345C8C7F&nm=Vending+Features&type=Publishing&mod=Publications%3A%3AArticle&mid=8F3A7027421841978F18BE895F87F791&tier=4&id=E759FF8FB5D0474DADEC4B0ACF341B11.

Scott, A. O. "The Screening of America." *New York Times*, November 23, 2008, MM21.

Seattle Daily Times. "Auto Dealers Complain of City 'Harassment.'" May 1, 1974, 18.

———. "Council Puts Limits on Peep Shows." January 18, 1966, 13.

———. "Legal Notices" (advertisement). December 14, 1975, E28.

Seattle Sunday Times. "Edison Old Bronx Studio Grinding Out 8 Films a Day." April 23, 1944, 2.

Seattle Times. "4 Cabarets Ordered Closed for Safety." May 10, 1960, 2.

Sharpe, Jennifer. "Rise and Fall of Scopitone Jukebox." *NPR*, August 6, 2009, accessed September 5, 2012. http://www.npr.org/templates/story/story.php?storyId=5630027.

Shippey, Lee. "Lee Side o' L.A." *Los Angeles Times*, November 23, 1940, A4.

Slotkin, Richard. *Gunfighter Nation: The Myth of the American Frontier*. Norman: University of Oklahoma Press, 1992.

Smoodin, Eric. "Introduction: The History of Film History." In *Looking Past the Screen: Case Studies in American Film History and Method*, edited by Jon Lewis and Eric Smoodin, 1–34. Durham: Duke University Press, 2007.

Sobchack, Vivian. "Lounge Time: Postwar Crisis and the Chronotope of Film Noir." In *Refiguring American Film Genres*, edited by Nick Browne, 129–169. Berkeley: University of California Press, 1998.

"Sono-vision" (advertisement). *Business Screen* 6, no. 5 (1945): 87.

"Sono-vision" (advertisement). *Business Screen* 7, no. 2 (1946): 7.

Sontag, Susan. *Against Interpretation*. New York: Picador, 2001.

Soundies Catalog 1942–1943.

Spigel, Lynn. *TV by Design: Modern Art and the Rise of Network Television*. Chicago: University of Chicago Press, 2008.

Spinrad, Leonard. "Movie Going Down Guatemala Way." *New York Times*, July 7, 1946, 41.

Spring, Katherine. *Saying It with Songs: Popular Music and the Coming of Sound to Hollywood Cinema*. New York: Oxford University Press, 2013.

Sterne, Jonathan. *The Audible Past: Cultural Origins of Sound Reproduction*. Durham: Duke University Press, 2003.

———. *MP3: History of a Format*. Durham: Duke University Press, 2012.

Stober, JoAnne. "Vaudeville: The Incarnation, Transformation, and Resilience of an Entertainment Form." In *Residual Media*, edited by Charles R. Acland, 133–155. Minneapolis: University of Minnesota Press, 2007.

Stowe, David. *Swing Changes: Big-Band Jazz in New Deal America*. Cambridge: Harvard University Press, 1994.

TIDE. "Soundies for Vets." July 1, 1944, 72–73.
Time. "Jimmie's Peep Shows." March 4, 1940, 67.
———. "Music: Soundies." September 16, 1940.
Times-Picayune. "On the Square." April 12, 1950, 23.
Townsend, Peter. *Pearl Harbor Jazz: Change in Popular Music in the Early 1940s*. Jackson: University Press of Mississippi, 2007.
Tucker, Sherrie. *Swing Shift: "All-Girl" Bands of the 1940s*. Durham: Duke University Press, 2000.
Turner, Victor. *The Ritual Process: Structure and Anti-Structure*. New Brunswick: Aldine Transaction Press, 2008.
Variety. "Brenner a Disc Jockey on TV with Soundie Films Instead of Wax." February 2, 1949, 37.
———. "'French Scop-i-tone' Is a La 'Soundies.'" September 27, 1961, 21.
———. "Further Analysis Cues Jukebox Take Nearer $150,000,000 A Year." August 21, 1940, 49, 60.
———. "Jerkbox?" March 22, 1944, 38.
———. "Kaiser Chain Yens 'Visual Disks' for TV Jockeys (V-J)." August 18, 1965, 62.
———. "Mills Novelty and Jas. Roosevelt's Classy N.Y. Preem for 'Soundies.'" October 23, 1940, 16, 18.
———. "Pictures: Cassette Machines Tested for Trailers." September 1, 1971, 20.
———. "Pictures: Two-Bits Services Girl-Watching Stags." June 10, 1964, 13.
———. "Roosevelt-Mills' Juke-Box Pix to Entail Cost of $1,000,000 a Yr." March 13, 1940, 4.
———. "Roosevelt Name Draws Publicity; Jukebox Operators Irritated." March 5, 1941, 45.
———. "Sight and Sound Jukeboxes Expected to Appeal Most to Hinterlanders Where Bands in Person Are a Rarity." December 4, 1940, 17.
———. "Yermi Stern's Juke-box Shorts Points Up New Gadgets Sundry Deficiencies." August 7, 1940, 16.
Wald, Elijah. *How the Beatles Destroyed Rock 'n' Roll: An Alternative History of American Popular Music*. Oxford: Oxford University Press, 2009.
Waller, Gregory. "Projecting the Promise of 16mm, 1935–1945." In *Useful Cinema*, edited by Charles R. Acland and Haidee Wasson, 125–148. Durham: Duke University Press, 2011.
Wasson, Haidee. "The Other Small Screen: Moving Images at New York's World Fair, 1939." *Canadian Journal of Film Studies* 21, no. 1 (Spring 2012): 81–103.
———. "Protocols of Portability." *Film History: An International Journal* 25, no. 1–2 (2013): 236–247.
———. "Suitcase Cinema." *Cinema Journal* 51, no. 2 (Winter 2012): 148–152.
Weigman, Robyn. "Black Bodies/American Commodities: Gender, Race and the Bourgeois Ideal in Contemporary Film." In *Unspeakable Images: Ethnicity and the American Cinema*, edited by Lester D. Friedman, 308–328. Urbana: University of Illinois Press, 1991.
Williams, Raymond. *Marxism and Literature*. New York: Oxford University Press, 1977.
———. *Television: Technology and Cultural Form*. London: Routledge, 1974.
Wolf, Arlene. "Milady Dreams of Post-War 'Utopia.'" *Canton Repository*, January 1, 1944, 10.
Wolfe, Charles. "Vitaphone Shorts and *The Jazz Singer*." *Wide Angle* 12, no. 3 (July 1990): 58–78.
Yanow, Scott. *Jazz on Film*. San Francisco: Backbeat Books, 2004.

Index

Page numbers in *italics* refer to illustrations.

About the Author

ANDREA J. KELLEY is an assistant professor of media studies at Auburn University's School of Communication and Journalism.